Essential Java∗

Essential Java*

Developing Interactive Applications for the World-Wide Web

JASON J. MANGER

McGRAW-HILL BOOK COMPANY
London · New York · St Louis · San Francisco · Auckland · Bogotá
Caracas · Lisbon · Madrid · Mexico · Milan · Montreal
New Delhi · Panama · Paris · San Juan · São Paulo
Singapore · Sydney · Tokyo · Toronto

Published by
McGRAW-HILL Book Company Europe
Shoppenhangers Road, Maidenhead, Berkshire, SL6 2QL, England
Telephone 01628 23432
Fax 01628 770224

British Library Cataloguing in Publication Data
The CIP data of this title is available from the British Library, UK.

ISBN 0–07–709292–9

Library of Congress Cataloging-in-Publication Data
The CIP data of this title is available from the Library of Congress, Washington DC, USA

McGraw-Hill

A Division of The **McGraw·Hill** *Companies*

1234   CL   9876

Typeset by Ian Kingston Editorial Services, Nottingham
and printed and bound in Great Britain at Clays Ltd, St Ives plc

Printed on permanent paper in compliance with the ISO Standard 9706

Contents

vi Contents

Preface

Up until now the World-Wide Web has faced a significant problem, namely that the information it contains is *static*. In essence you load a page, move back and forth a few times, and that's it – end of story. Static pages are now considered dull, and while it is possible to build a degree of interactivity into a hypertext page using existing HTML (hypertext mark-up language) facilities, the browsing of such pages does become rather tiresome.

In order to address the problem of *interactivity*, a new tool arrived on the Internet and with it brought *executable content* to the Web. **HotJava**™ was the tool, and in its wake there has been spawned a whole range of Java-related products. One very important product in this context is **Netscape Navigator 2.0**, the Web browser that this book is based upon. Netscape is the *de facto* standard browser that is estimated to be used by over 70 per cent of users on the World-Wide Web, and offers the user an unparalleled range of facilities which now includes **Java**™ support and a *scripting* language known as **JavaScript**™.

Java and JavaScript are quite different languages, although they share a common goal, namely to incorporate interactive, executable content within a hypertext page. Content is king on the Web. At a very simple level 'content' refers to the information contained within a hypertext document, i.e. the raw HTML and the data that it encapsulates. Ask Web developers what they mean by content and you get a quite different answer: content is *information*, *structure* and indeed the *interface* that presents the underlying information to the user. For the first time, hypertext documents can become hypertext applications.

And this is the key point. With Netscape 2.0 HTML documents can at last become *dynamic*. They can update themselves and they can be considered as applications in their own right, rather than simple repositories of text. Java and JavaScript applications can be 'interacted' with, or, alternatively, they can control themselves independently. Web-based hypertext documents share a similar content in that they are made up of the tag language HTML, out of which all Web pages on the Internet are constructed. In order to facilitate the use of languages such as Java and JavaScript, Netscape understands a newly modified HTML dialect.

Many of Netscape's *enhanced* HTML tags now accept additional attributes to process events such as field-value modifications and page-loading actions. Surprisingly, the inclusion of only two new HTML tags, `<applet>` and `<script>`, is all that is required in order to allow a Web page to contain the most complex and interactive interfaces imaginable.

Essential Java∗ is not an exhaustive treatment of the Java language, but rather an in-depth guide to the most important concepts in developing *executable content* for the Web.

Jason Manger (`wombat@spuddy.mew.co.uk`)
Surrey
February 1996

Acknowledgements

I would like to thank my new editor at McGraw-Hill Europe, Maria, for all of her hard-work on the *Essential Java* project. Maria is the only person I know who would listen to me rant on about the Net for hours on end while sipping cappuccino at various London cybercafés. She has promised to hit me very hard if I ever mention the word 'Java' (or any of its derivatives) to her again ;-) . My lips are sealed.

Thanks to everyone else at McGraw-Hill who oversaw this project, including Andrew, Julia, Tessa and Judith.

Introduction

Readership

The priority with this book has been to allow people with little programming knowledge to get to grips with the *Java* and *JavaScript* languages, and ultimately to become proficient in designing interactive hypertext-driven applications. The reader will find it helpful to have had some exposure to a programming language, although in saying this there are ample examples and line-by-line source code explanations in *Essential Java*∗ for the newcomer. Some previous exposure to HTML would also be useful. This book is biased towards Internet developers; HTML authors may want to examine JavaScript as a precursor to learning Java and all that it entails.

Software version information

This book is based upon the Java Developer's Kit (JDK) versions v1.0 beta-1 and v1.0 beta-2. All applets have been tested under these JDK versions. The beta JDK was essentially a *frozen* specification in terms of the classes and methods. Java applets (programs) that adhere to the beta JDK work with Netscape version 2.0, and more Java-aware browsers are sure to follow – it has been announced that Microsoft is now

1

licensing Java technology, as have IBM and a whole host of other companies. The Java applets you learn with this book can be used with *any* future 'Java-aware' browser.

JavaScript is presently a Netscape-based technology and only works with the 32-bit version of Netscape Navigator version 2.0. All of the JavaScript programs have been tested with **Netscape 2.0 beta-6**, the version that became available close to the completion of this book. JavaScript may undergo further changes, although these are not expected to be major. My own personal home page on the Web `http://www.gold.net/users/ag17/index.htm` has details of any changes, including all of the source code examples in the book.

What you will learn...

As mentioned, *Essential Java∗* is not an exhaustive treatment of the Java language – you can expect massive shelf-breaking volumes to appear as Java leaves beta-testing. With *Essential Java∗* you will learn all there is to know about developing interactive applications, since this is primarily what Java and JavaScript offer the end-user. The 'nuts-and-bolts' of designing user interfaces also makes up a large part of this book, where treatment of Java's Abstract Window Toolkit (Awt) is provided. In summary you can expect to learn how to:

- Program in the *Java* language
- Program in the *JavaScript* language
- Develop user interfaces with the Java Awt library
- Write hypertext documents that adhere to HTML 3.0 and the Netscape tag *extensions*

What this book will *not* teach you is how to become proficient in every aspect of the Java language. Only the salient features that allow interactive applications to be built are considered. Needless to say, in learning such skills you will be exposed to much of the Java language, although this book is not an exhaustive treatment of Java.

The **Introduction**, which is what you are reading now, contains details of readership, software versions and installation instructions, among other things. Read this chapter carefully if you need to find and install software such as Netscape 2.0.

Chapters 1–6 cover JavaScript, a scripting language originally developed by Netscape (and named *LiveScript*), and which is now endorsed by Sun – hence the change of name to *JavaScript*. JavaScript is based upon the Java language, but is a much looser implementation. It allows developers to embed scripts within their HTML documents that are activated when they are read into the Netscape Navigator browser. JavaScript may well be adopted by other browsers in the future; Microsoft and IBM have already licensed Java, so JavaScript should be integrated into more and more Web browsers over time. Using JavaScript you can write complete applications that interact with the user locally, and an abundance of source code examples are provided to help you on your way in this respect.

Chapter 7 is an introduction to the Java language and concentrates on core programming principles such as *applets* and *applications, classes, methods, operators, packages, code-blocks* and *flow control*. After reading this chapter you will have a good understanding of how Java programs are constructed and you will be able to write and compile your own Java programs.

Chapter 8 provides an in-depth treatment of Awt, the *Abstract Window Toolkit*. Awt is essentially a library of classes that perform graphical functions. With Awt you can design user interfaces using components such as windows, buttons, pick lists and text areas (for user input), as well as drawing images, and creating animations etc. Awt provides you with the framework to create interfaces into your Java programs and is an essential prerequisite for developing just about any GUI-based system in Java.

Chapter 9 is about threads, Java's mechanism for implementing multitasking operations. Using a thread you can invoke multiple processes to perform certain tasks, for example an image animation. Threads are useful, since they allow your Java programs to run smoothly without hogging the computer.

Finally, **Chapter 10** touches on Java's stream mechanisms. Streams are bidirectional flows of information between objects, such as files and, on a larger scale, remote Internet resources. Streams allow you to read and write to files and to load text and graphics from other computers located on the Internet onto your computer.

A series of appendices have also been provided, covering questions and answers, Java resources, an Awt function reference, mirror-site references (for Netscape and the JDK) and Netscape HTML/JavaScript colour codes.

Where should I start?

If you are a novice programmer, get to grips with the JavaScript language first. JavaScript is based upon Java and the skills you acquire here will boost your confidence. Existing C and C++ programmers will find Java a familiar environment in which to work. Java arrives with a number of standard applets that are basically pre-written routines.

■ Be on the look out for the **J** symbol in the chapters concerned with Java. Wherever you see this you can expect to find a quick recap, a tip, or just general advice.

■   Likewise, wherever you see the **N** symbol you can expect to find tips and explanations regarding the Netscape Navigator 2.0 Web browser.

What software will I need?

To develop programs in Java and JavaScript with the Netscape Web browser you will need a copy of:

■   The **Microsoft Windows 95** operating system (we are assuming that you are developing Java programs under this platform, although this book equally applies to other platforms that use the Java Development Kit)
■   **Netscape 2.0** (Windows 95; 32-bit versions are Java-enabled)
■   **Java Developer's Kit** (Windows 95 platform assumed, i.e. JDK 1.0b2 or the newer 1.0 release)

Microsoft Windows 95 is a commercial product, and is intended as an upgrade for systems such as **Windows 3.x**. Netscape Navigator will eventually be released as a commercial product also, although copies are available for non-profit use on the Internet from Netscape's FTP server at `ftp://ftp.netscape.com`. This book is based on Sun's beta-1 and beta-2 versions of the **Java Developer's Kit** (JDK), which allows applets to run in a Netscape 2.0 environment.

TIP
The earlier alpha versions of the Java run-time are redundant in that without considerable modification they only allow applets to run with the alpha release of the Windows 95 HotJava browser. Ensure that you develop using the most up-to-date JDK.

This book is based on the **Microsoft Windows 95** version of Netscape, and all of the screen displays have therefore been captured from this environment. Netscape 2.0 is available as both a 16-bit and a 32-bit application. Windows 3.x users *must* upgrade, since Java now uses facilities (e.g. multi-threading capabilities) that require a more advanced and robust operating system. Furthermore, the Microsoft Win32 extensions are not sufficient to run the Java run-time. Windows NT users can use the 32-bit version of Java, since their operating system is also based on a 32-bit architecture. The Java language is highly portable, so it is possible to move applets from platform to platform just as long as the host environment (Netscape 2.0 in this book) supports the Java run-time program.

A copy of **Netscape Navigator 2.0** or another browser that is 'Java-aware' will be required if you intend to develop and see Java programs. Netscape currently arrives in two *flavours*, one with Java capability and one without. Java and JavaScript only work with the 32-bit versions of Netscape 2.0 and cannot yet be used outside the Netscape environment. Other companies are now starting to license both Sun and Netscape technology, so we can safely expect other Web browsers to adopt Java and JavaScript in the near future.

TIP

Many Java applets can be run *locally* without an Internet connection, just as long as you use **Netscape Navigator 2.0**. Clearly, this will work only with applets that do not require network connections. In order to run Netscape locally you will need a null-WinSock package such as Netscape's `MOZOCK.DLL` file (which you should then rename to `WINSOCK.DLL`), or alternatively, install a TCP/IP stack such as the popular shareware package Trumpet WinSock and simply configure it not to dial into an Internet service provider. There have been problems running applets locally, since many of Java's features, such as image loading, have been made 'network-aware'. If you need to test applets, upload them to a Web server and then invoke them using an `http://` URL.

Installing Netscape 2.0 and the Java Developer's Kit

The following sections discuss the installation of the Netscape and Java software. Netscape Navigator is made freely available to individuals (please read the `LICENSE` file that accompanies the software). Netscape is a rather strange package, since it is neither freeware or shareware, but rather *demo-ware*. Netscape, as always, have provided evaluation copies of Netscape Navigator 2.0 during its progress through beta-testing. Such copies have expiry dates built into them. Netscape also offer commercial versions of their products. Sun currently offer the Java Developer's Kit (JDK) as freeware. Please read the licence agreement that arrives with the package for more details.

About the CD-ROM with this book

The CD-ROM that accompanies *Essential Java*∗ contains the 1.0b2 and 1.0 versions of the Java Developer's Kit, which will save you the time and trouble of downloading this system from the Internet. A number of applets and other documentation files accompany the JDK.

Installing Netscape Navigator 2.0

Netscape 2.0 for Windows 95 arrives as a self-extracting executable (`.EXE`) file and installation program. This section examines how to install Netscape on a Windows 95-based system.

Downloading Netscape 2.0

Netscape Navigator 2.0 resides at Netscape's Web server located at the address:

```
ftp://ftp.netscape.com/2.0
```

The directory in which the program resides is `/2.0` for Netscape version 2.0N. Enter the `windows` directory for the Microsoft Windows versions of the Netscape program. Netscape exists in a number of forms, both with and without Java support. The file you require for developing Java applications is the 32-bit version. Look for a filename beginning with `N32` and ending in `.EXE` (executable file).

You can use any FTP client to download this file; indeed you could also use the `ftp://` URL in your current version of Netscape (or other Web browser). Windows 95 now has a dedicated FTP client (`FTP.EXE`), which is installed along with the Dial-Up Networking module. You must have already installed the Microsoft 32-bit WinSock (TCP/IP stack) in order to use this facility.

When you invoke a command line FTP client, the `open` command should be used along with the name of the FTP site (`ftp.netscape.com` in this case) that you wish to contact; alternatively, quote the name of the FTP server after the `ftp` command. Once a connection has been made the FTP server will ask you for a username and password. Public FTP sites (or *anonymous* FTP sites as they are known) accept the username `anonymous` so that you can gain limited access to the server in order to download publicly available files, such as the Netscape program. When the server asks you for a password, simply enter your Internet email address in the form `user@host`.

You can now move to the appropriate directory and download Netscape, but be sure to enable *binary* mode for your file download (if you are using Netscape to download this file, binary mode will be invoked automatically). The `binary` command has been used since we are using an interactive FTP program, and the Netscape archive is an executable file (not a 'plain text' file). After this comes the `get` command, along with the name of the file to be downloaded. In the example we have used a *fully qualified* filename, i.e. one that points directly to the file we require.

When the file has been fully transferred to your computer the **ftp>** prompt will return, at which stage you should just type **quit** to end your FTP session. It can take approximately 30 to 40 minutes to download Netscape Navigator 2.0 with a V.34/V.Fast modem, depending on how busy the FTP server actually is.

Figure I.1 shows the initiation of an FTP (File Transfer Protocol) session within a DOS shell window to the site **sunsite.doc.ic.ac.uk** – a Netscape mirror site in the UK that I use to download the Navigator software. The FTP program is now included in Windows 95 as standard. The username **anonymous** is entered (**ftp** is also valid on most FTP servers), and I enter my full email address as a password in the **user@host** format, i.e. **ag17@cityscape.co.uk**. Access is then granted; notice the **ftp>** prompt, which awaits our next command. Refer to Appendix E for a list of Netscape mirror sites around the world.

Next I enable binary mode (with the **bin** command), change directory (**cd**) to where Netscape 2.0 is stored on this server (**cd /computing/information-systems/www/Netscape/2.0/windows**), and then I issue a **dir** (directory) command to see what file(s) are available. Notice the **n32e20.exe** file, which is the 32-bit version of Netscape Navigator 2.0. The file is then downloaded to our machine using the **get** command. If you need to save the file to another directory use the **lcd** command (local change directory) with the name of the local directory in which you want to save the Netscape program. For example, **lcd c:\temp** would save all subsequent files into the **c:\temp** directory on your computer's C drive (hard disk). Type **quit** to end the FTP session when the download is completed. You can then run the **n32e20.exe** program and install Netscape.

Figure I.2 illustrates all of these commands and the responses from the server (such responses have a numeric code prefixing them; all lines with **ftp>** represent commands typed to the FTP program in order to control the server).

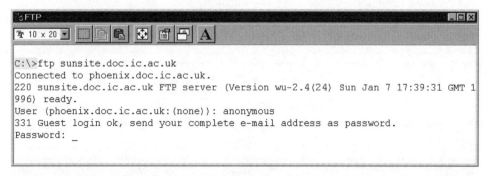

FIGURE I.1 *Starting an FTP session to a Netscape 2.0 mirror site.*

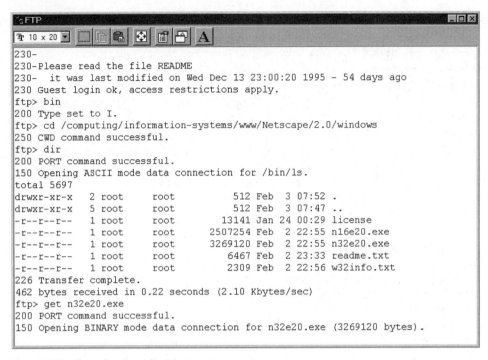

```
230-
230-Please read the file README
230-  it was last modified on Wed Dec 13 23:00:20 1995 - 54 days ago
230 Guest login ok, access restrictions apply.
ftp> bin
200 Type set to I.
ftp> cd /computing/information-systems/www/Netscape/2.0/windows
250 CWD command successful.
ftp> dir
200 PORT command successful.
150 Opening ASCII mode data connection for /bin/ls.
total 5697
drwxr-xr-x  2 root     root            512 Feb  3 07:52 .
drwxr-xr-x  5 root     root            512 Feb  3 07:47 ..
-r--r--r--  1 root     root          13141 Jan 24 00:29 license
-r--r--r--  1 root     root        2507254 Feb  2 22:55 n16e20.exe
-r--r--r--  1 root     root        3269120 Feb  2 22:55 n32e20.exe
-r--r--r--  1 root     root           6467 Feb  2 23:33 readme.txt
-r--r--r--  1 root     root           2309 Feb  2 22:56 w32info.txt
226 Transfer complete.
462 bytes received in 0.22 seconds (2.10 Kbytes/sec)
ftp> get n32e20.exe
200 PORT command successful.
150 Opening BINARY mode data connection for n32e20.exe (3269120 bytes).
```

FIGURE 1.2 *Downloading the Netscape program.*

Problems accessing Netscape's FTP server?

Netscape's server can become *very* busy (it is one of the most popular Internet sites) so you may have to keep reconnecting to their server if it has reached its maximum user-load. For this reason it is best to contact a *mirror site*. Mirror sites are duplicate file systems that exist in various countries around the world. For example, a UK user should contact the Netscape mirror site at `sunsite.doc.ic.ac.uk` rather than `ftp.netscape.com`, since the former is much nearer and response times will be significantly faster. Alternatively, look closely at the screen when you are denied access, since Netscape's FTP server will list all of the main mirror sites that exist.

TIP
Netscape's FTP server `ftp.netscape.com` is always busy and results in slow downloads. Try the machines `ftp2` through `ftp10` as well, or better still, use a *mirror site* that is located even nearer to home. (See Appendix E

for a list of Netscape mirror sites.) Netscape is normally stored immediately below the root directory in the directory named `/2.0`. Make sure that you enable *binary* mode for all downloads! Back up your copy of Netscape just in case you delete a component accidentally.

The installation of Netscape 2.0 is simplicity itself, since the main `.EXE` file now runs a setup system for the Netscape program. Copy the Netscape `.EXE` file that you have downloaded into a separate directory and then run it (either from a DOS prompt or from the *Start/Run* menu in Windows 95). After installing Netscape you should run the appropriate Netscape icon (the Windows 95 installation will create a new group window for you) and enter the *Options/Preferences* menu to provide details such as your email address and news server. The installation process will create a new folder group and Netscape icon (plus a link to the Netscape `READ.ME` file).

TIP

See Appendix E for a list of mirror sites that have Netscape 2.0. Mirror sites are duplicates of Netscape's FTP server, and can speed up your downloading operation considerably. There is also a clever Web page at Netscape's home server that will find the nearest mirror site with the latest copy of Netscape.

Installing Java

This section examines how to obtain and install the Java Developer's Kit. The JDK allows you to develop programs in the Java language, and contains the necessary tools and libraries to accomplish this.

TIP

The Java Developer's Kit is already on the CD-ROM that accompanies this book. Use the information in this section if you need to get the most recent JDK. You can find out which is the most recent JDK by visiting `http://java.sun.com` for version information (this is normally to be found on the first page at Sun's Java site).

Downloading and installing the JDK

If you intend to develop Java programs you will need access to the Java run-time program and libraries. These provide you with a development environment consisting of the Java compiler (`JAVAC.EXE`), interpreter (`JAVA.EXE`) and AppletViewer (`APPLETVIEWER.EXE`), as well as the Java class libraries, which contain all of the features that will enable you to build Java applications. Java was developed at Sun Microsystems, and their main FTP server is located at:

`ftp://ftp.javasoft.com`

The process of obtaining the Java run-time is similar to that for Netscape. The file is a self-extracting archive, as with Netscape. Using an appropriate FTP client, log in to `ftp.javasoft.com` and enter *anonymous* as a username. Then enter your full email address as a password. The version of the JDK for Windows 95 used for writing this book was named:

`JDK-beta2-win32-x86.exe`

although this will change as new releases are made available on the Internet.

TIP
This filename may change by the time this book is published. Whatever the filename, look for the characters `win32-x86`, which specify that the software is for a 32-bit version of Windows and runs on x86-based CPUs (i.e. 80486 and Pentium-based personal computers).

This file resides in the `/pub` directory. The file is just under 3 Mbyte in size. After you have downloaded the file, place it in the root directory of your hard disk (e.g. `c:\`), and then run the file. This will create a series of subdirectories below the directory `\JAVA` into which the various components of the Java development system will be installed. After the archive has finished executing you can back up and then delete it.

TIP
See Appendix D for a list of mirror sites that contain the JDK system.

Modifying your system's **PATH** and **CLASSPATH** variables

You should now alter your Windows 95 **PATH** variable (located in
AUTOEXEC.BAT) to include the directory **X:\JAVA\BIN**, where **X:** is your hard
disk drive letter. This latter directory is where the Java compiler and other utilities
are stored. You will need to use the utilities in this directory to make your own
Java applets. Including this directory in the **PATH** ensures that they can be
conveniently accessed from within any directory on your computer. For example
you could have the statement:

```
PATH=C:\DOS;C:\WINDOWS;C:\JAVA\BIN
```

TIP

You do not have to modify your **PATH** statement to include **\JAVA\BIN**,
although it makes sense in order to dispense with the need to keep typing
fully qualified pathnames to access the various Java tools (e.g. compiler,
interpreter and AppletViewer). To speed things up even more why not create
a DOS batch file, perhaps named **av.bat**, that invokes the AppletViewer.
This will save you typing in this horrendously long filename, for example:

```
c:\java\bin\appletviewer.exe %1
```

where **%1** represents the applet's HTML file that you want to invoke. Going
further still, you could of course rename **appletviewer.exe** to **av.exe**
;-). You can also 'launch' applets from the desktop using AppletViewer –
see Chapter 2 for more information on this.

TIP

Archie can be used to find files on the Web. Use a search engine such as
Infoseek (**http://www2.infoseek.com**) and search for **"archie"** to
find an Archie Web gateway.

TIP

The first release of the Java Developer's Kit (JDK) is now available on Sun's
FTP server (**ftp.javasoft.com**) in the directory **/pub** as the file
JDK-1_0-win32-x86.exe.

Support for ZIP files in the JDK

The JDK v1.0b2 introduced support for *compressed class files*, allowing classes to be imported from a ZIP-based archive (created using shareware packages such as WinZip or PKZIP), rather than unzipping every class – which can consume a large amount of disk space. The **JAVAC.EXE** compiler and run-time loader have been modified to deal with ZIP-based archives. Note that the JDK installation installs the compressed class system by default. A file called **CLASSES.ZIP** now includes all of the standard Java classes. You will need to add a system variable **CLASSPATH** to point to this file, for example:

```
SET CLASSPATH=.;X:\DEMO\CLASSES;X:\JAVA\CLASSES.ZIP
```

so that whenever you use a certain class within a Java program, the compiler uses **X:\JAVA\CLASSES.ZIP** to load the appropriate class file. Be sure to place your own *development* directory (where you are creating applets etc.) into the **CLASSPATH** variable also, as with **X:\DEMO\CLASSES** in the above example. The **CLASSES.ZIP** file is placed in the **LIB** subdirectory after decompressing the JDK archive.

If you do not want to use the **CLASSES.ZIP** file, but would prefer to see all of the classes, simply create a **CLASSES** directory below **\JAVA** and then unzip the **CLASSES.ZIP** file inside this. You can then back up and delete the **.ZIP** archive. Now you must modify your **CLASSPATH** statement to point to this directory, for example:

```
SET CLASSPATH=.;X:\DEMO\CLASSES;X:\JAVA\CLASSES
```

TIP
The '**.**' entry in the **CLASSPATH** statement is quoted so that the current directory is searched when a class is being located, effectively allowing applets to be developed in any directory of your choice, and not just those defined in the **CLASSPATH** variable.

If you want to use *both* ZIP-based archives and unzipped archives, simply alter the **CLASSPATH** directory to accommodate both the ZIP file and the directory name, for example:

```
SET CLASSPATH=.;X:\JAVA\CLASSES.ZIP;X:\DEMO\CLASSES
```

TIP
You can manage projects better by zipping up only those classes that are used in your applets/applications, but beware – the Java compiler cannot (yet) extract ZIP files that use PKZIP's proprietary *'compress'* format.

TIP
Netscape 2.0b4 also uses compressed classes. These are stored in the **CLASSES** subdirectory where Netscape is installed. Do not decompress this file, however, since this is not an installation requirement.

Adding a **HOME** variable and creating a **.hotjava** directory

Finally, many of the tools in the Java Developer's Kit look for a **HOME** directory in which saved configuration information is placed. Place a suitable (and permanent) entry for **HOME** in your **\AUTOEXEC.BAT** file as follows:

```
SET HOME=C:\JAVA
```

which uses **\JAVA** to save configuration information.

The actual configuration information that is saved is similar in format to a Windows **.INI** file. The directory **.hotjava** (note the '**.**' at the start) is used for this purpose, and should be placed in the directory pointed to by the **HOME** variable. For example, if **HOME** is set to **C:\JAVA**, ensure that you create a **.hotjava** directory within this directory, for example using the DOS command:

```
MKDIR C:\JAVA\.hotjava
```

You have now installed the JDK and are ready to develop Java programs.

Where do I go for more help?

Try McGraw-Hill's European home page at **http://www.mcgraw-hill.co.uk** – click on 'Computing' within the editorial information page. Or you can of course email me at **wombat@spuddy.mew.co.uk** for a chat. The appendices list a number of other Java resources where you can obtain all kinds of information on Java-related topics.

PART

1

JavaScript

CHAPTER

1

A JavaScript primer

In this chapter you will learn:

- What the JavaScript language can be used for
- How to embed JavaScript code in an HTML document
- What JavaScript objects and methods are
- What JavaScript expressions are

Developing executable content with JavaScript

JavaScript (also known as '*Mocha*', after Java, and the *Netscape Scripting Language* to others) is a programming language that allows executable content to be built into HTML documents. It is effectively a cut-down programming language based loosely upon Java, although not nearly as complex. JavaScript effectively bridges the gap between HTML authoring and Java programming, allowing non-programmers to develop executable content without becoming too deeply involved in a complex programming language.

More importantly, JavaScript is a *Netscape-aware* language; it is closely tied to the Netscape user interface. JavaScript programs are self-contained programs and are embedded within an HTML document. A JavaScript program is *interpreted* by the Netscape browser when a document containing a script is loaded, as opposed to Java applets which are stored separately from the HTML that invokes them, and which are compiled into a neutral 'byte-code' format using the Java compiler.

The only standard interactive mechanisms available to HTML authors in HTML 2.0 and 3.0 are hyperlinks and fill-out-forms. These HTML-based facilities have been considerably enhanced in Netscape 2.0, allowing full interaction with JavaScript programs. Programs written in JavaScript can perform a variety of tasks and can be as simple or as complex as is required. The Net-novice phrase 'HTML programming' results in many a *flame war* on the Internet, although it could now be argued (and probably will be) that, for the first time, HTML now does at least include some significant 'programmable content', albeit Netscape-enhanced. You can expect JavaScript to appear in many other Web browsers soon.

TIP

JavaScript was formerly known as *LiveScript* (named after Netscape's 'LiveWire' project to create a complete program development environment for the Web). Netscape developed JavaScript in late 1995, and to date some 30 companies have endorsed use of the JavaScript language and interpreter.

Java versus JavaScript

The main difference between Java and JavaScript lies in the size and complexity of the two languages. JavaScript is a looser implementation of Java – so variables can be left undeclared for example, and data-type casting is easier. In addition, JavaScript source code is not compiled, unlike Java applets: JavaScript is an *interpreted* language. The JavaScript interpreter reads JavaScript programs line by line and points out errors on this basis (rather than all at once, as with the Java compiler). Java source code must be compiled into byte-code format before it can be used, and hence JavaScript programs can be designed and tested much more quickly.

JavaScript, like Java, is also an *object-based* language, although it has no classes or inbuilt inheritance mechanisms, which Java uses as standard. Java programs consist of object *classes*, and are fully object-orientated. Both Java and JavaScript are also *secure* in that data cannot be written to a hard disk from an unknown source. The portability of both systems is a slightly different affair. Compiled Java code will run in any 'Java-aware' browser (currently Netscape and Sun's HotJava are the only such browsers). JavaScript requires the 32-bit version of Netscape 2.0 to function, although other browsers are expected to integrate JavaScript very soon (e.g. Microsoft's Internet Explorer).

What can I use JavaScript for?

All of the events generated by the Netscape Navigator browser, such as button clicking, field processing and page navigation, can be detected and acted upon by JavaScript. These events are important since they allow *structure* to be built into an application.

Rather than clicking randomly on hyperlinks, JavaScript can actually detect when a user leaves a particular page and can then invoke a suitable action. JavaScript is also very good at handling routine day-to-day tasks such as data validation, form processing, and string and numeric manipulation – tasks that are just not possible with the existing HTML dialects. It is particularly good at generating dynamic HTML, that is, HTML documents that are created by a JavaScript program rather than by the user. Documents can therefore control their own structure according to pre-defined rules. Most importantly, JavaScript can do away with static HTML pages. Here are the main uses of the JavaScript language:

- Generating HTML 'on-the-fly' from within a program
- Validating fields in an HTML form prior to submitting them to a server
- Obtaining *local* user input to control JavaScript actions
- Allow the user to make choices to invoke various actions within the browser
- Showing properly windowed messages to the user (e.g. warnings)
- Local form processing, local user input and other housekeeping tasks

Novice programmers will find it beneficial to learn JavaScript in order to prepare for the more complex and substantial Java language. JavaScript and Java are both programming languages in their own right and share similar facilities; indeed, the general *look and feel* of JavaScript has been closely modelled upon the Java language. Java code consists of *classes* and their *methods*, and is a more complex language than JavaScript because there is a requirement for declaring classes and writing class-methods.

It is important to distinguish the uses for each programming environment. The JavaScript language was never designed to be a replacement for Java; ideally it should be used to complement Java by allowing the overall environment for a Web application to be put together and presented to the user. Java is mainly used for 'heavy duty' work, such as the design of graphical user interfaces – see Chapter 8 on

Awt – while JavaScript is really a *foundation builder* that links together the building blocks of an application.

JavaScript is also far less strict in terms of syntax and type-checking. The Java compile-time system is made up of *classes* that are built by *declarations*. JavaScript is made up of a run-time system (i.e. no object code is produced) based upon a small number of primitive types, including the string, numeric and boolean types. Primitive types can also be composed into objects by setting their properties with the assignment operator. The key point to remember when developing scripts is that Web 'pages' are rapidly becoming a thing of the past; the emphasis now is on complete 'applications' that are *glued* together using technologies such as Java, JavaScript and HTML.

Using the new Netscape 2.0 `mocha:` URL

The `mocha:` URL (named after JavaScript's Java coffee connections) is new to Netscape 2.0, and allows JavaScript *expressions* to be entered and their results to be seen directly on the screen by the user. For example, you could type in a JavaScript function to see the output that it actually generates within the Netscape browser.

The `mocha:` URL can also be launched with an expression directly, e.g. `mocha:alert("Hello World!")` where `alert()` is the JavaScript function to invoke – in this case to display a warning box in its own window with the message *Hello World!*. The `mocha:` feature is not intended for use as a script debugging tool; rather it is a tool to allow simple JavaScript statements and expressions to be seen in *real time*.

The `mocha:` URL has also been implemented in Netscape 2.0N as the (more sensible) `javascript:` URL. Both work identically.

TIP
The `mocha:` URL is used to view the output of single JavaScript statements, such as function calls and the like. It cannot be used in conjunction with a JavaScript program loaded into Netscape, since the URL opens a new page (or rather *screen*) by default. It is possible to invoke `mocha:` within a Netscape `<frameset>..</frameset>` tag, although variables will not be accessible to the frame in which `mocha:` is invoked.

TIP
The output from `mocha:` can be confusing. In order to see the value of a JavaScript expression you should first assign it to a variable, for example:

```
var myVariable = expr("10 * 10");
```

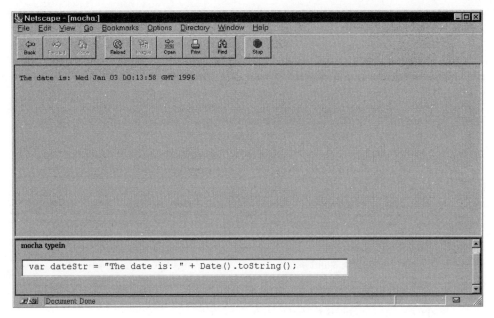

FIGURE 1.1 *The* `mocha:` *URL in action with a simple JavaScript string expression.*

Netscape will then examine the syntax of the expression, and print its value in the top half of the screen, along with the word `true` (most methods return `true` after being called successfully). Figure 1.1 illustrates the `mocha:` URL in action with a simple JavaScript expression.

Embedding JavaScript programs within HTML documents

JavaScript programs are either embedded within an HTML page. A new HTML tag called `<script>` has been introduced to Netscape 2.0, which allows the browser to reference the JavaScript program and then execute it accordingly. The HTML tag `<script>` is a container and requires a `</script>` to mark the end of the script body. The actual source code for a script is placed within the container accordingly.

Scripts can appear anywhere within an HTML document, but it is important to remember not to place literal HTML and JavaScript statements together – otherwise the results may not be as you intended. JavaScript statements can generate HTML dynamically, however, as will be shown in later sections. When Netscape encounters a `<script>` container it *parses* the contents of the container line-by-line. If at this stage an error is encountered it will be displayed on the screen, along with the line number of the offending statement.

TIP

It is recommended that JavaScript programs are placed within the HTML `<head>..</head>` container, since this is one of the first tags that is read into the browser. In theory, scripts can be placed anywhere within an HTML document (see examples below), although it is advisable to place your main script within the HTML document header container, as you will see in the many examples throughout this book. It really depends on what you are doing with your scripts. If scripts are used to create HTML dynamically, that is to say that you intersperse `<script>` containers throughout your HTML text to generate program or system values, this would be a quite valid arrangement. However, if you are defining functions to carry out various tasks, these are best placed within a single `<script>` container at the beginning of your document. You will learn all about JavaScript functions in the coming chapters.

The syntax for the `<script>` tag is as follows:

```
<script [language="JavaScript"]>
JavaScript-statements...
</script>
```

where `language` must currently be set to the value `"JavaScript"` (using the exact case shown) for all JavaScript scripts. The `language` attribute is optional in Netscape 2.0b6, but this may change in the future, so it is recommended that you use this attribute for all development in the meantime, at least. Examples of these syntaxes are shown later. The text that appears outside of the `<script>..</script>` container should all be pure HTML. You can have more than one JavaScript program within an HTML file's body; multiple JavaScript programs are executed in the order they appear in (in top-to-bottom fashion). JavaScript programs that are loaded into Netscape are evaluated after the HTML page that contains the `<script>..</script>` container has been loaded, and not before. Functions are loaded into memory and are only executed within Netscape when an event is generated, or when a call is explicitly made to a JavaScript function (or other user-defined function – *functions* being groups of JavaScript statements in this context).

TIP
JavaScript (like Java) is a case-sensitive language, so be sure to specify all strings using the exact case (e.g. `"JavaScript"` is not the same as `"Javascript"`).

For example, we could have:

```
<html>
<head>
<title>Title of document</title>
<script language="JavaScript">
document.alert("Welcome to my page!");
</script>
</head>
<body>
Here is the body text...
</body>
</html>
```

or we could have multiple scripts embedded within an HTML document, for example:

```
The date today is:<b>
<script language="JavaScript">
document.write(Date())
</script></b>.
The location of this document is: <b><tt><script
  language="JavaScript">document.write(document.location)
</script></b></tt>.<p>

<p>Here is a dynamically created HTML table:
<script language="JavaScript">
document.write("<dl><dd><table border><tr>
  <td>Cell 1</td>");
document.write("<td>Cell 2</td></tr>");
document.write("<tr rowspan=2><td>Cell 3</td></tr>");
document.write("</table></dl><p>");
</script>
<script language="JavaScript">
document.write("If it is a Friday");
if (Date().substring(0,3) == "Fri")
```

```
    document.write(" <blink><font color=Red>this</font>
    </blink> ");
else
    document.write(" this ");
document.write("word will be red and blinking.");
</script>
```

In fact, both of these examples are Netscape 2.0-compatible only, since the browser must support JavaScript in order to run these scripts. As you will see below, it is best to encapsulate the script within an HTML comment container so that the script does not appear literally within other browsers.

You won't yet understand the JavaScript statements shown in the examples above – these details are covered in this and later chapters (the examples merely illustrate *where* `<script>` tags are allowed to appear within an HTML document). As you will come to see, it is possible to use a single `<script>..</script>` container that contains a number of JavaScript *functions* that can carry out the same tasks as multiple scripts. However, if you need to create 'dynamic HTML' – as with the example above – the use of multiple scripts in this way is quite valid. As long as the results work locally for you with Netscape 2.0, they will also work for anyone using the same browser. Be sure to mention that your page is JavaScript-compliant (or Netscape 2.0-compliant) if you plan to use these features within your hypertext documents.

Ensuring backwards compatibility with other Web browsers

Literal use of the `<script>..</script>` container is *not* recommended, since HTML authors should never assume that a person reading their hypertext pages will be using a specific version of the Netscape browser (version 2.0 in this case). The problem of browser versions plagues the Web community and arises from the fact that different browsers now have different (indeed vastly different) capabilities. JavaScript does actually have the ability to detect the client browser being used via a dedicated system variable, although the Web browser must of course be 'JavaScript-compatible' in the first place in order to detect such instances! We therefore end up with the archetypal *chicken-and-egg* style problem. It is important to remember that Netscape 1.x is already the browser of choice for over 70% of Web users currently using the Internet (according to recent independent studies) and it can be safely assumed that most of these people will upgrade to version 2.0 in the near future, if not already.

Because Netscape 2.0 is designed to understand the `<script>` tag, it can prepare itself for any source code that it will need to run as a result. More importantly, Netscape 2.0 allows JavaScript code to be included *within* an HTML comment and still be properly interpreted. As you may know already, HTML comments take the general form:

```
<!— this is an HTML comment on a single line —>
```

HTML versions 2 and 3 allow a comment to span multiple lines, for example:

```
<!—
this is an HTML comment container spanning
four lines
—>
```

In order to overcome the problem of browsers other than Netscape 2.0 reading JavaScript embedded files *all* JavaScript code should be placed within an HTML comment container. The `<script>` and `</script>` container tags should *not* be commented, however. In this way, non-Netscape 2.0 browsers will simply ignore the script and its output will never be seen (other Web browsers will ignore tags they do not recognize). Java applets can overcome this similar problem because the applet source code is physically separated from the file that invokes it. This is clearly not the case with a JavaScript embedded HTML file. A non-Netscape 2.0 browser that parses the `<script>` tag will ignore it, simply because the tag isn't recognized. Our newly modified 'JavaScript-aware' HTML file now resembles that shown below, and is said to be *backwards compatible* with other Web browsers:

```
<script language="JavaScript">
<!-- Start of script statements:
[JavaScript statements]
<!-- End of script statements -->
</script>
```

When Netscape 2.0 encounters a `<script>` tag, it is evaluated immediately and all functions and variables are placed into storage. We shall of course be examining such functions later on, so that you can build your own JavaScript programs from scratch.

TIP
Place your JavaScript code within a pair of HTML comments, otherwise people who are using Netscape version 1.x (or another non JavaScript-aware browser) will see the literal statements that make up the program.

Testing your JavaScript programs with Netscape

In order to test your JavaScript programs simply load the HTML file containing the script into Netscape 2.0. You can do this in one of two ways:

- Use the *File/Open* option to open a local file from disk, i.e. the JavaScript/HTML file
- Use the Netscape `file:` URL to open a local file directly

In the case of the second option, simply enter a URL of the form:

```
file:///drive|/directory/filename
```

For example:

```
file:///c|/JavaScript/examples/button1.html
```

which will load the HTML file named `button1.html` from the directory `c:\JavaScript\examples`. The \ and / slashes can be used interchangeably as directory-level separators, although the `file:///drive|` part must be left intact. The file will then be read into Netscape, and you will see the status bar message change to *Reading File...* accordingly. If any errors are detected they will be shown to you on the screen in a window. Note the line number of the offending message in such instances so that you can quickly locate and correct the error. Netscape 2.0 also understands the shorter `file:` URL (originally implemented in Netscape 1.2) of the form:

```
file:/drive|/directory/filename
```

 TIP
Any errors that exist in a JavaScript program will be shown via a dialog box when the script is read into the Netscape browser. All errors cause the program to be stopped at that point, perhaps even stoppping execution. There are no *warnings* as such in JavaScript.

Dealing with JavaScript errors

JavaScript issues an *alert* whenever an error is detected within a script. Scripts in `<script>..</script>` are read into memory before being executed and are parsed for syntactical errors. If an error is detected Netscape provides a small dialog box with the name of the file in which the error occurred (along with a URL

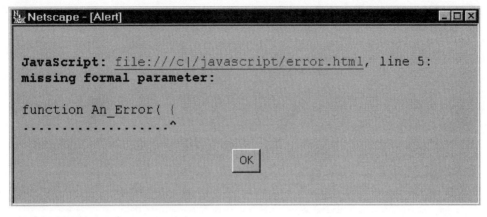

FIGURE 1.2 *A typical JavaScript alert.*

to actually load the file if required), a description of the offending error, and a line number where the error occurred. Figure 1.2 illustrates a typical JavaScript alert.

In order to clear an alert simply press the OK button provided. Multiple alerts will be displayed if there are multiple errors. Netscape will then load the body of your hypertext document, although if an error has been trapped and you still try to use your application, it clearly will not function correctly until the error has been dealt with. In Figure 1.2 we can see the error message `missing formal parameter`, which in this case means that we have missed out a right-hand bracket in the JavaScript `function` statement.

JavaScript's error-message descriptions can be difficult to understand, since they are often expressed in a programming nomenclature, although over time you will quickly acquire the skills to find and correct such errors.

A JavaScript language primer

JavaScript is not unlike many existing programming languages and has many similar features. In essence, however, JavaScript was designed with simplicity in mind. The JavaScript language is made up of three main items:

- User-defined and system variables
- JavaScript statements, objects and methods
- Expressions and operators

Variables are containers for values, and can be system or user-defined. Statements are groups of Java keywords that perform specific actions and which are used to control the flow of execution within a program and to perform tasks such as iteration. For example, a simple statement could take the form:

```
document.write("<b>Hello World!</b>");
```

which uses JavaScript's `write()` method to display the emboldened string **Hello World!** in the Netscape browser (HTML tags can be included to achieve whatever layout/appearance effects you require). Here is another statement that assigns the value of 365 to the variable `days`:

```
days = 365;
```

Objects include basic system types such as strings and date values, and are said to have *properties* and *methods*. Properties are values that belong to an object; for example, JavaScript's `Math` object has values for many mathematical constants (e.g. `Math.PI` returns the value for π. *Methods* are similar to *functions* found in other languages. They perform specific actions on data; for example, `Math.sin(8.69)` returns the sine value of the value `8.69`. Some methods return values, while others do not (i.e. they just perform a specific action and exit). JavaScript's built-in objects and methods are covered in greater detail in Chapters 3 and 5 respectively.

JavaScript variables and literals

Variables are classified as system- and user-defined values. In the course of a JavaScript program you will make use of variables to store values and make calculations. Variables can store a variety of values, including:

- Strings: groups of characters
- Numeric values: *integers* and *real* numbers
- Boolean values: *true* and *false* values

A **string** is a collection of characters enclosed in single (`'`) or double quotes (`"`). For example, `"McGraw-Hill"` is a string value, as is `"42"`. In the case that numbers are stored as string values, it is still possible for JavaScript to carry out numeric calculations on them, as described in more detail below. A string can also contain a number of embedded codes that control basic formatting as well, as shown in Table 1.1.

For example, if the string `"Hello\nWorld"` is encountered, the output would in fact appear on two lines when shown on the screen within the browser because of the `\n` (new line) code in the middle. To attract attention to a message you can use `\a`, which sounds an audible 'beep'.

TABLE 1.1 *Embedded string formatting codes*

Code	Meaning
\n	New line character
\t	Tab character
\r	Carriage return code
\f	Form feed code
\a	'Alert' code (issues an audible beep)
\b	Backspace (delete) key

When using strings, be sure to use the same type of quote to encapsulate the string, i.e. the statement:

```
MyString = "Invalid';
```

is not valid under JavaScript and will cause a run-time error.

Numeric values can either be *integer* (whole numbers) or *floating point* values. For example 0, –5 and 38 are integers, while 8.68 and 2.71828 are floating point or *real* numbers.

Boolean, or logical, values are used for *true/false* situations and can only hold the literal values **true** and **false** under JavaScript.

Creating user-defined variables

JavaScript is a loosely implemented language, and variable creation is no exception. Furthermore it is not necessary to state the *type* of the variable in JavaScript. Variables themselves must start with either an alphabetic character (a–z or A–Z) or an '_' underscore character, after which the variable name can contain a combination of letters, numbers and underscores. For example, all of the following variable names are valid in JavaScript:

- ■ `tempVar`
- ■ `NumberOfHits`
- ■ `Days_in_month`

In JavaScript a user-defined variable can be created in one of two ways:

- ■ Using the **var** statement with the assignment operator (=)
- ■ Using an assignment operator (=) to create a variable

The JavaScript **var** statement (meaning 'create **var**iable') is used both to create and to initialize a variable with a given value. The assignment operator (=) is used to store an initial value in the variable, and is optional in JavaScript. For example we could have the statement:

```
var daysInYear = 365;
```

which creates a numeric variable called **daysInYear** that holds the initial value **365**. It is also possible to create a variable without using the **var** statement, for example:

```
Age = 28;
```

although in this instance it is not absolutely clear whether the variable **Age** is in fact a newly created variable; we could have already created the variable **Age** elsewhere in our script and be *overwriting* it with a new value. For the sake of clarity, all new variables should be created using the **var** statement. You do not have to use **var** to refer to such variables, of course. The value contained *within* a variable is termed the *literal representation* of that variable, or just the 'literal', i.e. 28 is the literal of the variable **Age** in the previous example.

It is also possible to create a variable *without* assigning it an initial value, for example:

```
var TempVar;
```

At this stage **TempVar** has no data type. The type of the variable (string, integer etc.) can be set as and when you need to use the variable. In contrast, in languages such as C the type of a variable must be set before using it. Note that in JavaScript you cannot refer to a variable until it has been created – either by using **var** or by assigning a value to a variable directly. It is also possible to change the data type of a variable by reassigning it an appropriate value, although this is not recommended because of the possibility of confusion at a later stage.

TIP
The **var** statement can also be used in the following way:

```
var name="Jason", email="ag17@cityscape.co.uk";
```

thereby allowing multiple variable definitions to be placed on a single line.

Arrays

Arrays are an ordered set of values that are associated with a single variable identifier. In fact, many of the standard object properties in JavaScript are arrays. In JavaScript an array is referenced using the expression:

```
arrayName[index]
```

where `arrayName` is the name of the array, and `index` is a numeric index variable that specifies an *element* within the array. For example, `arrayname[0]` is the first element (note that array indices start at zero (0) in JavaScript). The actual elements of an array can be of any data type, for example strings, numbers, and even other JavaScript objects, such as date objects.

Consider the JavaScript function `MakeArray(n)` shown below, which is used to create n array elements. This function works by using a `for` loop to create the number of array entries that we require (and sets the value of each array to zero to begin with):

```
function MakeArray(n) {
    this.length = n;
    for (var x = 1; x <= n; x++) {
      this[x] = 0;
    }
  return this;
}
```

We could invoke the `MakeArray()` method as follows:

```
myAnimals = new MakeArray(3);
```

which in turn would create three array variables, namely `myAnimals[0]`, `myAnimals[1]`, and `myAnimals[2]` respectively. Notice how the `new` statement has been used to create an instance of the array we require. We can now assign values to our array using the following assignment statements:

```
myAnimals[0] = "Wombat";
myAnimals[1] = "Dingo";
myAnimals[2] = "Koala";
```

Here is a more extensive JavaScript program that uses arrays to print out the properties of a number of JavaScript objects (more can be found on JavaScript's standard objects and properties in Chapters 3 and 5):

```html
<html>
<head>
<script language="JavaScript">
<!—
function MakeArray(n) {
  this.length = n;
  for (var x = 1; x <= n; x++) {
    this[x] = 0;
  }
  return this;
}
function writeData() {
var counter;
  var JavaObjs = new MakeArray(4);
  var objName  = new MakeArray(4);
  JavaObjs[1] = window;
  JavaObjs[2] = document;
  JavaObjs[3] = history
  JavaObjs[4] = Math;

  objName[1] = "window";
  objName[2] = "document"
  objName[3] = "history";
  objName[4] = "Math";
  document.write("<table cellpadding=4 border=1>");
  for (counter = 1; counter <= 4; counter++) {
    document.write("<tr><td align=middle><b>" +
      objName[counter] + "</b></td>");
    for (i in JavaObjs[counter]) {
      document.write("<td align=middle>" + i + "</td>");
    }
    document.write("</tr>");
  }
  document.write("</table>");
}
writeData();
<!—>
</script>
</head>
<body>
</body>
</html>
```

The script above prints the properties of four common JavaScript objects that every hypertext document is automatically given. The results are written into an HTML table for readability using JavaScript's `document.write()` method.

Data type conversions

With JavaScript you do not have to specify the type of a variable when you initially declare it. Furthermore, JavaScript will automatically convert an expression to the data type of the left-hand operand. This is best illustrated with an example. Consider the case where we have declared the following JavaScript variables:

```
var Days = "334";
var DaysinDec = 31;
```

If we now issued the statement:

```
DaysNow = Days + DaysInDec;
```

it would set the value of the variable `DaysNow` to `"33431"` and *not* the numeric value of the expression 334+31. This is because JavaScript converts the variable `DaysinDec` (which initially was a numeric value) into a string value because the left-hand operand (variable `Days`) is also a string value. The end result is that the right-hand operand (`DaysinDec`) is concatenated with the first variable. If you wanted to add the values together in the *numeric* sense, the value of `Days` should be numeric to start with. In the context of our example, the statement:

```
MyValue = DaysinDec + Days;
```

would yield the value 365 because the left-hand operand (the variable `DaysinDec` in this instance) is numeric to begin with).
  Some statements cannot be handled by JavaScript of course; for example:

```
ErrorVal = 365 + "Wombat";
```

since `"Wombat"` cannot be converted into a numeric value. However, the statement:

```
OkVal = 365 - "10";
```

would work, since the left-hand operand is numeric and the value `"10"` (a string) would be converted to a number accordingly.

Using JavaScript expressions

Expressions are combinations of variables, operators and methods that evaluate to a single value. We have already seen examples of expressions that use the assignment operator in the previous section. More advanced expressions in JavaScript include:

- Arithmetic expressions (which evaluate to a single number, e.g. `33`)
- String expressions (which evaluate to a single string value, e.g. `"Marsupial"`)
- Logical or boolean expressions (which evaluate to either `true` or `false`)

Conditional expressions

Conditional expressions include comparisons against the value of certain JavaScript and user-defined variables. The `? (condition) val1 : val2` statement can be used for this purpose; for example:

```
timeType = (hour > 12) ? "PM" : "AM"
```

would assign the string value `"PM"` to the variable `timeType` if the variable `hour` is greater than (>) 12; otherwise `timeType` takes the value `"AM"` instead – thus checking the status of a 24-hour clock in this case.

Assignment expressions

Assignment expressions use operators to assign values to variables. The operators in JavaScript include those shown in Table 1.2.

All of these assignment operators assign values to a left-hand operand based on the value of the right-hand operand. The basic assignment operator (=) assigns the value of the right-hand operand to its left-hand operand; thus:

TABLE 1.2 *Some Javascript operators*

Operator	Meaning
=	Assignment
+=	Add a value and assign
+	Add a value
-=	Subtract a value and assign
-	Subtract
*=	Multiply a value and assign
*	Multiply a value
/=	Divide a value and assign
/	Divide a value

```
x = 45;
```

makes variable **x** take the numeric value 45, while:

```
x = x * 10;
```

increases the value of **x** ten times. Many of JavaScript's assignment operators are shorthand operators. Thus we could have used the statement:

```
x *= 10;
```

instead of the previous (and longer) statement to increase the value of variable **x** by ten times its current amount. All of the other operators work in a similar way.

Simple arithmetic

Simple arithmetic operators include + (addition), − (subtraction), * (multiplication) and / (division). These are used with operands as need arises, for example:

```
hoursInAyear = 24 * 365;
MinutesinAYear = hoursInAyear / 60;
```

Incrementing and decrementing

JavaScript also supports ++ and —— to increase and decrease values by 1. For example:

```
days ++;
```

increases the value of the numeric variable **days** by 1, whereas the JavaScript statement:

```
days ——;
```

decreases the value of the variable **days** by 1.

Comparison operators

JavaScript's comparison operators are identical to those found in other programming languages, and include those shown in Table 1.3.

Notice how the equality operator is == as opposed to a single equals sign (a single equals sign is the assignment operator in both Java and JavaScript). The inequality operator is != in JavaScript, as in the C programming language (mainly because the logical *not* operator in JavaScript is the single exclamation mark). It is therefore possible to test whether a boolean variable is true or false using a conditional expression such as:

TABLE **1.3** *Comparison operators*

Operator	Meaning
==	Equality (equal to)
!=	Inequality (not equal to)
>=	Greater than or equal to
<=	Less than or equal to
>	Greater than
<	Less than

```
if (!selected)
  // 'selected == false' statements
else
  // 'selected == true' statements
```

Used within a JavaScript while loop (to be examined later) we could have the following JavaScript code:

```
<html>
<head>
<script langauge = "JavaScript">
<!——
var stopLoop = false;
var counter = 1;
while (!stopLoop) {
  document.write(counter, " x 10 = ", counter * 10,
  "<br>");
  counter++;
  stopLoop = (counter > 12) ? true : false;
}
<!——>
</script>
</head>
<body>
</body>
</html>
```

which implements a simple multiplication table script. The variable stopLoop is initially set to false, and the while loop keeps running while stopLoop is not true (i.e. !stopLoop). When stopLoop is set to true (after 12 iterations of the loop in this case) the loop terminates and the program exits. You will read more about program loops later, although you can see how the JavaScript **!** operator can be used to good effect. The

```
stopLoop = (counter > 12) ? true : false;
```

statement translates to: *'If the variable counter is greater than 12, set variable stopLoop to true; otherwise set variable stopLoop to false'*, and is a shorthand notation for the longer version:

```
if (counter > 12)
   stopLoop = true;
else
   stopLoop = false;
```

Logical operators

JavaScript's logical operators are **&&** (logical *and*) and **||** (logical *or*) respectively. They are used with boolean values. For example, if we had the three assignment statements:

```
age1 = true;
age2 = false;
age3 = true;
```

the JavaScript expression:

```
age1 || or age2
```

would yield a **true** value, since the expression uses the logical 'or' operator, and only one of the values in the or-expression has to yield **true** in order for a **true** value to be returned. The 'and' operator (**&&**) requires that all values in the expression yield **true** for a **true** value to be returned; thus the expression:

```
age1 && age2
```

would yield a **false** result, since the boolean variable **age2** is set to **false**. You can of course mix values by bracketing off the appropriate parts; for example:

```
if (age1 && age2) || age3 {
   yes();
}
else {
```

```
    no();
}
```

translates to 'Invoke the **yes ( )** function if **age1** and **age2** are both **true** or if just **age3** is **true**; otherwise execute the **no ( )** function'.

String operators
The string operators in JavaScript are + and +=, which can be used to join strings together; for example, if we had the statements:

```
part1 = "Java";
part2 = "Script";
```

then the JavaScript statement:

```
part3 = part1 + part2;
```

would place the string value "**JavaScript**" in the variable **part3** .

Creating user-defined JavaScript objects
The JavaScript language adheres to a simple object-based model in which an *object* is a construct with *properties* that are themselves JavaScript variables. Each object can have a number of *methods* that are associated with it. Aside from JavaScript's built-in objects, it is also possible to implement user-defined objects using JavaScript.

Under JavaScript an object's properties are accessed using the notation:

```
objectName.property
```

where **objectName** is the name of the JavaScript object and **property** is the name of the property we need to access. Properties are defined by assigning them an initial value. For example, we could have an object called **browser** that has the properties **name** and **platform**. You could then assign properties to the newly created **browser** object using JavaScript statements such as:

```
browser.name = "Netscape 2.0";
browser.platform = "Windows 95";
```

Objects are created by using the JavaScript **function** statement. You will learn all about functions later on, although in this context we would need the following source code to create and initialize the **browser** object:

```
function browser(name, platform) {
```

```
   this.name = name;
   this.platform = platform;
}
...
nscap = new browser("Netscape 2.0", "Windows 95")
```

The special object named `this` is used in JavaScript to refer to the current object. Within the scope of the `browser()` function the value of `this` refers to the current function, hence `this.name` is really a shorthand notation for `browser.name`. The `browser` function here simply defines the structure for a browser object and assigns the values to the `name` and `platform` properties. The statement that actually creates an *instance* of the `browser` object can be seen at the end of the example, where the `nscap` variable calls the `browser()`. Notice the use of the `new` statement to create the object (taken from the Java language). In order to refer to values within an object (i.e. a property of that object) we could use the expression:

```
nscap.platform
```

which in this case would yield the value `"Windows 95"`. Objects can have properties that are other objects. For example, if we had a simple `person` object defined as the following:

```
function person(name) {
   this.person = name;
}
```

we could then create some new `person` objects (named `p1` and `p2`) using the statements:

```
p1 = new person("Jason");
p2 = new person("Maria");
```

Extending the example, if we now had a new object called `emailAddress` that associated an email address with a `person` object, defined as follows:

```
function emailAddress(name, address) {
   this.name = name;
   this.address = address;
}
```

and we created two new `emailAddress` objects as follows:

```
e1 = new emailAddress(p1, "jason@somewhere.com");
e2 = new emailAddress(p2, "maria@sometime.com");
```

we could now ascertain the email address for the person *Jason* using the notation:

```
e1.name.person;
```

You could even create an entirely new JavaScript function to display all of a person's details, as illustrated below with the **showDetails** function:

```
function showDetails() {
  var persDet = "Name: " + this.name + "\n" +
    "email: " + this.address;
  document.write(persDet);
}
```

TIP
A function that is not passed any parameters is defined using an open and closed bracket notation, e.g. **showDetails()**.

By altering the function definition for **emailAddress** to include a reference to the **showDetails** function as follows:

```
function emailAddress(name, address) {
  this.name = name;
  this.address = address;
  this.showDetails = showDetails;
}
```

we can now call the **showDetails** function using the statement:

```
e1.showDetails();
```

Since variable **e1** is associated with an **emailAddress** object (see earlier) that itself refers to a **person** object via the variable **p1**, we can then retrieve the following information:

```
Name: Jason
Email: jason@somewhere.com
```

CHAPTER

2

JavaScript statements

This chapter examines the nuts and bolts of the Java language: JavaScript statements. Statements perform a number of tasks, such as the flow of control within a program and the testing of conditions. In this chapter you will learn how to:

■ Structure your JavaScript programs
■ Create user-defined functions and pass function arguments
■ Control program flow using JavaScript's conditional statements
■ Perform iterative tasks using JavaScript's looping constructs
■ Create user-defined objects with JavaScript

The JavaScript language is made up mainly of *statements*. Statements are made up of a series of language verbs that perform specific tasks. For example, statements control the flow of execution through a program and the creation of variables and user-definable functions, among many other things. JavaScript statements can be delimited with a semicolon (;) for readability, although this remains optional (except in the case where multiple statements are contained within a text-string, i.e. in an event-handler attribute).

// Comment
Syntax: `// Comment`

The `//` (double-slash) statement allows a comment to be entered into the script. Use this statement for single-line comments only.

/* Comment */
Syntax: `/* Comment */`

Similarly, the `/* ... */` can also used for inserting comments into scripts and can be used to span comments over multiple lines, for example:

```
/*
** This is a JavaScript comment on three lines
*/
```

break
Syntax: `break;`

The `break` statement is used with JavaScript's `while` and `for` loops. It terminates the loop at the point the statement is reached, passing control to the next statement immediately after the loop. Consider the small JavaScript program example shown below:

```
<script language="JavaScript">
<!-- hide the script
function Test() {
  var index = 1;
  while (index < 12) {
    if (index == 6)
      break;
    index++;
  }
// The 'break' statement brings us here
}
  <!-- end of script -->
</script>
```

In this example, the variable `index` is initialized to 1, and a `while` loop is set to run while the value of the `index` variable is less than 12 (`index < 12`).

However, the `if` statement in line 3 of the script checks to see if `index` equals 6 (`index == 6`), and when it does the `break` statement terminates the `while` loop. The end result is that the `while` loop will always terminate after six loop iterations, and control will pass to the next statement, as indicated by the final comment in the script. The variable `index` is incremented (`++`) to ensure that it increases in size by one upon each loop iteration.

continue

Syntax: `continue;`

The `continue` statement is used to terminate the execution of a block of statements that exist within a `for` or `while` loop. The `continue` statement continues execution of the loop with the next iteration. In contrast to the `break` statement, it does not terminate the execution of the loop at the point that it is encountered. In a `while` loop it jumps back to the condition, while in a `for` loop it jumps to the update expression.

for

Syntax:

```
for ([initial-expression;] [condition;]
[update-expression]) {
  Statement(s)...
}
```

The `for` statement allows statement *iteration* to be implemented in JavaScript. It is one of the two looping statements in the JavaScript language, the other being `while`. The `for` statement can be used to iterate single or multiple statements. If multiple statements (known as a *code block*) are to be iterated, the `{` and `}` brackets must encapsulate the statements; a single statement can simply be placed by itself without bracketing.

The three parameters to the `for` statement are all optional, and are used to control the execution of the loop. If they all are used a semicolon (`;`) must separate each part, as specified in the syntax description above. In order to start the loop, an `initial-expression` statement is commonly used to initialize a numeric counter variable that is used to track the loop's progress. `Condition` is used to set the scope of the loop, principally the condition under which the statements in the loop are executed, and is also optional. If omitted this evaluates to a `true` condition (useful for infinite loops). The `condition` is evaluated upon every iteration of the loop.

Control passes to the next JavaScript statement (after the loop) when this condition is met.

Finally, we have the **update-expression** which is used to update the loop counter (as normally set in **initial-expression**). Note also that the JavaScript statement **continue** can be used to jump directly to the **update-expression** part of the loop. For example, we could have a loop that sends HTML-formatted text to the browser using the JavaScript **writeln()** function (see the later sections for more detail on JavaScript string functions):

```
<script language="JavaScript">
<!—— hide the script
function Test() {
  var String1 = '<hr align="center" width=';
  for (var size = 5; size <= 100; size+=5)
    document.writeln(String1 + size + '%">');
}
<!—— end of script ——>
</script>
```

In this example, our script outputs a series of horizontal rules (**<hr>**) that increase in size from 5 per cent to 100 per cent in increments of 5 (**+=5**) – making exactly 20 iterations in total. The variable **String1** stores the HTML tag and is updated within the loop to include a new width value via the variable **size**. The end result of each iteration is a new **String1** value that contains a series of **<hr>** tags that increase in width. When the variable **size** reaches 100 the loop exits. Since only one statement is included in the loop, code-block bracketing is not required.

for .. in

Syntax:

```
for (indexVar in objectName) {
  Statement(s)...
}
```

Another variation of the **for** loop is the **for..in** loop, which is used to loop over the properties within the object identified by the variable **objectName**. The index variable **indexVar** stores the current value that has been returned. For example, here is a simple script that shows all of the properties of the JavaScript **window** object:

```
<script language="JavaScript">
<!——
function write_data() {
```

```
document.write("<table cellpadding=4 border=1>" +
               "<tr><td align=middle>" +
               "<b>window</b></td></tr>");
for (i in window) {
   document.write("<td>" + i + "</td>");
}
document.write("</tr></table>");
}
write_data();
<!——>
</script>
```

Notice how the **for** statement loops over the **window** property, and the results are placed into an HTML table structure for readability. The function **write_data()** houses the body of the script in this example, and is called using the final statement in the script so that the results can be seen.

function name(arguments, ...)
Syntax:

```
function functionName(arguments, ...) {
   Statement(s)...
}
```

Functions are found in many programming languages. In essence, a function is a group of JavaScript statements that performs a specific task and then returns a value. The value returned may be formed by some calculation that the function is designed to perform. The **{** and **}** brackets define the *scope* of the function, i.e. the statements that make up the function. Functions can also accept *arguments* – values that are passed to the function for use within it. Multiple arguments are separated by a comma (**,**). In order that a function returns a value, the optional **return** statement should be used with an appropriate value. You can omit the **return** statement if your function does not return a useful value. For example, we could create a very simple function to multiple two numbers together:

```
function multiply(number1, number2) {
   return number1 * number2;
}
```

In the script above the function **multiply** accepts two arguments, **number1** and **number2** – the two numbers that we want to multiply together. The function itself consists of only one statement, namely the **return** statement, which is used to return a value from a function (although optional, since not all functions have to return specific values). The value returned in this instance is the first number multiplied (∗) by the second. In order to call the function with some arguments we could use a file structured as follows:

```
<script language="JavaScript">
<!— hide the script from other browsers
function multiply(number1, number2) {
  return number1 * number2;
}
var result = multiply(10, 10);
document.write(result);
<!—end—>
</script>
```

The script above writes out the result 100 (10 multiplied by 10) on the browser's screen. Clearly, functions come in all shapes and sizes; try to use them to process repetitive tasks so that you alleviate the duplication of source code. This example also shows that statements can exist outside of functions, although it should be avoided if possible – try to call functions using JavaScript's event-handling attributes (described in greater detail later).

As an extension of the previous example consider this script, which performs the same operation except that it displays a more readable final result. Notice how the two arguments passed to the `multiply()` function are strings, rather than literal numbers. This allows the numbers to be output as a string:

```
<script language="JavaScript">
<!— hide the script from other browsers
function multiply(number1, number2) {
  document.write(number1 + " multiplied by "
    + number2 + " = "
    + (number1 * number2));
}
multiply("10", "10");
<!— end of script —>
</script>
```

TIP

Notice how numbers stored as strings are passed to a function that carries out numeric calculations. JavaScript's loose data type casting makes this possible, and it can be very convenient for the programmer, since there is no need to keep changing between string and numeric data types.

Functions are read into Netscape as soon as they are encountered, but are not executed immediately (unless a specific statement to invoke a function is encountered). In this way you can store up statements ready to execute according to user events that happen later on, e.g. user input or page loading. If you need to execute some JavaScript functions without giving the user the choice, simply include them outside of any `function` statements, as in the previous example which calls the function `multiply()` without asking the user.

TIP
It is advisable to place your JavaScript programs in the `<head>..<./head>` container of your hypertext document. This will ensure that all of your functions and other JavaScript statements are read into memory as soon as the document is loaded into Netscape. Even though I have done it above, it is best to try to avoid issuing statements *outside* the scope of a function. Try to use one of JavaScript's event-handling attributes instead (covered later) to invoke the function from a user interface object, such as a button. Of course, there will be some cases where you will *have* to invoke functions in a compulsory way, particularly where there is no way to invoke the action you require through a user-controllable object. As a rule of thumb you may want to make functions that are optional controllable by the user.

if .. else
Syntax: if (condition) { statements1 } [else { statements2 }]

The `if .. else` statement is a conditional statement that allows blocks of JavaScript statements to be executed depending on a user-defined condition. The `condition` part of the `if` statement is an expression that when held `true` executes the JavaScript statements in the code block `statements1`.

A code block must be enclosed in { and } brackets; single statements do not require this, however. The optional `else` part of the `if` statement allows the code block identified by `statements2` to be executed if the main `if` statement's `condition` is held `false`, i.e. if the condition is not met. It is also possible to *nest* `if` statements inside each other.

The example JavaScript program below defines a function called `Validate()` that uses an `if` statement to check a person's age entered via an HTML form. (You will learn all about form processing with JavaScript later.) The `onClick` attribute of the `<input>` tag is new to Netscape 2.0 and allows JavaScript statements (and therefore functions) to be called when a form button is clicked upon. In JavaScript it is possible for a form field within an HTML document to be referenced using the expression `this.form.fieldname`, where `this.form` refers to the current form and `fieldname` is the field in the form we need to reference (as identified by the `name` attribute). A JavaScript function that is passed the name of a form field uses the `value` keyword to obtain the value of the field passed to it, as in the `Validate()` function below:

```
<html>
<head>
<script language="JavaScript">
<!— hide the script from other browsers
function Validate(form) {
  if (form.value >= 50) {
    alert("You do not qualify for this policy");
  }
  else {
    // More statements etc...
  }
}
<!— end of script —>
</script>
</head>
<body>
<form name="myForm">
Name: <input type="text" size=30 name="name">
Age:  <input type="text" size=5  name="age"><hr>
<input type="button" value="Submit details"
   onClick="Validate(this.form.age)">
</form>
</body>
</html>
```

This script is slightly different from previous examples in that it calls a JavaScript function from within the **<body>** part of the HTML document. Remember that you cannot mix JavaScript statements and HTML tags together within the **<script>..</script>** container. Anything placed within an HTML **<body>..</body>** container will of course still be displayed, so bear in mind how your output will look when outputting such text. In the example, the function `Validate()` checks the form field named **age**. If the value entered into this field is less than 50 the user is shown further details, otherwise they are told that there is a problem and the `alert()` function in JavaScript displays a suitable warning message in a window. Other statements can now be placed accordingly, depending on the actions you require.

return

Syntax: `return value;`

The `return` statement is used within a `function` to return a specific `value` or expression. Its use is optional within JavaScript functions. For example, a function could return a boolean (`true`/`false`) value, which could then be used by an `if` statement:

```
...
function CheckAge(age) {
  if (age > 65)
    return false;
  else
    return true;
}
...
if CheckAge(this.form.age) {
  // True returned so OK.
}
  else {
// False returned, so not OK.
}
```

Likewise, a JavaScript expression could also be returned by a function, for example:

```
return (hours / 60);
```

this

Syntax: `this.objName;`

The `this` statement is used to refer to the object `objName` in a method. For example, a field within an HTML form could be referenced by using the notation `this.form.fieldname`. The `this` statement is very useful in the creation of new objects, as well as referencing properties from within JavaScript functions. It is also used to identify an object unambiguously by *binding* it within the scope of the current object. For example, a `<form name="myForm">` tag is a form object with the name `myForm`; therefore any reference to `this.form.objectName` refers to the current HTML form, where `objectName` is the name of an object within the form, e.g. a text area field.

TIP

The `this` statement *cannot* be used outside the scope of a JavaScript function, otherwise a run-time error will occur.

---

var

Syntax: `var VarName [= value|expression];`

The **var** statement creates a new variable identified by **VarName**. The variable will be either *global* or *local* depending on the location of the **var** statement. The programmer may assign a literal value or an expression to the variable created.

It is possible to omit the **var** statement when assigning a value to a variable, although variables created without **var** are made into *global* variables. For example, in the script below, the variable **myVar** is defined twice with two unique values, once within a function and once outside a function. Since both variables are created using **var**, both values can be obtained by specifying the **this** statement. Hence, **this.myVar** is the value **"Hello 1"** (**this** applies to the script as a whole in this instance), while **myVar** by itself is **"Hello 2"**.

```
<script language="JavaScript">
<!—
var myVar = "Hello 1";
function Test() {
  var myVar = "Hello 2";
  document.writeln(this.myVar + "\n");
  document.writeln(myVar);
}
Test();
<!—>
</script>
```

However, if we omit the **this** statement two **"Hello 2"** values are printed, since the value of **myVar** is taken from the scope of the current function.

Finally, by omitting the **var** statements completely, to leave the following:

```
<script language="JavaScript">
<!—
myVar = "Hello 1";
function Test2() {
  myVar = "Hello 2";
```

```
    document.writeln(this.myVar + "\n");
    document.writeln(myVar);
}
Test2();
<!—>
</script>
```

the first instance of the variable **myVar** will be used throughout, since it will be assumed as a *global* variable with scope of the *entire* script. Thus **myVar** will first take the value "**Hello 1**", which will then be overwritten in function **Test()** with the value "**Hello 2**". Here are some further examples of **var** in general use:

```
// Creates a local variable call '_TempVar' and
// assigns no initial value:
var _TempVar;

// Creates the local variable 'Days' and assigns it the
// value of a simple numeric expression:
var Days = (365 / 12);

// This is the same as the previous, except Days is now
// a global variable:
Days = (365 / 12);

// Creates the local variable 'name' whose value is
// taken from the hypothetical Getname() function:
var name = GetName("Jason");
```

TIP

The *scope* of variables created with **var** (and by direct assignment) depends on the whereabouts of the statement. If **var** is used outside of a function, the variable will be accessible to the entire application, although variables created *within* functions are only available for use within that function, i.e. they are *local* to the function, rather than *global*, for example:

```
<script language="JavaScript">
<!— start
function TestFunction() {
var LocalVar = "Hello";
}
document.writeln(LocalVar);
```

```
<!-- end -->
</script>
```

would result in the error `"LocalVar is not defined"` since `LocalVar` has been referenced outside of the `TestFunction()` function in which it was originally defined.

TIP

Use `var` for local variables defined *within* the scope of a JavaScript function.

while

Syntax: `while (condition) { statements }`

The `while` statement is the second looping statement in the JavaScript language, the first being the `for` loop. With `while` it is possible to keep executing one or more JavaScript `statements` *until* a particular `condition` is reached. If a code block is to be executed the code segment must be bracketed using { and }.

For example, the script below uses a `while` loop to implement a simple multiplication table. The table required is submitted to the `TimesTable()` function (and could be made user-definable by providing an input field via a form as in earlier examples). The `while` loop iterates 12 times, while the value of variable `begin` is less than or equal to 12. The table is finally output with some simple HTML-formatting tags using the standard JavaScript function `write()`. The `prompt()` method has been used to allow users to input a number of their choice for the multiplication table to be generated:

```
<html>
<script language="JavaScript">
<!-- hide the script from other browsers
function TimesTable(number) {
  begin = 1;
  document.write("Times Table for: <b>" +
                 number + "</b><hr><pre><dl>");
  while (begin <= 12) {
    document.write("<dd>" + begin + " x " +
    number + " = " + number);
    begin++;
  }
```

```
    document.writeln("</dl></pre>");
  }
  TimesTable(prompt("Enter a number",10));
  <!— end of script —>
  </script>
  </html>
```

with

Syntax: with objectName { statements }

The with statement makes the object identified by objectName the default object for the JavaScript statements in the code block statements. For example, we can use the with statement using the JavaScript Math object as follows:

```
  with (Math) {
    document.writeln(PI);
    document.writeln(sin(1.5));
  }
```

which allows us to do away with using the Math prefix when referring to Math methods such as sin() (the JavaScript sine function), as well as using standard object constants such as PI, or we could use the with statement with the document object as follows:

```
  with (document) {
    writeln("Some <b>HTML-formatted</b> text");
    write("<hr>");
  }
```

which saves prefixing the document object into the write() and writeln() methods.

CHAPTER

3

JavaScript's standard objects

JavaScript offers the programmer a family of approximately 20 standard object types, each of which have a set number of *properties* and *methods*. Objects provide access to the building-blocks of your HTML document. In JavaScript each HTML tag that you create is represented by a JavaScript object. In this chapter you will learn how to:

- Understand the concepts behind JavaScript's objects, methods and properties
- Integrate HTML tag objects with event handlers
- Extract values from form elements, such as text fields, text areas, checkboxes and radio buttons
- Manipulate and create string objects
- Create user-defined buttons that invoke JavaScript functions
- Access mathematical methods and properties

JavaScript's object types

Table 3.1 lists the object types that are currently supported in JavaScript.

TABLE 3.1 *Object types supported in JavaScript*

Object type	Object name in Netscape 2.0	Object description and tag
Anchor object		Used to access HTML `<a name>..</a>` anchors
Button object		Used to access HTML `<input type="button">` buttons
Checkbox object		Used to access checkbox elements within an `<input type="checkbox">` HTML tag
Date object		Used for both date and time manipulations
Document object	`document`	Refers to the current hypertext document loaded into Netscape
Form object	`form`	Refers to the current HTML `<form>` container, allowing form elements to be accessed
History object	`history`	Refers to Netscape URL history and standard navigation buttons. Used for document movement and URL recall operations
Link object		Used to access a hyperlink created with an HTML `<a href>..</a>` tag
Location object	`location`	Contains information on the current 'document location' e.g. URL-based information
Math object	`Math`	Contains mathematical constants and functions
Password object		Provides access to an HTML `<input type="password">` password text field
Radio button object		Used to access an HTML `<input type="radio">` radio button
Reset object		Used to access an `<input type="reset">` buttons within an HTML form
Selection object		Used to access an item in a `<select>` container (selection list)

TABLE 3.1 *(contd)*

Object type	Object name in Netscape 2.0	Object description and tag
String object		Used for text string manipulation. All text strings in JavaScript are treated as string objects (e.g. `"Wombat"` is a string object)
Submit object		Used for access to an HTML `<input type="submit">` button within an HTML form
Text object		Used to access an `<input type= "text">` text field
Text area object		Used to access an HTML `<textarea>` text container
Window object	`window`	Used to refer to the current Netscape window

Using JavaScript objects

Some objects, such as the `Date` and `Math` objects are built into the JavaScript interpreter, while others relate to specific tags within an HTML page. For example, the text object allows you to access a text field defined with the HTML tag `<input type="text" size=20>`. In order to identify an object two things have been done.

First, a new `name` attribute has been added to many of the existing HTML tags so that these tag objects can be specifically referred to. For example, the tag:

```
<input name="nameField" type="text" size=20>
```

is not *just* a text field. Now it is treated as a text field *object*. With JavaScript HTML your tags, and the values within them, become the actual objects that you are actually manipulating.

Secondly, JavaScript provides the developer with object *properties*. Properties are the components of an object. For example, the `document` object has a property called `bgColor` that represents the background colour of the current document – as set by the HTML `<body bgcolor="#rrggbb">` tag. It is also important to note that HTML tag attributes get *mapped* onto JavaScript properties automatically by Netscape. There is more on this later in the chapter.

 TIP
HTML tags become HTML *tag objects* in JavaScript.
   You will also have noticed that not all JavaScript objects directly relate to HTML tags; for example the `Math` object. In such cases the name of the object must be quoted verbatim when referring to the object in your JavaScript program, as you will see in later examples.

The listings in this section contain a description of each Netscape object, as shown in Table 3.1, along with the properties and methods of that object and the HTML syntax that is applicable. Many HTML tags have also been modified to accept *event handling attributes*. These attributes allow JavaScript code blocks (or even complete JavaScript functions) to be invoked on a particular object, allowing them to become interactive. For example the HTML `<body>` tag now accepts an event attribute named `onLoad` that executes a JavaScript function as soon as a document is loaded:

```
<body onLoad="InitFunction()">
```

calls the JavaScript function `InitFunction()` as soon as the current document is loaded.
   You can cross-reference all of the object details in this chapter to other sections of the book in order to find out just what each method, property and event handler does. Since individual HTML tags now create JavaScript objects, the HTML syntax for a variety of tags has also been provided.

Object methods

All of JavaScript's 20 or so objects have a number of *methods* that are associated with them. Methods perform specific functions upon objects, for example a string object could be changed to lower case using the JavaScript assignment statement:

```
myString = "JAVASCRIPT".toLowerCase();
```

where `"JAVASCRIPT"` is the string object and `toLowerCase()` is a method that converts a string to lower case. In this example the variable `myString` would be assigned the value `"javascript"`.

Object properties

Another term used in the context of object-driven programming is *property*. Many of the objects in JavaScript have *default properties* and these can be referred to by placing a period (.) after the object name and then following this with the name of the property. For example, all string objects have a default property called `length` which returns the length of the string object. So, in the context of the previous example, the JavaScript statement:

```
strLen = myString.length;
```

stores the value 10 in the variable `strLen` (which is the length of the string object `"JAVASCRIPT"`). Every object that you create will have one or more default properties.

Consider the following HTML document stored at the hypothetical URL `http://www.web.com/doc.htm`:

```
<html>
<head>
<title>This is my document</title>
</head>
<body bgcolor="#0000bb" fgcolor="#ffff00">
<form name="myForm">
<input type="text" name="Person" size=35><br>
</form>
</body>
</html>
```

As soon as this example document is loaded into Netscape a number of object properties will be created, including properties within the `document` object, such as:

```
document.title="This is my document"
document.fgColor=#ffff00
document.bgColor=#0000bb
document.href="http://www.web.com/doc.htm"
```

which reflect the contents of the tags and their attributes within the document. JavaScript will also create a `forms` property (not to be confused with a `form` *object*, where the object refers to the current form) that is an array of forms that exist within the current hypertext document. The `forms` property belongs to the `document` object. We could now refer to our form as `document.forms[0]`, where 0 means the first form in the current document. If you had two `<form>` containers within the current document, `forms[1]` would refer to the second, and so forth. All of these properties are set automatically by JavaScript, according to the tag objects embedded within your HTML document. Chapter 4 explains all of these properties in detail.

Anchor objects

Properties
- `name`

Methods
None

Event handlers
Not applicable

HTML syntax
```
<a name="AnchName">
anchText
</a>
```

Object description
An *anchor* is an object within an HTML document that is the *target* for a hyperlink. Anchors are created using a tag of the form `<a name="anchName">anchText</a>`, where `anchName` is the name of the anchor and `anchText` is some descriptive text that identifies the anchor's address, such as a section title.

In order to activate the anchor an `<a href="#refName">LinkName</a>` tag is required, where `refName` is the name of the anchor that the user wants to move to and `LinkName` is the text that is the visible hyperlink that the user can click upon in order to activate the link. The hash (#) specifies that the anchor is local, i.e. that it exists within the scope of the current document. Anchors that exist in external HTML documents are referenced using the notation `filename#anchorName` e.g. `file2.html#sec2`.

JavaScript can reference the anchors within a hypertext document loaded into Netscape using the `anchors` property of the `document` object, which contains an array of entries for each anchor that is defined within the current hypertext document.

Button objects

Properties
- `name`
- `value`

Methods
■ `click`

The `click()` method can be used to activate a button object.

Event handlers
■ `onClick`

The `onClick` attribute can be specified in the `<input type>` tag, and allows a JavaScript statement or function to be invoked when the button is pressed (see the later example).

HTML syntax
```
<input type="button"
  [ name="ButtonName" ]
  [ onClick = "Eventhandler" ]
  value="ButtonText">
```

Object description
A button object is a clickable component within an HTML form. Buttons can activate JavaScript events such as function calls, or they can invoke one or more JavaScript statements (using `Eventhandler`).

For example, we could have the following HTML document, which presents a button to the user and which has a JavaScript function – `ButtonFunction()` – that handles the button-press (this is known as an *event handler* in JavaScript terminology):

```
<html>
<head>
<title>Button Demo</title>
<script language="JavaScript">
<!-- start of script:
function ButtonFunction() {
  alert("You pressed the button!");
}
<!--end-->
</script>
</head>
<body>
<form>
<input name="MyButton" type="button" value="Press me!"
  onClick="ButtonFunction()">
</form>
</body>
</html>
```

Checkbox objects

Properties
- ■ `name`
- ■ `checked`
- ■ `defaultChecked`

Methods
- ■ `click()`

Event handlers
- ■ `onClick`

HTML syntax
```
<input type="checkbox"
  [ name="CheckboxName" ]
  [ onClick = "Eventhandler" ]
  [ checked ]
  value="ButtonText">
```

Object description

Checkbox objects allow yes/no selections to be made by the user. They appear in Netscape as a square box which can be checked either *on* or *off*. Checked boxes have crosses in them. The `checked` property is a boolean property that returns a true value when a given checkbox is selected; `defaultChecked` returns a true value when the optional `checked` attribute has been specified. The `checked` attribute allows a checkbox to appear selected when it first appears (i.e. the default selection).

Consider the following example, where two checkboxes have been defined. The first checkbox has an `onClick` event associated with it, so clicking on this box will invoke the JavaScript function named `CBFunction()`. The second checkbox is not associated with any JavaScript-based event:

```
<html>
<head>
<title>Checkbox Demonstration</title>
<script language="JavaScript">
<!-- Start of Java script
function CBFunction() {
  alert("You checked Option 1!");
}
```

```
<!— End of script —>
</script>
</head>
<body>
<form>
<input name="cb1" type="checkbox"
onClick="CBFunction()">Option 1
<input name="cb2" type="checkbox">Option 2
</form>
</body>
</html>
```

Date objects

Properties
None

Methods
- getDate()
- getDay()
- getHours()
- getMinutes()
- getSeconds()
- getTime()
- getYear()
- parse()
- setDate()
- setHours()
- setMinutes()
- setMonth()
- setSeconds()
- toString()

Event handlers
Not applicable

HTML syntax

```
dateVar = new Date(parameters);
dateVar.method()
```

Object description
Date objects are built into the JavaScript language and allow date and time functions to be accessed. In JavaScript the system date is held internally as the number of milliseconds since 1 January 1970, 00:00:00 (known as the *epoch* date, where 1000 milliseconds is equal to one second). **Date** objects have the greatest number of supporting methods in JavaScript, including methods to set and extract every field from a **Date** object.

From the syntax it can be seen that the **new** statement creates a new instance of a **Date** object. The **parameters** argument can include any one of the following:

- An empty parameter list, e.g. **Date( )**, which simply extracts today's date and time
- A string representing the date and time in the form: "Month day, year time"; for example, **"March 1, 1996 12:00:00"** (note that the time is in 24-hour format)
- A set of values for the year, month, day, hour, minute and seconds; for example, the string **"96,3,1,12,30,0"** is the same as 1 March 1996, 12:30:00 p.m.
- A set of integer values for only the year, month and day; for example **"96, 3, 1"** is the same as 1 March 1996. The time elements will all be set to zero if omitted

So, for example, we could create a new **Date** object using today's (local) date and time with the JavaScript statement:

```
todayDate = new Date( );
```

Likewise, we can create a **Date** object with a different date by passing the necessary parameters to the object directly, for example:

```
theDate = Date(96,3,1,12,30,0);   // 1 Mar 1996 12:30:00
```

As a more extensive example, here is an HTML/JavaScript application that prints a date header at the top of an HTML document. Note that **Date** objects are not string objects, and must be coerced to a string before they are displayed (this can be done using the **toString( )** method of the **Date** object):

```
<html>
<head>
<script language="JavaScript">
<!— start of script
function showHeader() {
```

```
      theDate = Date().toString();
      document.writeln("<html><table width=100% border=1>" +
        "<tr><td width=50% align=left><b> Date</b>: " +
        theDate + "<td><td align=right></td></tr>" +
        "</table><p>");
        // etc ...
    }
    showHeader();
    <!— end of script —>
    </script>
    </head>
    </html>
```

Here is another HTML/JavaScript application that uses the **Date** object to extract the current hour and uses this to change the background pattern of the current document using Netscape's **<body background>** tag:

```
<html>
<script language="JavaScript">
<!— start of script
theTime = new Date();
theHour = theTime.getHours();
if (theHour < 18) // 6pm local time
  document.write("<body background="day.gif"
text="#0000FF>");
else
  document.write("<body background="night.gif"
text="#FFFFFF>");
<!— end of script —>
</script>
This is the text of the body...
</body>
</html>
```

Notice how the script is used to create the first **<body>** tag. The final **</body>** tag is output literally within the document, which is quite valid since all of the necessary HTML tags are output in the correct order. Using similar code you can load different backgrounds according to a certain day or hour, or you could alter your page layout (including images) according to the same criteria. For example, in the previous example the image file **night.gif** is used as a background when the time is later than 6 p.m.; otherwise the graphic **day.gif** is used instead. Both of these files are assumed to exist in the same directory as the HTML file that references them. You can of course refer to any image stored on the Internet using a URL of the form `http://host/imagefile`, where `imagefile` is a file in either GIF or JPEG format (both of which Netscape 2.0 supports).

The use of dates to determine a background image would have been impossible in earlier versions of HTML without the use of a CGI script. JavaScript clearly does away with the need for a script in this instance.

Document objects

Object name
    document

Properties
- alinkColor
- anchors
- bgColor
- fgColor
- forms
- lastModified
- linkColor
- links
- loadedDate
- location
- referrer
- title
- userAgent
- vlinkcolor

Methods
- clear()
- close()
- open()
- write()
- writeln()

Event handlers
- onLoad
- onUnLoad

HTML syntax
```
<body background="ImageURL"
  bgcolor="#backgroundColour"
```

```
      fgcolor="#foregroundColour"
      link="#hyperlinkColour"
      alink="#activelinkColour"
      vlink="#visitedlinkColour"
      [ onLoad="Eventhandler" ]
      [ onUnLoad="Eventhandler" ]>
   [HTML text ...]
   </body>
```

Object description

The document object contains information on the current hypertext document that is loaded into the Netscape browser. A document object is created in HTML using the <body>..</body> container. The properties of the **document** object relate to the <body> tag's attributes; for example, **bgColor** is set in the <body> tag with the bgcolor="#rrggbb" attribute.

All of the properties for the **document** object reflect the elements that a hypertext document can contain, including anchors, forms, titles and hyperlinks. Items such as forms and hyperlinks, of which there can be many, are stored in properties structured as arrays. Please refer to Chapter 4 for more information on these.

Here is a simple HTML document that displays a message using JavaScript's **alert()** method when it is initially loaded into Netscape:

```
<html>
<head>
<title>Welcome</title>
<script language="JavaScript">
<!-- Beginning of script
function WelcomeMsg() {
   alert("This document requires Netscape Navigator\n" +
         "2.0 or above. Please maximize your window." +
         "for optimal viewing. Thank you.");
}
<!-- End of script -->
</script>
</head>
<body bgcolor="#0000FF" fgcolor="#FFFF00"
   onLoad="WelcomeMsg()">
<hr>
<!-- etc. -->
</body>
</html>
```

The `onLoad` and `onUnLoad` event handlers are useful for catching page-entry and page-departure events within the Netscape browser. You could offer the user the option of entering a particular document, or you could control which documents users next visit when they exit or enter a particular page etc.

Form objects

Properties
- action
- elements
- method
- name
- target

Methods
- submit()

HTML syntax
```
<form name="formName"
    [ target="windowName" ]
    [ action="CGIscriptURL" ]
    [ method="GET | POST" ]
    [ onSubmit = "Eventhandler" ]>
    <input type=...>
    <textarea>...</textarea>
    <select>...</select>
</form>
```

Event handlers
- onSubmit

Object description
Form objects allow the user to provide input into a number of fields within a hypertext page, and then either process these values locally or submit them to a server for further processing.

Forms can contain text fields, text areas, radio buttons, checkboxes, selection lists and buttons. A form is created using the HTML `<form>..</form>` container. The `onSubmit` event handler allows the user to ascertain when the form has been submitted. Forms are 'submitted' by including an `<input type="submit">` tag. The `target` attribute specifies a window in which to see server responses i.e. the feedback after submitting the form to a server. The `GET` and `POST` values of the `method` attribute specify the *mode* in which the form is submitted to the Web server (the POST method submits the form data as a body of text on the standard input stream, whereas GET method forms submit their data via an environment variable called QUERY_STRING which is set on the server, allowing the form data to be extracted). These variables are part of the CGI (Common Gateway Interface) standard. See http://hoohoo.ncsa.uiuc.edu/cgi for more on the CGI standard.

Forms can be accessed by specifying the name of the form (after naming the form with the name attribute), or by using the document.forms[n] property.

As an example, here is a simple HTML form with two text fields that uses an onSubmit event handler to catch the pressing of a *submit* button. The JavaScript function FormHandler() then uses the document and forms property to print the values entered by the user into the form. Notice how the name of each field has been suffixed with the value property. The value property allows the value of a form field to be accessed:

```html
<html>
<head>
<script language="JavaScript">
<!-- Start of script
function FormHandler() {
  alert("Name: " +
        document.forms[0].name.value + "\n" + "email: " +
        document.forms[0].email.value);
}
<!-- End of script -->
</script>
</head>
<body>
<form onSubmit="FormHandler()">
Name: <input type="text" name="name" size=35>
Email: <input type="text" name="email" size=30><hr>
<input type="submit" value="Submit details">
</form>
</body>
</html>
```

History objects

Object name
    history

Properties
    ■ current

■   `length`

Methods
■   `back()`
■   `forward()`
■   `go()`

HTML syntax

`history.methodName(args)`

Event handlers
   None

Object description
History objects contain information about the documents (i.e. URLs) that the user has visited with Netscape. Netscape has a *Go* menu that contains the current history list, and this option is reflected in the JavaScript method of the same name – `go()`. For example, we could make the user return to the document that was loaded two clicks ago using the JavaScript statement:

`history.go(-2);`

noting the use of a negative number to specify past documents. To move forward, issue an unsigned number: for example `history.go(2)` moves forward two documents – assuming two documents are ahead of the currently loaded document in the history buffer and can be retrieved. The expression `history.length` can be used to determine the size of the current Netscape history buffer.

Link objects

Properties
■   `target`

HTML syntax

```
<a href="locationURL"
   [ name="LinkName" ]
   [ target = "windowName" ]
   [ onClick = "Eventhandler" ]
   [ onMouseOver = "EventHandler" ]>
Hyperlink-text...
</a>
```

Event handlers
- onClick
- onMouseOver

Object description
A link object is a string of text encapsulated in an HTML `<a href="URL">..
</a>` container. Hyper-references, or *hyperlinks* as they are more commonly known, allow movement between documents by specifying a URL (uniform resource locator) to load when the hyperlink is clicked upon by the user. A simple link object can be created using the HTML `<a href>` tag, for example:

```
<a name="hlink1" href="http://www.gold.net">Go to
   GoldNet</a>
```

which renders the text *Go to GoldNet* as a hyperlink (by default this will be underlined and coloured blue in Netscape) and specifies that the resource named as `http://www.gold.net` be loaded when the hyperlink is clicked upon. The `onClick` event handler allows a hyperlink to activate a JavaScript function, while `onMouseOver` allows a JavaScript function to be activated when the user *hovers* over an active hyperlink with the mouse. For example, we can display a status bar message for users contemplating selecting a hyperlink with:

```
...
<a name="yahoo" href="http://www.yahoo.com"
   onMouseOver="self.status='Visit Yahoo';
   return true">
Yahoo!
</a>
```

TIP
Note that all link objects are also `Location` objects (see below).

Location objects

Object name
   location

Properties
- hash

- host
- hostname
- href
- pathname
- port
- protocol
- search

Methods
- assign()
- toString()

Event handlers
None

HTML syntax

```
location.propertyName
```

Object description
A location object contains information on the current URL – the current document
loaded into the Netscape browser. Location objects are useful for extracting
location information from the current URL, such as the Web server hostname and/or
pathname. For example, you can extract the current hostname of the server you are
connected to into a variable and print it out in the browser using the following
JavaScript statements:

```
currentUrl = location.hostname;
document.writeln("You are connected to: <b>" +
  currentUrl +"</b>");
```

or better still (using one line of code fewer):

```
document.writeln("You are connected to: " +
  location.hostname + "</b>");
```

Here is another script and HTML file that uses the hostname property to display a
simple welcome message to a user when they load the document:

```
<html>
<head>
<script language="JavaScript">
```

```
<!— hide script
function Welcome() {
  alert("Welcome to the XYZ Company at " +
        location.hostname +
        "\n\nPlease maximize your browser's window " +
        "for optimal viewing. We support Netscape 2.0.");
}
Welcome();
<!— End of script —>
</script>
</head>
<!— etc. —>
<body>
This is the body text for the document...
</body>
</html>
```

Math objects

Object name
  Math

Properties
  ■ E
  ■ LN10
  ■ LN2
  ■ PI
  ■ SQRT1_2
  ■ SQRT2

Methods
  ■ abs()
  ■ acos()
  ■ asin()
  ■ atan()
  ■ cos()
  ■ exp()
  ■ log()
  ■ max()
  ■ min()
  ■ pow()
  ■ round()

- ■ `sin()`
- ■ `sqrt()`
- ■ `tan()`

Event handlers
   None

Syntaxes:
- ■ `Math.propertyName`
- ■ `Math.methodName()`

Object description
The math object offers the JavaScript developer a number of mathematical constants and methods that can be used for various calculations. Mathematical constants are accessed using statements of the form:

```
piVal = Math.PI;   // The value of 'Pi'
```

which places the value for *pi* into the variable `piVal`. `Math`'s methods can be applied to specific values, for example:

```
x = Math.pow(2,12);   // Calculate 2 to the power of 12
```

Refer to Chapter 5 for details of all mathematical methods and the arguments that they accept.

Password objects

Properties
- ■ `defaultValue`
- ■ `name`
- ■ `value`

Methods
- ■ `focus()`
- ■ `blur()`
- ■ `select()`

Event handlers
   None

HTML syntax

```
<input type="password"
  [ name="ObjectName" ]
  [ value = "defaultValue" ]
  [ size = NumofChars ]>
```

Object description

A password object is a text field within an HTML form that uses an <input type="password"> tag. Password fields allow text entry, but shield the input by substituting asterisks (*) for each character typed, thus stopping sensitive information from being made visible on screen. For example:

```
<form name="PassForm">
Enter password: <input type="password" name="PassField"
  size=10>
</form>
```

creates a ten-character password field that the user can now enter text into.

Radio button objects

Properties

- checked
- defaultChecked
- index
- length
- name
- value

Methods

- click()

Event handlers

- onClick

HTML syntax

```
<input type="radio"
  [ name="ObjectName" ]
  [ checked ]
  [ onClick="EventHandler" ]
  value = "buttonValue"> [RadioText ...]
```

Object description

The radio button object exists as one or more radio buttons within an HTML form, and is created using an `<input type="radio">` tag. Radio buttons offer a selection of *yes/no* options, only one of which can be chosen when they exist as a group. It is important to remember that the `name` attribute should be the same for *each* radio button that is created, unlike checkboxes. This is required since it is not possible to select more than one radio button in a group. When a radio button object is created the object becomes an indexable array which you can access using the appropriate number. For example, the form:

```
<form>
<input type="radio" name="select" checked>Good
<input type="radio" name="select">Bad
<input type="radio" name="select">Ugly
</form>
```

creates three radio buttons. In order to find out whether or not the first radio button is selected you can use the `checked` property as follows:

```
document.forms[0].select[0].checked
```

If this expression returns a true value you know that this button is selected (only one button can be selected in any one group, remember). In this instance `select[0]` is the first radio button – array indexes always start at zero in JavaScript. The `checked` attribute has also been used in the first radio button to select a default button. This would also have the effect of enabling (setting true) the `defaultChecked` property if the form was submitted at this stage.

As a further example, consider the following HTML form, which defines three radio buttons and an event handler to process the user's selection:

```
<html>
<head>
<script language="JavaScript">
<!— Start of script
function FormHandler() {
  if (document.forms[0].pge[0].checked)
    document.forms[0].result.value = "Poor";
  if (document.forms[0].pge[1].checked)
    document.forms[0].result.value = "Good";
  if (document.forms[0].pge[2].checked)
    document.forms[0].result.value = "Excellent";
}
```

```
<!— End of script —>
</script>
</head>
<body>
<form onSubmit="FormHandler()">
<input type="text" size=20 name="result"><hr>
  Please enter a rating:<br>
<input type="radio" name="pge"
  onClick="FormHandler()" value="poor" checked>1<br>
<input type="radio" name="pge"
  onClick="FormHandler()" value="good">2<br>
<input type="radio" name="pge"
  onClick="FormHandler()" value="excellent">3<hr>
</form>
</body>
</html>
```

This script uses an `onClick` event handler in the `<input>` tag to update a text field as soon as the user has clicked on a radio button. The JavaScript function `FormHandler()` tests the `checked` property of each radio button in turn (`pge[0]`, `pge[1]` and `pge[2]`) and then assigns a value to the `result` field (a text field in the form created using an HTML `<input type="text">` tag) accordingly.

It is possible for `<input type="radio">` tags to include a `value` attribute. If this is the case we can restructure our example as:

```
<html>
<head>
<script language="JavaScript">
<!— Start of script
function FormHandler() {
  if (document.forms[0].pge[0].checked)
    document.forms[0].result.value =
    document.forms[0].pge[0].value;
  if (document.forms[0].pge[1].checked)
    document.forms[0].result.value =
    document.forms[0].pge[1].value;
  if (document.forms[0].pge[2].checked)
    document.forms[0].result.value =
    document.forms[0].pge[2].value;
}
<!— End of script —>
</script>
```

```
</head>
<body>
<form onSubmit="FormHandler()">
<input type="text" size=20 name="result"><hr>
  Please enter a rating:<br>
<input type="radio" value="Poor" name="pge"
  onClick="FormHandler()" checked>1<br>
<input type="radio" value="Good" name="pge"
  onClick="FormHandler()">2<br>
<input type="radio" value="Excellent" name="pge"
  onClick="FormHandler()">3<hr>
</form>
</body>
</html>
```

which uses the `value` attribute within the `<input>` tag and then uses the `value` property of the radio button object to access this.

Reset button objects

Properties
■   name
■   value

Methods
■   click()

Event handlers
■   onClick

HTML syntax
```
<input type="reset"
  value="ButtonText"
  [ onClick="Eventhandler" ]>
```

Object description
The reset object provides a clickable *reset button* within an HTML form. A reset button is used to clear the contents of every field within the scope of the current form. This is a convenience feature that saves the user from manually deleting a form's contents before entering new data.

Selection list objects

Properties
- defaultSelected
- index
- selected
- text
- value

Methods
- click()

Event handlers
- onChange
- onBlur
- onFocus

HTML syntax
```
<select name="objectName"
  [ size="NumberofChars" ]
  [ multiple ]
  [ onBlur = "Eventhandler" ]
  [ onChange = "Eventhandler" ]
  [ onFocus = "Eventhandler" ]
<option [ selected ] OptionText >
</select>
```

Object description

A selection object represents a `<select>..</select>` container within an HTML form. The `options` property of the `Selection` object can be used to gain access to the items within the selection object. The individual selection items are created using the HTML `<option>` tag. The `multiple` attribute specifies that all of the items are to be made visible (only one is by default). The `selected` attribute in the `<option>` tag specifies that this option is currently selected when the selection list initially appears. For example, we could have the following selection items:

```
<form name="SelectForm">
Which Web browser do you use?<br>
<select name="browser" onChange="ChangeFunc()">
<option selected>Netscape Navigator
<option>Microsoft Explorer
<option>NCSA Mosaic
```

```
</select>
```

Whenever a new selection is made the **onChange** event handler is called and in turn invokes the JavaScript function named **ChangeFunc()**. For more details see the entry for the **text** property in Chapter 4 to find out how to retrieve the item that has been selected by the user.

String objects

Properties
■ length

Methods
■ anchor()
■ big()
■ bold()
■ charAt()
■ fixed()
■ fontcolor()
■ fontsize()
■ indexOf()
■ italics()
■ link()
■ small()
■ sub()
■ substring()
■ sup()
■ toLowerCase()
■ toUpperCase()

Event handlers
None

Syntaxes
■ StringObject.methodName()
■ StringObject.PropertyName

Object description
A string object consists of a series of alphanumeric characters (for example **"JavaScript"**) and has one property, namely **length**. So, for example, if you had a string variable called **Name**, defined with the statement:

```
var Name="Java"
```

the value of the JavaScript expression:

```
Name.length
```

would yield the numeric value 4.

If we have a variable called `Name` with the value `"JavaScript"`, the statement:

```
result = Name.toUpperCase();
```

would place the value `"JAVASCRIPT"` in the variable `result`. Similarly, the statement:

```
result = Name.toLowerCase();
```

would yield the value `"javascript"`. Literal strings can also be converted; for example:

```
result = "JAVASCRIPT".toLowerCase();
```

stores the value `"javascript"` in the variable named `result`. The string `"JAVASCRIPT"` is treated as a string object in JavaScript.

The `substring(start,end)` method returns a substring of a string, where `start` is the starting position of the string and `end` is the ending position. Character positions start at zero (0) in JavaScript and then work their way upwards.

TIP
String positions start at zero (0) in the JavaScript language.

If it happens that the value of `start` is greater than that of `end` then the `substring()` method returns a substring starting at position `end` and ending at character position `start`, and the end-result will be the same. In the case that `start` and `end` are the same value an empty string (`" "`) is simply returned. For example, the JavaScript statement:

```
result = Name.substring(0,4);
```

yields the value "Live", as too does the statement:

```
result = Name.substring(4,0);
```

If the **end** parameter is omitted from **substring** JavaScript assumes that you want it set at **length+1**, i.e. the end of the string. So in the case of the statement:

```
result = Name.substring(4);
```

JavaScript would set the value of **result** to "String".

TIP
You can use the new **mocha:** URL in Netscape 2.0 in order to try out such expressions directly. This can be useful to see the results of string processing methods such as **substring()**.

Strings can also contain the special value **null**, which represents a string that is currently undefined, i.e. which has no current value. Note that **null** is not the same as an empty string (i.e. " ").

Submit button objects

Properties
- name
- value

Methods
- click()

Event handlers
- onClick

HTML syntax

```
<input type="submit" value="ButtonText">
```

Object description
The submit object represents the submit button on an HTML form. Submit buttons are provided via the HTML tag **<input type="submit">** and are used to send the contents of the current form to a server for further processing. The server that does the processing can be named in the **action** attribute of the **<form>** tag in

which the submit button resides. Submitting a form always results in the current page being reloaded.

Text and text area field objects

Properties
- defaultValue
- name
- value

Methods
- blur()
- focus()
- select()

Event handlers
- onBlur
- onChange
- onFocus
- onSelect

HTML syntax (text field)

```
<input type="text"
   [ name="objectName" ]
   [ value="defaultValue" ]
   [ size="NumberofChars" ]
   [ onBlur="Eventhandler" ]
   [ onChange="Eventhandler" ]
   [ onFocus="Eventhandler" ]
   [ onSelect="Eventhandler" ]>
```

HTML syntax (text area container)

```
<textarea [ name="objectName" ]
          [ rows = rows ]
          [ cols = columns ]
          [ onBlur="Eventhandler" ]
          [ onChange="Eventhandler" ]
          [ onFocus="Eventhandler" ]
          [ onSelect="Eventhandler" ]>
[ Default-Text ... ]
</textarea>
```

Object descriptions

A text object is created using the HTML form tag `<input type="text">`. It is a field that allows alphanumeric characters to be entered by the user. Text area objects are different in that they allow multiple-line input, and are different in that they are structured as a container. The HTML example below illustrates two fields, the first an ordinary text field, and the second a text area field. Whenever the contents of the text area change the JavaScript function `MyFunc()` is invoked:

```
<html>
<head>
<script language="JavaScript">
<!— Start
function MyFunc() {
   alert("The text area field changed!");
}
<!— end —>
</script>
</head>
<body>
<form name="TextForm">
Enter some text: <input type="text" size=40
   name="sometext"><br>
Enter some more text: <textarea rows=40 cols=10
   name="tarea"
   onChange="MyFunc()">
</form>
</body>
</html>
```

In order to access the data in a text field, use the `value` property. In context to the above example the JavaScript expression:

```
document.forms[0].sometext.value
```

would yield the text held in the text field named `sometext`. Text areas are accessed in the same way. Both field types can be dynamically updated by assigning values to each respective field. The `defaultValue` property refers to the `value` attribute of the `<input type="text">` tag, and for the text area field the text placed between the `<textarea>` and `</textarea>` tags.

Window objects

Object name
```
window
```

Properties
- ■ `frames`
- ■ `parent`
- ■ `self`
- ■ `top`
- ■ `status`
- ■ `defaultStatus`

Methods
- ■ `alert()`
- ■ `close()`
- ■ `confirm()`
- ■ `open()`
- ■ `prompt()`

Event handlers
- ■ `onLoad`
- ■ `onUnLoad`

Syntax
- ■ `window.PropertyName`
- ■ `window.methodName()`

Object description
The window object is the top-level object in JavaScript, since all documents and their components must exist within a window. Therefore the current window is always assumed, and you do not have to reference it when you assign methods and access properties from this object. The properties `self` and `window` are both valid when referring to the *current* window. Likewise, a window can be closed with `close()`, `self.close()` or `window.close()`.

TIP
Netscape 2.0 introduces a concept known as *frames*. These are individual regions of a window that can have scroll bars. They can be used to display separate documents (e.g. different URLs within the same window area).

JavaScript can reference a frame using the `frames` property. Refer to the section on the `frames` property in Chapter 4 for more information.

C H A P T E R

4

JavaScript's standard properties

Javascript has a number of *standard properties* that contain values that are set according to the Netscape browser's working environment. Every element created with an HTML tag has an associated *property* that allows the JavaScript author to ascertain which elements and values are set in the current hypertext document. In this chapter you will learn:

- How to use JavaScript to access Netscape properties (such as colours) and form elements (such as text field values or a checkbox's status)
- How to update Netscape's environment by modifying a property
- How to use mathematical constants and other JavaScript properties

JavaScript's standard properties

JavaScript has approximately 50 standard properties – values that belong to various objects and which are used to determine their behaviour. All objects have properties, and this section documents each property and the objects that it acts upon.

A good tip to remember is that you can dynamically change some of Netscape's standard properties by simply assigning the property a new value; for example:

```
document.bgColor="#0000FF";
```

would change the current document's background colour to blue (see the `bgColor` property for more details). This saves having to use specific HTML tags to achieve the same effects. Look out for properties that can be set in this way.

`alinkColor` property
Description: Active hyperlink colour
Applies to object(s): `document`

This property represents the colour of an active hyperlink within the current hypertext document as set by the `<body alink="#RRGGBB">..</body>` tag, where `"#RRGGBB"` is a hexadecimal-encoded red–green–blue triplet representing the active link colour combination, `"#0000BB"` being the default (blue in this case), for example:

```
document.alinkColor="#ff0000"; // Active-links are red
```

`anchors` property
Description: An array of hyperlinks that exist within the current hypertext document
Applies to object(s): `document`

`bgColor` property
Description: The background colour of the currently loaded hypertext document
Applies to object(s): `document`

This property represents the background colour of the current hypertext document as set by the `<body bgcolor="#RRGGBB">..</body>` tag, where `"#RRGGBB"` is a hexadecimal-encoded red–green–blue triplet representing the background colour, for example:

```
document.bgColor="#0000FF"; // Blue background colour
```

You could phase in a series of colours using a simple `for` loop, for example:

```
<html>
<head>
<script language="JavaScript">
<!---
var thisNum = "40";
for (var i = 1 ; i <= 20; i++) {
   document.bgColor = "#C0C0" + thisNum;
   thisNum += 10;
}
<!——>
</script>
</head>
<body>
Body text goes here...
</body>
</html>
```

Notice how the addition operator += works with a number that is stored as a string. This allows us to alter a colour triplet dynamically within a loop, thus outputting a series of **document.bgColor** assignments statements (which in turn alter Netscape's background colour). By altering the value of **thisNum** you can control the rate at which new colours appear.

checked property
Description: A boolean value indicating whether or not a checkbox or radio button object is checked
Applies to object(s): **checkbox** and **radioButton**

The **checked** property returns a boolean value indicating whether or not a radio button or checkbox object is selected, i.e. 'checked' by the user.

defaultChecked property
Description: A boolean value indicating whether or not the default checkbox/radio button object is checked
Applies to object(s): **checkbox** and **radioButton**.

The **defaultChecked** property returns **true** if the checkbox or radio button being examined is the default button, as set by the **checked** attribute (see **<input type="radio|checkbox">** syntax).

`defaultSelected` property
Description: A boolean value indicating whether or not the default option in a `<select>` tag is selected
Applies to object(s): `selection`

This is a boolean property that returns `true` if an `<option selected>` tag within an HTML `<select>..</select>` container is currently selected by the user, i.e. if the default selection has been made.

`defaultStatus` property
Description: The default status bar message
Applies to object(s): `window`

The `defaultStatus` property contains the default status bar message that appears in Netscape (not to be confused with the `status` property – see later).

`defaultValue` property
Description: Default text field value
Applies to object(s): `text`, `textArea`, and `string`

Contains the default contents of a text field according to the value supplied by the `value` attribute.

`E` property
Description: Euler's constant
Applies to object(s): `Math`

Contains the value of Euler's mathematical constant e, the base of the natural logarithms (2.718...), for example:

```
exp = Math.E;  // Store e in variable exp
```

`elements` property
Description: Form elements array
Applies to object(s): `form`

The `elements` property is an array of objects that contain each element of an HTML form (in the order that they are defined within the HTML file), such as the text fields, text areas, and radio and/or checkboxes. Note that the index starts from zero. The `formName` variable is taken from the `forms` property (see below) and is also an array that represents the form number within the current HTML document. So, for example:

```
document.forms[0].elements[0]
```

refers to the first element in the first form of the current document. The term
`document.forms.length` would therefore contain the number of forms in the
current hypertext document.

`fgColor` property

Description: The foreground colour of the currently loaded hypertext document
Applies to object(s): `document`

This property represents the foreground colour of the current hypertext document as
set by the `<body fgcolor="#RRGGBB">..</body>` tag, where `"#RRGGBB"` is
a hexadecimal-encoded red–green–blue triplet representing the current foreground
colour. For example:

```
document.fgColor="#FFFF00";
```

sets the current document's foreground colour to yellow.

`forms` property

Description: An array of forms within the current document
Applies to object(s): `document`

The `forms` property is an array containing each form that is defined within the
current HTML document. For example, `document.forms[0].field1.value`
yields the value of the field named `field1` that existed within the first form of the
current document. Consider the longer example shown below, which defines a series
of forms using the HTML `<form>...</form>` container. By using the `forms`
property it is possible to dynamically update a form field with a new value:

```
<html>
<head>
<title>Multiple form Test</title>
<body>
<form>
Field 1 <input name="field1" type="text" value=
  "Field 1"><br>
</form>
<form>
Field 2 <input name="field2" type="text" value="Field 2">
</form>
<form>
```

```
<input name    = "button1"
       type    = "button"
       value   = "Update field 1"
       onClick = "document.forms[0].field1.value =
                  'Updated!'"><p>

<input name    = "button2"
       type    = "button"
       value   = "Update field 2"
       onClick = "document.forms[1].field2.value =
                  'Updated!'">
</form>
</body>
</html>
```

There are no JavaScript functions in this example; the actual code is embedded inside an **onClick** event attribute within an <input> tag. The <input> tags are buttons in this instance, and clicking on them updates each field of the first two forms defined within the current document. Remember to use the **value** property when assigning values directly to fields within an HTML form. Omitting the **value** property effectively means that you are referring to the variable identifier, and not the value held *within* it (this will also result in a run-time error).

frames property

Description: Frame elements array
Applies to object(s): **window**

The **frames** property is an array of frames that exists within the current window. Frames are regions of a window that can contain separate HTML documents (and therefore separate URLs) and are a Netscape 2.0 feature that will probably become *standard* HTML in the near future. Frames can have their own properties, such as background colours and bitmaps, and can be navigated autonomously by the user. It is also possible for one frame to update another, as will be demonstrated in this section.

To refer to the first frame within a frameset document you would use the expression:

```
window.parent.frames[0]
```

where **parent** refers to the <frameset> container – the parent of each frame. The **parent** property is used specifically with frameset documents. The number of frames in the current HTML document will be returned by **window.frames.length**. A frameset document is created using the Netscape container:

```
<frameset rows=rowsize cols=colsize>
<frame name=frameName src=Filename>
</frameset>
```

where `rowsize` and `colsize` are strings that specify the size of each of the frames and can be a mixture of percentages or literal pixel values (e.g. `50%` or `150` (pixels)), and `name` names the frame. Frames are named to allow them to be the destination for a hyperlink. The `<a href>..</a>` container now has a `target` attribute that allows a frame to be specified so that the file it loads is the frame you require. The `Filename` value is the name of an HTML file to load into the frame. For example:

```
<frameset rows="50%, 50%">
<frame src="http://www.mcgraw-hill.co.uk">
<frame src="http://www.gold.net/users/ag17/index.htm">
</frameset>
```

loads the home page of the Web site `www.mcgraw-hill.co.uk` into the first frame and the page `index.htm` in the directory `/users/ag17` from the Web site `http://www.gold.net`.

As you can see, a frameset document has no *body* as such, but instead specifies a series of frames and the documents (i.e. HTML files) that are then loaded into them. For example, consider the HTML document below, `test1.htm`, which is a frameset document that defines two frames. The files actually loaded into each frame are called `test2.htm` and `test3.htm` respectively. The `src` attribute of the `<frame>` tag specifies the file to load into the frame. The sizes of the frames are equal (both are set to `50%` in this instance). When this document is loaded into Netscape two regions within the Netscape display area will be created.

```
<!—test.htm—>
<html>
<head>
<title>HTML Frame Example</title>
</head>
<frameset rows="50%, 50%">
  <frame src="test2.htm">
  <frame src="test3.htm">
</frameset>
</html>
```

Now assume that `test2.htm` contains the following HTML and JavaScript program:

```
<!—test2.htm—>
<html>
<head>
<script language="JavaScript">
<!— start of script
var theDoc = window.parent.frames[1].document;
function ShowHtml(expr) {
  theDoc.writeln(expr+"<p>");
}
<!— end of script —>
</script>
</head>
<body bgcolor="#ABCDEF">
<form name="myForm">
Please enter some HTML. The results will be shown in the
  lower frame.
<textarea name="HtmlExpr" cols=65 rows=6>
</textarea><br>
<input name  = "button1"
    type     = "button"
    value    = "See HTML"
    onClick = "ShowHtml(document.myForm.HtmlExpr.value)">

<input name  = "button2"
    type     = "button"
    value    = "Clear frame"
    onClick = "theDoc.close() ; theDoc.open() ;
               theDoc.close()">
</form>
</body>
</html>
```

In particular, notice how we define a global variable, `theDoc`, which refers to the second frame (`frames[1]`, remembering that frame numbers begin at zero):

```
var theDoc = window.parent.frames[1].document;
```

This expression refers to the document in the second frame of the current window. The **parent** property *must* be used in such instances since it refers to the `<frameset>` document, i.e. the parent of both frames in this instance. We can now use the value of **theDoc** to address the second frame within the Netscape browser.

The file `test3.htm` could just be left as an empty HTML document. A frame document must exist when referenced with the `src` attribute, so it must exist in order that it can be loaded into the frame:

```
<!--test3.htm-->
<html>
<head>
</head>
<body>
</body>
</html>
```

The only JavaScript function within `test2.htm` is `showHtml()`, which simply writes out an argument that is passed to it. The argument (`expr`) in this case is just some HTML-formatted text:

```
function ShowHtml(expr) {
   theDoc.writeln(expr+"<p>");
}
```

Since the variable `theDoc` is a *handle* to the document in the second frame, the `writeln()` method in this function acts upon this frame. The actual value of `expr` is determined by what the user enters into an HTML text area container defined in `text2.htm` as:

```
<textarea name="HtmlExpr" cols=65 rows=6>
</textarea>
```

The name `attribute` is important since it allows a text area *object* to be created. We can now reference the text within this text area field, as in the example where two buttons are defined. The first button simply calls the `showHtml()` function and passes the text area field to it as an argument:

```
<input name = "button1"
   type     = "button"
   value    = "See HTML"
   onClick = "ShowHtml(document.myForm.HtmlExpr.value)">
```

With the second button we simply provide a way of clearing the frame. In Netscape 2.0 beta 5 the `clear()` method does not perform any action on a frame, hence the use of the `open()` and `close()` methods to clear the frame (this combination works in beta 5):

```
<input name = "button2"
   type    = "button"
   value   = "Clear frame"
   onClick = "theDoc.close() ; theDoc.open() ;
              theDoc.close()">
```

Both buttons use an **onClick** event attribute to invoke a JavaScript function or statements.

The end-result of this program is to allow HTML expressions to be entered by the user and their results placed into a separate frame within the browser. All of the files are assumed to exist in the current directory, although they could be accessed via any Web server using the **http://** URL service type. This simple example could easily be extended to place just about any text into an alternative frame. Another salient point of the example to note is the naming of the **<form>** container using the **name** attribute. Without this attribute you must refer to the form using the **forms** property, for example:

```
<form>
...
<input name  = "button1"
   type    = "button"
   value   = "See HTML"
   onClick = "ShowHtml(document.forms[0].HtmlExpr.value)">
...
</form>
```

Notice how the **forms** property (an array) has been used to refer to the first form within the current hypertext document. Since there is only one form defined in this document, the value of **forms[0]** will correctly reference it. See the earlier section on the **forms** property for more examples. Figure 4.1 illustrates the HTML expression program in action with a simple table and an image. The image name **about:logo** is an internal GIF image that displays the Netscape 'N' logo. You can find details of other internal images (and other useful internal icons) at my home page at **http://www.gold.net/users/ag17/index.htm**.

TIP

Each frame in Netscape 2.0 can be selected by clicking on an empty region within the frame. A border will then appear around the selected frame and you can use Netscape's *View/Reload frame* option to reload the document that is currently active within the frame.

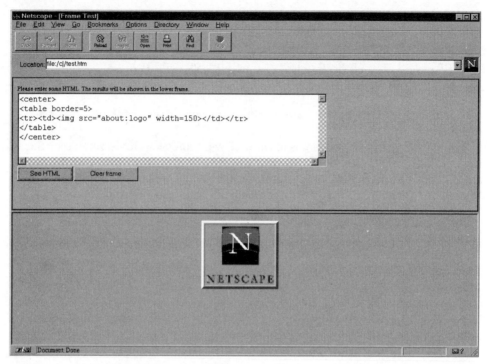

FIGURE 4.1 *The HTML expression program in action.*

hash property
Description: The anchor name following the # sign
Applies to object(s): `location`

The `hash` property is used to extract a local hyperlink from an HTML `<a href>` tag.

host property
Description: The hostname and port property
Applies to object(s): `location`

Contains the hostname and port of the current URL in the format `host:port`

hostname property
Description: The current URL hostname
Applies to object(s): `location`

Contains just the hostname from the currently loaded URL. For example, if `http://www.wombat.com` is loaded into Netscape, the JavaScript statement:

```
hname = location.hostname;
```

would store the string value `"www.wombat.com"` into the variable `hname`.

`href` property
Description: The current URL property
Applies to object(s): `location`

`Location.href` contains the current URL, as loaded into Netscape.

`lastModified` property
Description: Document modification date
Applies to object(s): `document`

This property contains the date on which the current hypertext document was last modified.

`length` property
Description: Object lengths
Applies to object(s): `history`, `radioButton`, `string`, `anchors`, `forms`, `frames`, `links` and `options`

For a `history` object the length of the history list is returned; for a `string` object the length of the string (in characters) is returned (`null` strings return a zero length); for a `radioButton` object the number of radio buttons is returned. For `anchors`, `frames`, `forms`, `option` and `link` objects the number of elements in each structure is returned.

`linkColor` property
Description: Hyperlink colour
Applies to object(s): `document`

The `linkColor` property contains the current hypertext document's hyperlink colour, expressed as a hexadecimal-encoded red–green–blue triplet of the form `"#RRGGBB"`, as set by the HTML `<body link="#RRGGBB">..</body>` container. You can assign a value directly to this property to change its colour.

`links` property
Description: Array of hyperlinks in the current document

Applies to object(s): `document`

The `links` property is an array of hyperlinks that exist within a hypertext document. Hyperlinks are created in HTML using the `<a href=URL>linkText</a>` container tag. It is `linkText` that is stored within the `links` array. You can use the `links` property to provide an index of hyperlinks. For example, consider the frameset HTML document shown below, perhaps named `index.htm`:

```
<!—index.htm—>
<html>
<head>
<title>A sample hyperlink indexer</title>
</head>
<frameset rows="50%,50%">
  <frame src="links.htm">
  <frame src="empty.htm">
</frameset>
</html>
```

where `empty.htm` is an HTML file with an empty body, for example:

```
<html>
<head>
</head>
<body>
</body>
</html>
```

which will be used as a *repository frame document* for our hyperlink index. The file `links.htm` is where all the action happens and resembles the following:

```
<html>
<head>
<script language="JavaScript">
<!—
function showLinks() {
  // Refer to each frame using the variables theDoc1
  // and theDoc2:
  var theDoc1 = window.parent.frames[0].document;
  var theDoc2 = window.parent.frames[1].document;
  var counter = 1;
```

```
theDoc2.writeln("Index of hyperlinks in the main
   document:<p>");

// Output the link-index to the second (lower) frame:
for (var n = 0; n < theDoc1.links.length; n++) {
   theDoc2.writeln(counter, ". <a href="+
   theDoc1.links[n] + ">" +
      theDoc1.links[n] +
      "</a><br>");
   counter++;
   }
}
<!——>
</script>
</head>
<body onLoad="showLinks()">
My home page is <a href="http://www.gold.net/users/ag17/
   index.htm">here</a>,
and Netscape's is <a href="http://home.netscape.com">
   here</a>.
Here is yet another hyperlink to
<a href ="http://www.microsoft.com">Microsoft's</a>
   home page.
</body>
</html>
```

First of all we define some variables to point to each frame. Refer to the section on the `frames` and `parent` properties at this stage if you do not understand these concepts. When the file `links.htm` is loaded, an `onLoad` event embedded within the `<body>` tag invokes the JavaScript function `showLinks()`. The `onLoad` event is triggered *after* the current document is loaded. The file `links.htm` has a number of example hyperlinks created using `<a href>` tags. These hyperlinks are accessed using a simple `for` loop using the `links` array property, and are output into the lower frame for the user to see. You could omit the `onLoad` attribute and invoke the list using another component, such as an HTML button.

For more information on frameset documents, see the section on the `frames` property. The `parent` property simply references the original `<frameset>` tag and must be used when addressing specific frames within an HTML document.

LN2 property
Description: The natural logarithm of 2
Applies to object(s): `Math`

A mathematical constant, here the natural logarithm of 2 (~0.693).

LN10 property

Description: The natural logarithm of 10
Applies to object(s): Math

Another mathematical constant, here the natural logarithm of 10 (~2.303).

location property

Description: The full URL of the current document
Applies to object(s): document

The document.location property contains the full URL of the current hypertext document.

method property

Description: Form posting method property
Applies to object(s): form

Contains the form transmittal method "post" or "get" , as set via the method attribute of the HTML <form>..</form> container.

name property

Description: Object name property
Applies to object(s): applet, button, checkbox, form, password, radioButton, reset, submit and text

The name property is defined in nearly every Netscape HTML tag via the name attribute. It is used to return the name of the object. In the case of submit, reset and button objects the name property returns the value attribute, i.e. the name of the button (since reset, submit and button are all visible buttons with text placed within them).

options property

Description: A list of options in a <select> tag
Applies to object(s): selection

The options property contains details of the elements within an <option> tag of an HTML <select>..</select> container. It is an array of such objects, so for a selection object named browser the expression:

```
browser.options[0]
```

would store the first `<option>` selection value. The number of selection objects can be returned using the `length` property, i.e. `browser.options.length`. See also the `selected` and `text` properties for more information.

`parent` property
Description: The parent frame window property
Applies to object(s): `window`

In a *frameset* document (i.e. one that defines a framed window using the Netscape HTML `<frameset>..</frameset>` container), the `parent` property returns the name of the parent window. For example:

```
window.parent.frames[0].document
```

where `frames` is the name of the standard property that refers to the frames within the current frameset document, and `document` is the current document property. This expression addresses the document loaded into the first frame of the current frameset document, so you could write HTML-formatted text into a frame using the JavaScript statement:

```
window.parent.frames[0].document.writeln("Some
  <b>HTML</b> text");
```

It is better to define a variable with the name of the document and frame that you want to write into, and then use this with methods such as `writeln()`; for example:

```
var theDoc1 = window.parent.frames[0].document;
var theDoc2 = window.parent.frames[1].document;
...
theDoc1.writeln("Frame 1"); // Writes to frame 1
theDoc2.writeln("Frame 2"); // Writes to frame 2
```

See the entry for the `frames` property for further information on using frame-related properties.

`pathname` property
Description: Pathname/URL information property
Applies to object(s): `location`

The `pathname` property returns the file or path after the third slash ('/' or '\') in the current URL. For example, if the current URL is `http://www.gold.net/ users/ag17/index.htm`, the expression:

```
location.pathname
```

returns `"users/ag17/index.htm"`.

PI property
Description: Mathematical constant π (*pi*)
Applies to object(s): `Math`

The mathematical constant π (~3.1416).

port property
Description: URL port number
Applies to object(s): `location`

The `port` property returns the current port number from the URL (if specified). For example, if the current URL was `http://www.somehost.com:8080/index.html` the value of `location.port` would be `8080`.

protocol property
Description: Protocol access method
Applies to object(s): `location`

Returns the protocol access method, based upon the current URL (including colon), e.g. `http:`, `gopher:` or `news:`.

selectedIndex property
Description: A numeric value representing the `<option>` selected in a `<select>` container
Applies to object(s): `selection`

The `selectedIndex` property is used in conjunction with a selection object created using the HTML `<select>..<option>..<select>` container. Options placed within a `<select>` container are stored in JavaScript as an array, so in order to ascertain which option has been selected the `selectedIndex` property must be used. Properties such as `text` and `value` can then be used to extract actual option values. Please refer to the section on the `text` property for a full example.

self property
Description: Current window property
Applies to object(s): `window`

The **self** property refers to the current **window** object. This property can be used to make code more readable and to avoid ambiguity.

status property
Description: Transient status bar message
Applies to object(s): **window**

The **status** property represents a transient message in the Netscape status bar at the bottom of the current window (not to be confused with the **defaultStatus** property, which stores the default status bar message). For example, we could have the following JavaScript/HTML document:

```
<html>
<body>
<a href="http://www.gold.net/users/ag17/index.htm"
  onMouseOver="self.status='Please click me!';
    return true">
  <img src="image1.gif" border=0>
</a>
</body>
</html>
```

This script defines an image (**image1.gif**) as a hyperlink and then launches the URL in the **<a href>** tag when the hyperlink is clicked upon. As the user moves over the hyperlink the message *"Please click me!"* is displayed (this stays in the status bar until a new message replaces it).

target property
Description: The window targeted for form response
Applies to object(s): **form** and **link**

The **target** property returns the value placed in the **target** keyword of the HTML **<form>** tag. This specifies a window that is to be used for any feedback after the form has been submitted, and works in conjunction with a **<frameset>** tag.

text property
Description: The text after an **<option>** tag
Applies to object(s): **selection**

The **text** property contains the text placed after an **<option>** tag within a **<select>..</select>** container, and could be used to extract the option that has been selected by the user.

In order to write a script to access and process selection lists you will have to make use of three different JavaScript properties. The first is the `selectedIndex` property. This contains the actual option selected by the user. By itself, `selectedIndex` is useless until it is used with the `options` property (which contains an array of `<options>`s that are contained within an HTML `<select>..</select>` container. Finally, we need the `text` property to retrieve the text of the option, as specified immediately after the `<option>` tag. Consider the following JavaScript application:

```
<html>
<head>
<script language="JavaScript">
<!--
function showSelection() {
  var idx = document.forms[0].uj.selectedIndex;
  alert('You selected: ' +
    document.forms[0].uj.options[idx].text);
}
<!-->
</script>
</head>
<body>
<form>
Have you ever used JavaScript before?
<select name="uj">
<option selected>No
<option>Yes
</select>
<hr>
<input type="button"
  value="Submit!"
  onClick="showSelection()">
</form>
</body>
</html>
```

This document has a single JavaScript function named `showSelection()`, and is activated when the user clicks on a button within an HTML form. `showSelection()` creates a variable named `idx` which contains the index number of the option selected (options are stored as arrays in JavaScript). The expression that does this is:

```
document.forms[0].uj.selectedIndex;
```

where **forms[0]** refers to the first form within the current document (see the earlier section on the **forms** property), and **uj** is a selection list object created with an HTML **<select name="uj">..</select>** container.

In order to ascertain which option has been selected, the **selectedIndex** property has been used. This property only works with selection list objects, and returns a number according to the **<option>** selected by the user. Now that we have this number stored away, we can use it in an expression that specifies the **text** property, namely:

```
document.forms[0].uj.options[idx].text
```

which in this case uses the **idx** variable to *index* the **options** array property, and thus return the option selected. The **value** property can also be used to access a **value** attribute stored with the **<option>** tag so that more complicated values can be returned, rather than simple option descriptions (this feature was not implemented within beta 5, however).

title property
Description: Document title
Applies to object(s): **document**

The **title** property contains the document title as set by the **<title>..</title>** container within the current HTML file loaded into Netscape.

value property
Description: The value of a field
Applies to object(s): **button, checkbox, reset, submit, radioButton, password, selection, text** and **textArea**

The **value** property returns a string value based upon the **value** attribute when used with **button, reset** and **submit** objects. With a checkbox the string value **"on"** is returned if an item is checked, and **"off"** if unchecked. Radio buttons and selection lists will return the literal value of the **value** attribute that they are created with; **text** and **textArea** objects will yield a verbatim copy of the string (or strings) entered within them.

vlinkColor property
Description: The colour of a 'visited' link
Applies to object(s): **document**

The `vlinkColor` property returns a hexadecimal-encoded red–green–blue triplet that represents the colour of all visited hyperlinks. A *visited* hyperlink is one that has been clicked upon in the past, and which is stored in the Netscape URL history file `NETSCAPE.HST`. Visited link colours are initially set using the HTML `<body vlink="#RRGGBB">` tag, or, if not specified here, internally in Netscape's *Options/Preferences* menu.

`window` property
Description: The current window
Applies to object(s): `document`

Refers to the current window. See also `self`.

CHAPTER

5

JavaScript's standard methods

JavaScript provides the developer with an impressive range of methods that perform a variety of fundamental tasks. Methods are analogous to *functions* or *procedures* in other programming languages, and control just about every action within a JavaScript program. In this chapter you will learn:

- How to create *dynamic* HTML documents that are reflected in the Netscape browser using JavaScript's `write()` and `writeln()` methods
- How to obtain user input using JavaScript's `prompt()` method
- How to access date and time variables

Using JavaScript's standard methods

JavaScript arrives with an extensive set of standard methods, some of which we have already seen in earlier sections. By integrating these methods into your JavaScript applications you can control the objects that appear within a hypertext document to a much greater degree.

Some JavaScript methods return specific values, such as `true` and `false`, and some do not. For each method the syntax, return value and object family is also shown. Methods are said to fall into a particular object class: for example, `abs()` is a `Math` object method. JavaScript's object families were discussed in Chapter 3. Be sure to note the syntax description when referring to each method; some methods require their object family name to be prefixed onto them.

abs()
Syntax: `Math.abs(val)`
Returns: The absolute value of the numeric argument `val`
Object family: `Math`

The absolute value of a number is that number with any preceding sign removed. For example, the value **−5** has an absolute value of **5**, which can be seen using the simple script:

```
<html>
<head>
<script language="JavaScript">
<!-- start:
x = -5;                              // Negative value
document.writeln(Math.abs(x));  // ... now positive
<!-- end -->
</script>
</head>
</html>
```

acos()
Syntax: `Math.acos(val)`
Returns: Arc cosine value of `val`
Object family: `Math`

`acos()` is a mathematical method that returns the arc cosine (in radians) of the numeric argument `val` that is passed to it.

FIGURE 5.1 *The* `alert()` *dialog from the JavaScript example.*

alert()

Syntax: `alert(string | expression);`
Returns: Nothing
Object family: `window`

The `alert()` method allows a string of text to be displayed within a window on the user's screen. The window is autonomous from Netscape and can be moved by the user, although not shut down. An exclamation mark icon will be shown by the side of the message and an `'OK'` button will be provided to clear the message from the screen. HTML-formatted text will be shown literally within `string` and should not therefore be used. Since `window` is a top-level object, you do not need to prefix the `alert()` method with `'window'`; `alert()` is allowed by itself. In order to break up lines in the alert box use the `\n` (*new line*) code; for example:

```
alert("\nWelcome to my Home Page!\n\nThis page " +
      "requires Netscape 1.1 or higher.");
```

would display some text on two separate lines within a window, as shown in Figure 5.1.

Notice how Netscape places the title `"JavaScript Alert:"` at the top of the text to distinguish the message from a standard Windows 95 dialog box. This text cannot be removed and is provided automatically by Netscape.

TIP
Codes such as `\n` are best used in JavaScript functions that output HTML-formatted text into the browser. An example is the `document.writeln()` function, explained later on in this chapter.

Functions that display text within a window, such as `alert()` and `confirm()` (discussed below) only understand \n.

`alert()` is useful as a validation mechanism, for example by defining a function that validates a particular field of an input form, for example:

```
function validateName(name) {
  if (name.length > 30) {
    alert("Names must be less than 30 characters.");
    name.value = ""; // Reset the name
  }
}
```

We can then include the `validateName` function within an HTML form field, such as:

```
<form name="myForm">
<input type="text" name="PersonsName"
  onBlur="validateName(form.PersonsName)">
...
</form>
```

The `onBlur` attribute is new to Netscape 2.0 and allows a JavaScript function, here `validateName()`, to be called when the focus from a text field is lost – in this case when the user moves out of the `PersonsName` field within the form. Notice how the `form` object precedes the name of the text field that we are passing to the `validateName()` function. Event-handling attributes are covered in more detail later on in this chapter.

TIP

The `alert()` method can also display the value of an expression, which can be useful for debugging purposes, for example:

```
alert(null == "");
```

will return `false`, since the expression does not hold true. (It is useful to note also that `null` is a special value that means that a string object has no value; it is not the same as an empty string, however, as this statement will demonstrate.) You can also include other methods within `alert()` boxes; for example:

```
alert("The date is " + Date()
```

---

anchor()

Syntax: `stringObj.anchor(anchName);`
Returns: Nothing
Object family: `string`

Anchors are targets for HTML `<a href="#anchorName">..</a>` tags. They are points within a hypertext document that can be moved to using a hyperlink that addresses the anchor. Anchors are useful for creating indexes and for providing the user with a way of moving within a document (or documents). Anchors can exist locally (within the same file) or externally (within other files). The target for an anchor can also be a URL, such as another Web server on the Internet.

The `anchor()` method is used to make a string object (`StringObj`) into a named anchor, where `anchName` is the name for the anchor. Consider the following example:

```
<html>
<head>
<script language="JavaScript">
<!—
anchorName = "Section1";
anc        = anchorName.anchor(anchorName);

document.writeln("Click <a href=#Section1>here</a> " +
                 "for section 1.");
/*
** More of the current document appears here
*/

// Section 1:
document.writeln("<a name=" + anchorName + ">" +
                 "<h1>Section 1<hr></h1></a>");
document.writeln("This is the text for section 1.");
<!—>
</script>
</head>
<body>
```

```
<hr>
</body>
</html>
```

which implements a named anchor using the `anchor()` method to create the anchor `"Section1"` (noting that spaces are not allowed in anchor names), where the variable `anchorName` is a string object that contains the name of the anchor, and `anc` is an anchor object that creates the anchor. By clicking on the hyperlink named *here*, users are then positioned at the anchor named `"Section1"`, effectively moving them to that part of the document just as if they had navigated their way manually to this region of the document using the cursor keys etc. If you need to specify an anchor in another HTML file, use the syntax:

```
<a href="filename.html#anchorName">..</a>
```

The `<a href>` code can also be replaced by a JavaScript equivalent, namely the `link()` method, which is used to create a hyperlink. See the later section on `link()` for more information.

asin()

Syntax: `asin(val)`
Returns: The arc sine of the argument passed as `val`
Object family: `Math`

The `asin()` function is passed a numeric value (specified in radians) and produces the arc sine of that value.

atan()

Syntax: `atan(val)`
Returns: The arc tangent of the argument `val`
Object family: `Math`

back()

Syntax: `history.back()`
Returns: Nothing
Object family: `history`

The `history.back()` method simulates the pressing of the *Back* button in Netscape, allowing the previous hypertext document to be loaded. This method performs the same action as a `go(-1)` method. If you use the reload button in

Netscape with a document containing a `back()` statement, Netscape will continue to load the previous URL from the history buffer, i.e. you will retrieve a unique document upon each reloading. You could implement a simple *Back* and *Forward* button of your own in JavaScript as:

```
<html>
<body>
<form>
<input type="button" value="Back"
  onClick="history.back()">
<input type="button" value="Forward"
  onClick="history.forward()">
</form>
</body>
</html>
```

where the `forward()` method invokes the opposite action to `back()`. Emulating Netscape's *Back* and *Forward* buttons can be useful to allow the user to retain basic page navigation controls when a window has its toolbar disabled. Disabling Netscape's main toolbar allows a larger display area to be used – especially if Netscape's directory buttons and location field are disabled. Netscape's toolbars can be disabled by opening a new window using an `open()` method with the `toolbar=no` attribute. See `open()` for more details.

big()
Syntax: `string.big()`
Returns: Nothing
Object family: `string`

Use `big()` with a string to make that string appear in a large font. This makes use of Netscape's `<big>..</big>` tags; for example:

```
document.writeln("This is " + "big".big() + " text");
```

would place the word `"big"` in a `<big>..</big>` container, thus making this word appear in a larger font than the rest of the sentence. Notice how the string object `"big"` has been placed literally in the text; this could be replaced with a string variable if required, of course.

The actual font size rendered by a `<big>` tag will depend on the settings in Netscape's *Options/Preferences/Fonts* setup screen, and will be relative to the base font set within Netscape's Preferences.

blink()

Syntax: `string.blink()`
Returns: Nothing
Object family: `string`

Use `blink()` with a string to make that string blink. This makes use of Netscape's HTML `<blink>..</blink>` container.

```
document.writeln("This is " + "blinking".blink() +
  " good!");
```

blur()

Syntax: `objName.blur()`
Returns: Nothing
Object family: `password, text, textArea`

`blur()` removes focus from a given object (`objName`). *Focus* is the term applied to the object that is currently selected, e.g. a text field within an HTML form.

B()

Syntax: `string.B()`
Returns: Nothing
Object family: `string`

This method makes the specified string object **bold** by encapsulating the string in HTML `<b>..</b>` (bold) tags. Ensure that the case of the function is kept as shown. (This function may become `bold()` in later releases of Netscape.) For example, we could have:

```
myVar = "bold";
document.writeln("This is "+ myVar.B() + " text");
```

which writes the string "This is **bold** text" into the Netscape browser.

charAt()

Syntax: `string.charAt(index);`
Returns: A character at the string index indicated by the numeric value of `index`
Object family: `string`

`charAt()` is used to return a character at a given position within a string. For example:

```
myString = "Wombat";
m_Pos = myString.charAt(2);
```

would set the variable **m_Pos** to the value **"m"**. Note that strings start at position **0** in JavaScript.

clearTimeout()

Syntax: **clearTimeout(id)**
Returns: Nothing
Object family: Not applicable

The **clearTimeout()** method clears the timeout event identified by the timeout identifier **id**. A timeout is basically a countdown to a user-defined event. See **setTimeout()** for more information and an example.

click()

Syntax: **formObject.click()**
Returns: Nothing
Object family: **checkbox, radioButton, reset** and **submit**

The **click()** method allows a simulated button-click to be invoked on the form element named as **formObject**. **click()** works with checkboxes, radio buttons, reset buttons and submit buttons. If **click()** is used on a button, the value of the **name** attribute for the button must be used. Checkboxes and radio buttons can be activated and deactivated with **click()** by quoting the **name** attribute of the checkbox in question. For example, a button defined as:

```
<input name="myButton" type="button" value="Click me!">
```

could be automatically clicked with the JavaScript statement:

```
document.forms[0].myButton.click()
```

as could a checkbox, radio button, submit or reset button. Submit buttons submit an HTML form to a server for processing (or rather, to a CGI script on the server) and are created using an **<input type="submit" ...>** tag. Reset buttons clear the fields within an HTML form and are created using an **<input type="reset" ...>** tag.

close()

Syntaxes:
- **window.close()**
- **document.close()**

Returns: Nothing
Object family: `document, window`

The `close()` method can be used with either `window` or `document` objects.

Document objects
With a `window` object the `close()` method closes a data stream opened using the `document.open()` method, and then writes all of the data in the stream into the browser window. Streams are used for displaying HTML-formatted text. Streams are continuous *chunks* of text that are written into the browser in one go. Multiple `write()` or `writeln()` methods that are used to write data into the browser are considered as continuous streams of text. Streamed text will also appear more quickly in the Netscape browser.

Window objects
When used with a `window` object the `close()` method simply closes the current browser window. New browser windows can be opened using the `window.open()` method.
    Refer to the section on the `open()` method for more information.

confirm()
Syntax: `confirm(String);`
Returns: `true` (for OK button) and `false` (for CANCEL button)
Object family: `window`

The `confirm()` function displays a user-defined message within a window and presents OK and CANCEL buttons that the user can click on. The function returns a boolean (logical) value depending on the button pressed by the user, which can be used as a test condition for a task or action. For example, we could have the following code:

```
var result = confirm("Are you sure?");
if (result == true) {
  alert("You clicked on the 'OK' button");
}
else {
  alert("You clicked on the 'CANCEL' button");
}
```

In this small JavaScript example, the variable `result` is assigned the value returned from the `confirm()` function. Upon clicking an appropriate button, an `if` statement shows a simple message indicating the button pressed (although of course

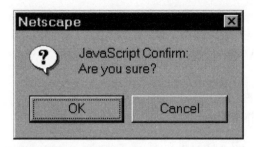

FIGURE 5.2 *The* `confirm()` *dialog in the JavaScript example on p. 116.*

any valid JavaScript statements can be placed in these code blocks). Figure 5.2 illustrates the `confirm()` window from the above example. Notice how the text *"JavaScript Confirm:"* is placed in the window so that you know that this dialog originates from the Netscape JavaScript interpreter.

It is possible to shorten your code somewhat when using `if` statements with the `confirm()` function. Consider the following code, for example, where the `confirm()` function has been integrated into an `if` statement in the same line:

```
var result;
if ((result=confirm("Are you sure?")) == true) {
  // User pressed on 'OK' button
  alert("You pressed OK");
}
```

However, to be even more compact you can omit the '==' testing criterion completely, for example:

```
if (confirm("Are you sure?")) {
  // User pressed on 'OK' button
  alert("You pressed OK");
}
```

since `confirm()` is a boolean method and specific variables do not need to be set in order to test the value that it actually returns.

cos()
Syntax: `cos(val);`
Returns: The cosine of the argument `val`
Object family: `Math`

escape()

Syntax: `escape(character)`
Returns: The hexadecimal value for the ASCII code of the of the `character` argument.
Object family: Not applicable

The `escape()` method allows the ASCII code of a non-alphanumeric (alphabetic) character in the ISO Latin-1 character set to be returned in the format `%nn`, where `nn` is the numeric ASCII code. The value of `nn` is stored in hexadecimal (base 16). For example:

```
var exclamVar = escape("!")
```

would store the value `"%21"` into the variable `exclamVar` since 21 is the hexadecimal representation of the decimal number 33, and the ASCII code for 33 is an exclamation mark (!). To convert hexadecimal values to decimal (base 10) numbers, use JavaScript's the `unEscape()` method.

eval()

Syntax: `eval(arithmetic-expression)`
Returns: The value of the evaluated expression as a number
Object family: None. The `eval()` method is not associated with any object as such, but is built in to the JavaScript language

`eval()` takes an arithmetic expression as an argument and returns the result of the expression as a number. For example:

```
price = 868;
calcVat = eval(price * 1.175);
```

adds `17.5%` to the variable `price` and places the result in the variable `calcVat`.

exp()

Syntax: `exp(val)`
Returns: The exponent of the numeric argument `val`
Object family: `Math`

This mathematical method returns Euler's constant (e) to the power of the argument `val`.

```
e = exp(1); // Returns 2.71828...
```

The `Math.E` property returns the same value as exp(1).

focus()
Syntax: `obj.focus();`
Returns: Nothing
Object family: `password`, `text`, `textArea`

This function moves the focus to the object `obj`, that is to say that object `obj` becomes the currently selected object within the browser. For example, a text area field created and named using the HTML `<textarea>..</textarea>` tag could be given the focus so that the cursor appears within that field ready for the user to enter or change a value within it.

fontcolor()
Syntax: `string.fontcolor(RGB-color)`
Returns: Nothing
Object family: `string`

This method sets the colour of a string using the `<font color="#rrggbb">..` `</font>` tags in Netscape. The argument `RGB-color` is a red–green–blue triplet specified in hexadecimal notation, `#FFFF00` being yellow and `#0000FF` being blue, for example.

fontsize()
Syntax: `fontsize(size)`
Returns: Nothing
Object family: `string`

The `fontsize()` method allows text to be changed in size. This is done by encapsulating a string in Netscape `<fontsize=size>..</fontsize>` tags. For example, to print a string of text with a font size of 14 points the following statement could be used:

```
document.writeln(MyString.fontsize(14));
```

where `MyString` is a string object (i.e. a string variable). There is also a `size` attribute in the `<font>` tag (a Netscape HTML extension) that can be used. `<fontsize>` was not implemented in Netscape beta 4, but should be included in future versions. You could of course use the `<font size=size>..</font>` tag, if required.

forward()
Syntax: forward()
Returns: Nothing
Object family: history

Use the forward() method to simulate the pressing of the Netscape *Forward* button. The Forward button is a navigation button in Netscape's toolbar that allows the user to move between previously loaded documents. This method is the same as issuing a go(1) statement. See also the back() method.

getDate()
Syntax: dateObject.getDate()
Returns: The day of the month (a number between 1 and 31) for the date object named dateObject
Object family: Date

This method can be used to extract the current day number from the current month. Be sure to apply the function to a Date object, such as that provided by the JavaScript Date() method. For example:

```
theDate = new Date("August 8, 1996 08:08:08");
theDay = theDate.getDate();
```

would store the value 8 in the variable theDay.

getDay()
Syntax: dateObject.getDay()
Returns: The day of the week for the date object named dateObject. The following integer values are returned from getDay(): 0 – Sunday; 1 – Monday; 2 – Tuesday; 3 – Wednesday; 4 – Thursday; 5 – Friday; and 6 – Saturday.
Object family: Date

For example:

```
theDate = new Date("December 28, 1995 11:00:00");
DayNum = theDate.getDay();
```

would store the value 4 into the variable DayNum, since 28 December 1995 fell on a Thursday.

getMinutes()
Syntax: dateObject.getMinutes()

Returns: The minutes in the date object named as `dateObject`
Object family: `Date`

For example, if we had:

```
theDate = new Date("December 28, 1995 11:33:00");
Mins = theDate.getMinutes();
```

The value `33` would be stored in the variable `Mins`.

`getSeconds()`
Syntax: `dateObject.getSeconds()`
Returns: The seconds in the date object named `dateObject`
Object family: `Date`

`getTime()`
Syntax: `dateObject.getTime()`
Returns: The number of milliseconds since the JavaScript epoch date (1 January 1970 00:00:00)
Object family: `Date`

`getTimezoneOffset()`
Syntax: `dateObject.getTimezoneOffset()`
Returns: The time zone difference (in minutes) between local time and GMT
Object family: `Date`

For example, we could have:

```
theDate = Date();
Localtime = theDate.getTimezoneOffset();
```

`getYear()`
Syntax: `dateObject.getYear()`
Returns: The year value from the date object `dateObject`
Object family: `Date`

`go()`
Syntax: `object.go(val | "String")`
Returns: Nothing
Object family: `history`

`go()` is a `history` method that moves the user to a different hypertext document based upon the current Netscape document history. The method can be passed one of two arguments: (i) an integer value `val` that represents the number of history entries to move backwards or forwards (use negatively signed integers for backwards movement, e.g. `-3`); or (ii) a `String` representing a URL to move to based upon that string matching a substring of the `String` argument. That is to say, you can search for a URL in the history list using a substring search, upon which Netscape will then load the URL for that history entry (strings are not case-sensitive). For example:

```
history.go(-3);
```

would move backwards three history entries, according to the current Netscape document history, whereas:

```
history.go("users/ag17");
```

would search the current Netscape history for a string containing "users/ag17" and then load that URL accordingly, e.g. `http://www.gold.net/users/ag17/index.htm`. If multiple URLs are matched, only the first is returned.

indexOf()

Syntax: `stringObj.indexOf(char, [index])`
Returns: The index (an integer) representing the position of the first character, `char`, optionally starting from position `index`
Object family: `string`

`indexOf()` is a string-based function that is used to search for instances of a particular character in a text string. For example:

```
aString = "wombat@marsupial.somehost.au";
PosAt = aString.indexOf("@");
```

would place the value 6 in to the variable named `PosAt`, since the character '@' lies at position six within the string stored in variable `aString`, remembering that in JavaScript index positions start at zero (0). So, for example, we could extract the hostname from the above string using:

```
HostName = aString.substring(PosAt, aString.length);
```

which uses JavaScript's `substring()` method to extract the part of the string we need. The `index` argument is used when you want to start the search from a specific character within a string – you could use `indexOf()` to ascertain this value, of course.

I()

Syntax: `StringObj.I()`
Returns: Nothing
Object family: `string`

Changes the appearance of the string object named `StringObj` so that it is *italicized*. The effect is made using an HTML `<i>..</i>` (italics) container that encapsulates the `StringObj` object. The `italics()` method has also been proposed.

lastIndexOf()

Syntax: `StringObj.lastIndexOf(char | [,index])`
Returns: The index within the calling string of the last occurrence of the specified character
Object family: `string`

The calling string is searched in a backwards manner, optionally starting at position `index` (which can range from `0` to `StringObj.length-1`).

link()

Syntax: `stringObj.link(UrlString)`
Returns: Nothing
Object family: `string`

The `link()` method makes the string object `locString` into an HTML hyperlink by encapsulating the string within an HTML `<a href>..</a>` container. The method is used to dynamically create hyperlinks from within JavaScript programs, rather than using HTML. The `UrlString` object must therefore be a valid URL, and `stringObj` is the text for the hyperlink, i.e. the text that the user sees within Netscape. For example, we could use the following JavaScript code to create a hyperlink to the URL `http://www.gold.net/users/ag17/index.htm`

```
<html>
<head>
<script language="JavaScript">
<!-- start script
myUrl = "http://www.gold.net/users/ag17/index.htm";
ref   = "here";
document.writeln("Click " + ref.link(myUrl) +
```

```
                           " to visit my home page.");
      <!— end of script —>
      </script>
      </head>
      <body><hr></body>
      </html>
```

In this case the variable `ref` is a string object that contains the single word `"here"`, and which represents the text of the hyperlink that the user will click on. The actual URL is stored in the string object named `myUrl`; therefore the expression `ref.link(myUrl)` creates the link we require. In order to display the link within the current HTML document, the `document.writeln()` method is used.

In order to provide an anchor for a *local* hyperlink, i.e. a link to another part of a document, use a URL of the form `filename#anchorname` (or just `#anchorName` for the current document) with the `anchor()` method – see earlier in this section.

log()
Syntax: `log(val)`
Returns: The natural logarithm (base e) of the numeric argument `val`
Object family: `Math`

max()
Syntax: `max(val1, val2)`
Returns: The larger numeric argument, `val1` or `val2`
Object family: `Math`

The `max()` method should be used to return the greater of two arguments. For example:

```
number1 = 100;
number2 = 101;
largest = max(number1, number2);
```

places the value `101` into the numeric-variable `largest`.

min()
Syntax: `min(val1, val2)`
Returns: The lesser numeric argument, `val1` or `val2`
Object family: `Math`

`min()` works in the opposite manner to the `max()` method, as described above.

open()

Syntaxes:
- ```
  window.open("URL", "windowName",
  ["WindowFeatures,..."]);
  ```
- ```
  document.open( [ "MIME-type" ] );
  ```

Returns: Window ID value (for `window.open()` method)
Object family: `window` and `document`

The `open()` method in JavaScript works in two modes, the first for document-based objects and the second for window-based objects. Note that issuing an `open()` by itself is equivalent to calling `document.open()`.

Window-based objects

`window.open()` opens a new browser window, rather like selecting the *New Web Browser* option from the *File* menu in Netscape. The `"URL"` argument is a URL that you want to load when the window is opened, such as the address of another Web site (`http://`) or a local file (`file://`). If the `"URL"` argument is left blank, `window.open()` opens a blank window.

The `"windowName"` argument allows the newly created browser window to be allocated a title, and if left blank the Netscape default is used (this simply shows the words 'Netscape' and the URL of the currently loaded document).

`windowFeatures` is an optional argument that specifies the windows appearance. A comma-separated list of values controls this. Table 5.1 illustrates the values that can be used (note that no spaces are allowed).

The values in Table 5.1 all default to `yes` and the new window size emulates the previous window (if left unspecified). The ordering of attributes is not important. The `copyhistory` attribute copies the previous Netscape history into the current window, while `directories` enables or disables the standard Netscape directory buttons that link into Netscape's Web server at `http://home.netscape.com` (e.g. the *Net Search* button).

For example, we could create a new window measuring 500 pixels by 300 pixels with the following JavaScript code:

```
myUrl = "http://www.gold.net/users/ag17/index.htm";
window.open(myUrl, "My home page!",
  "width=500,height=300");
```

where `myUrl` is the URL that we want to load into the new window, and `"My home page!"` is the title for the new window. The window's features are specified in the last argument; all of the standard window features are kept in this case – only the `width` and `height` of the window are changed.

TABLE **5.1** *windowFeatures arguments*

Attribute	Values		Description
`toolbar`	`[=yes|no]`	`[=1|0]`	Toolbar mode (on/off)
`location`	`[=yes|no]`	`[=1|0]`	Location bar (on/off)
`directories`	`[=yes|no]`	`[=1|0]`	Directory buttons (on/off)
`status`	`[=yes|no]`	`[=1|0]`	Status bar (on/off)
`menubar`	`[=yes|no]`	`[=1|0]`	Menu bar (on/off)
`scrollbars`	`[=yes|no]`	`[=1|0]`	Scroll bars? (yes/no)
`resizable`	`[=yes|no]`	`[=1|0]`	Resizable window? (yes/no)
`copyhistory`	`[=yes|no]`	`[=1|0]`	Copy the history? (yes/no)
`width`	`= pixelwidth`		Window width
`height`	`= pixelheight`		Window height

TIP

In order to write HTML-formatted text into a window, simply use JavaScript's standard methods, such as `document.writeln()`, remembering to **name** the new window and then **prefix** each statement with the window name that you want the text displayed in.

Here is another example, which houses the `open()` method in a JavaScript function. The window is named so that it can be referenced at a later stage using JavaScript's `writeln()` method. You must name a window by assigning it to a variable if you want to target it specifically at a later stage:

```
function CreateNewWindow(url, name, options) {
  myWin = window.open(url, name, options);
  myWin.document.writeln("A <b>new</b> window!");
}
```

In this function declaration, the arguments `url`, `name` and `options` are passed to the `open()` method verbatim. We could thus call this function using the statement:

```
CreateNewWindow("", "Demonstration"!",
width=600,height=400");
```

which in this case does not specify a URL to load, but instead writes the HTML-formatted text 'A **new** window!' into the window. You can create and reference as many windows as you like in this way.

TIP
If you place a `<title>..</title>` container in the text within a newly created window, this will override the `windowName` argument that is passed to the `open()` method.

TIP
Why not put all of the window options in a single string and pass this to the `open()` method? This makes the method more readable, and saves line space; for example:

```
winOpts = "width=500,height=250,scrollbars=0";
window.open("", "Blank window", winOpts);
```

JavaScript's event-handling features can also be put to good use with windows. For example, a button in an HTML form could activate a window showing some options or a help screen:

```
<html>
<head>
<script language="JavaScript">
<!— start:
function HelpWin() {
  w = window.open('helpfile.htm', 'newWin',
  'toolbar=no,menubar=no,width=300,height=300')">
}
<!— end —>
</script>
</head>
<body>
<form name="HelpForm">
<input type="button" name="HelpButton" value="Help!"
onClick="HelpWin()";
</form>
</body>
</html>
```

In this case the button `HelpButton` invokes the JavaScript function `HelpWin()`, which creates a new browser window with the arguments specified. You can replace the function with whatever you require, of course. The HTML file `helpfile.htm` is then read into the window and displayed.

The `window.close()` method can be used to close the new window once the user has finished with it, so you may want to include the following in the file you read into the window (`helpfile.htm` in this case):

```
<form>
<input type="button"
  value="Exit help window"
  onClick="window.close()">
</form>
```

which closes the current window, i.e. the window in which the document containing this `<form>` is located. A window can also be closed by clicking on the cross in the upper right-hand corner of the window (a standard feature in Windows 95).

If you want to create a window and document *on-the-fly* simply omit the URL argument and use `write()` to place text in the window. For example, using the following JavaScript function:

```
function windowOpener() {
  m = window.open("","Display window",
    "toolbar=no,directories=no,menubar=no");
  m.document.write("<title>My window</title>");
  m.document.write("<body>Here is my body text</body>");
  m.document.write("<form><input type='button' " +
    "value='Exit' onClick='window.close()'>" +
  "</form>");
}
```

The `windowOpener()` function creates a new window and writes some HTML-formatted text (including a button to close the window) directly into it.

Remember that you can stop the user from meddling with any of Netscape's menus and other options by creating a *minimalist* window, i.e. a window with all menus and options disabled – effectively allowing the user only to browse the text within the current window, as in the previous example, which disables the Netscape toolbar, menu bar and directory buttons.

 TIP
Remember to use single quotes inside HTML constructs that use double quotes, such as in `onClick` event handlers (as in the example above). In

fact, you *can* use the same type of quotes just as long as you 'escape' them using the \ character, for example:

```
<input type="button" name="myButton"
  value="Click!"
  onClick="alert(\"Hello World!\")">;
```

Such 'escaping' is widely deployed in many scripting languages to remove any *special properties* from a given character – in this case it allows the same type of quote to be used within an `onClick` event-handler attribute. Personally, I would use the single-quote mechanism.

Document-based objects

`document.open()` is used to collect a text stream consisting of a series of `document.write()` or `document.writeln()` statements. These statements write HTML-formatted text directly into the Netscape browser. A `document.close()` statement must then be used to close the stream and load the data immediately into the browser.

The `MIME-type` argument is optional, and if specified dictates the format of the file being written into the browser. MIME, or Multipurpose Internet Mail Extensions, is a naming standard for specifying different file formats. For example, in Netscape 2.0 the MIME-type for a GIF image is `image/gif`, whereas an HTML document is referred to as `text/html`. If you click on Netscape's *Options* menu, select *General Preferences* and then click on the *Helpers* tab you will see a long list of MIME types that are currently supported, including *plug-in* MIME-types; `text/html` is the default MIME-type for the `document.open()` method. Netscape 2.0 understands the following MIME-types:

- `text/html` – specifies a document containing ASCII text with HTML formatting
- `text/plain` – specifies a document containing plain ASCII text
- `image/gif` – specifies a document constituting a GIF image
- `image/jpeg` – specifies a document constituting a JPEG image
- `image/xbm` – specifies a document constituting an X bitmap image

In order to use a plug-in, for example a VRML viewer such as Chacho Communications' VR Scout VRML plug-in, the MIME-type `x-world/vrml` could be specified. This would load the plug-in application and use it as the destination for any `write()` or `writeln()` methods.

For example, here is a simple JavaScript function, `textStreamWin()`, which creates a new window and writes an HTML-formatted text stream into it:

```
function textStreamWin() {
   str = "Here is some <b>HTML-formatted</b> text";
   w = window.open("","Example window", "toolbar=no");
   w.document.open();
   w.document.write("<hr>");
   w.document.write(str);
   w.document.write("<hr>");
   w.document.close();
}
```

It isn't necessary to use `document.open()` and `document.close()` for *every* piece of HTML-formatted text that you write into the Netscape browser. The main benefit of streams is that they offer a performance advantage.

parseInt()

Syntax: `parseInt(string, radix)`
Returns: An integer based on the parsing operation on the argument `string`
Object family: Not applicable

The `parseInt()` function is used to convert a string to a different radix (or *base*). Bases include hexadecimal (16), octal (8) and decimal (10). The `string` argument is the number to parse, for example a hexadecimal number such as `"FF"` (decimal 255). `parseInt()` is useful for number conversions. If `parseInt()` encounters a character that is not a numeral in the specified radix it ignores the character and all successive characters and returns a value based upon the conversion up to that point. If the first character in `string` cannot be converted to a number within the specified radix, `parseInt()` returns zero. All values returned by `parseInt()` are truncated to integers, i.e. whole numbers. For example:

```
parseInt("12", 10)
```

returns 12, since the `radix` argument is 10 and thus a decimal number is returned (the unaltered value 15 in this instance). The expression:

```
parseInt("12.68", 10)
```

also returns 12, since `parseInt()` always returns an integer (a whole number).
   When converting hexadecimal numbers, the numerals A to F are used for numbers above 9 .e.g. 10 = A, 11 is B, 12 is C and so on. Thus the expression:

```
parseInt("F", 10)
```

returns the value 15 since **F** is 15 in decimal (base 10).

pow(val1, val2)
Syntax: pow(val1, val2)
Returns: val1 to the power of val2
Object family: Math

The power function is represented in JavaScript by the **pow()** method. For example:

```
tenTimesten = pow(10,10);   // Same as 10 * 10
```

prompt()
Syntax: prompt("message", input-default)
Returns: A string entered by the user
Object family: window

The **prompt()** method is JavaScript's primary data input method, allowing keyboard input from the user to be stored in a variable. The **prompt()** method provides a window and input field automatically when it is invoked. The **"message"** argument represents a string to display when showing the initial input prompt, and **"input-default"** is a default value that is placed within the input field. For example, we could define and invoke a simple JavaScript function as follows:

```
function goSomewhere() {
   // Ask the user to i/p a URL, and suggest a default:
   goHere = prompt("Where do you want to go?",
                   "http://wombat.doc.ic.ac.uk");

   // Load the URL into a new window:
   myWin = window.open(goHere, "", "width=600");
}
```

You can make your code more compact by omitting the assignment of a variable to the **prompt()** method. For example, in the previous example you could use a statement of the form:

```
window.open(prompt("Where do you want to go?",
                   "http://wombat.doc.ic.ac.uk"), "",
                   "width=600");
```

which integrates **prompt()** directly into the **open()** method.

round()

Syntax: `Math.round(val)`
Returns: The argument, `val`, rounded to the nearest integer (whole number)
Object family: `Math`

The `round()` method is used to round a number. The rules for rounding are as follows: If the argument `val` has a fractional part greater than or equal to `0.5` the number is rounded to `val+1` , otherwise `val` is returned without the fractional part, i.e. as an integer. For example:

```
MyValue1 = 68.5;
MyValue2 = 68.3;
rounded1 = Math.round(MyValue1);   // Result: 69
rounded2 = Math.round(MyValue2);   // Result: 68
```

select()

Syntax: `object.select();`
Returns: Nothing
Object family: `text, textArea, Password`

Highlights an input area of an HTML form (a text field, password field or text area).

TIP
Selection and focus are not the same thing in JavaScript. Use both `select()` and `focus()` to select *and* then allow user input within a form field.

setDate()

Syntax: `dateObject.setDate(day)`
Returns: Nothing
Object family: `Date`

The `setDate()` method is used to set the day of the month for the date object `setDate()`, for example:

```
myDate = new Date("7 August, 1996 12:00:00");
myDate.setDate(8);
```

changes the day from 7 August to 8 August (updating variable `myDate` in the process), where `day` is a value ranging from 1 to 31.

setHours()
Syntax: `dateObject.setHours(hours)`
Returns: Nothing
Object family: `Date`

Sets the hours in the date object `dateObject`, in much the same way as with the previous example, which set the day number in a month (hours = `0-23`)

setMinutes()
Syntax: `dateObject.setMinutes(mins)`
Returns: Nothing
Object family: `Date`

Sets the minutes in the date object `dateObject` (mins = `0-59`).

setMonth()
Syntax: `dateObject.setMonth(month)`
Returns: Nothing
Object family: `Date`

Sets the months in the date object `dateObject`, where `month` is a value ranging from `1-12`.

setSeconds()
Syntax: `dateObject.setSeconds(secs)`
Returns: Nothing
Object family: `Date`

Sets the seconds in the date object `dateObject`, where `secs` is a number ranging from `0-59`.

setTimeout()
Syntax: `setTimeout(expression, msecs)`
Returns: Timeout identifier for the current timeout
Object family: Not applicable

The `setTimeout()` function invokes a JavaScript statement, such as a function call (`expression`) after a specified number of milliseconds (`msecs`), where 1000 milliseconds is equivalent to one second. Timeouts are essentially countdown mechanisms that allow user-defined events to be activated after a certain period of elapsed time. A timeout can only be halted with `clearTimeout()`.

Consider the JavaScript application below, which displays a username and password field (for access into another page, perhaps), and then allows the user 30 seconds to enter a value and submit the password. After 30 seconds have elapsed, the program then reloads the previous page using JavaScript's `document.back()` method.

```
<html>
<head>
<script language="JavaScript">
<!— start:
function TimerFunc() {
   // Create a timeout in 30 seconds to reload the
   // previous hypertext page:
   setTimeout('document.back()', 30000)
}
<!— end —>
</script>
</head>
<body onLoad="TimerFunc()">
<font size="+3"><i>Password Screen...</i><hr></font>
<form name="PassForm"
method="post"
action="http://www.somehost.com/cgi-bin/checkpass">
Please enter your username
<input name="username" type="password" size=10><br>
Please enter your password
<input name="passw" type="password" size=10><p>
You will be returned to the previous page in 30
seconds.<p>
<input type="submit" value="Submit!">
</form>
</body>
</html>
```

In this program the function `TimerFunc()` is automatically invoked when the user loads the current document – notice the `onLoad` event attribute in the `<body>` container. `TimerFunc()` uses `setTimeout()` to run the JavaScript command `document.back()` after 30 000 milliseconds (or 30 seconds). The user is presented with a username and password field. The `action` attribute of the `<form>` specifies that the CGI script `http://www.somehost.com/cgi-bin/checkpass` is run when the form is finally submitted. The executable CGI script `checkpass` will check the username and password and perhaps send back a new hypertext page for access to another part of the system.

Here is another program that uses JavaScript's timeout methods to implement a real-time clock that can be placed in any of your hypertext pages for added effect.

```
<html>
<head>
<script language="JavaScript">
<!— start of script:
function showTime() {
  // Get the current time and extract the hours, minutes
  // and seconds:
  var timeNow = new Date();
  var hours   = timeNow.getHours();
  var minutes = timeNow.getMinutes();
  var seconds = timeNow.getSeconds();

  // Alter the time format so that it is a 12 hour clock:
  var timeString = "" + ((hours > 12) ? hours - 12 :
    hours);

  // Break up the time as HH:MM:SS, making sure that
  // each field has at least two digits:
  timeString  += ((minutes < 10) ? ":0" : ":") + minutes;
  timeString  += ((seconds < 10) ? ":0" : ":") + seconds;

  // Add an AM/PM indicator based on the current hour:
  timeString  += (hours >= 12) ? " p.m." : " a.m.";

  // Update the time-field in the document:
  document.htmlClock.timeField.value = timeString;

  // Update the clock in 1 seconds time:
  timerID = setTimeout("showTime()", 1000);
}
<!— end of script —>
</script>
</head>
<body onLoad="showTime()">
<form name="htmlClock">
<input type="text" name="timeField" size=14>
</form>
</body>
</html>
```

The program defines a single function, `showTime()` that creates a `Date` object called `timeNow` – notice the `new` statement – and then extracts the hours, minutes and seconds using JavaScript's `getHours()`, `getMinutes()` and `getSeconds()` methods. We then ensure that the clock is a 12-hour clock by taking away 12 hours from the `hours` variable in the case that it is greater then 12 (e.g. if `hours` was `16` (4 o'clock) we would calculate `hours` − `12`, which is just the value `4`). `Date` objects include 24-hour times by default. The time is then placed in the format `HH:MM:SS` and we ensure that the `minutes` and `seconds` variables have at least two digits in them so that they adhere to the `HH:MM:SS` format described earlier.

Finally, an `a.m.` or `p.m.` indicator is added based upon the condition that the `hours` variable is greater than `12`. All of these values are placed into a string called `timeString`, whose value is then assigned directly into a field in our document for the user to see. A field named `timeField` exists within a form in the body of the document, and is used to display the value held in the variable `timeString`. The value of `document.htmlClock.timeField.value` is assigned the value of `timeString`, which results in the field being instantly updated. Finally, we update the timeout to run the whole function again in one second's time, thus ensuring that the clock updates every second.

Notice how the behaviour of the `showTime()` function is *recursive*, since it calls itself in order to update the timeout value. Effectively, `showTime()` will call itself forever (or until Netscape is terminated or we move to a new URL).

setYear()
Syntax: `dateObject.setYear(year)`
Returns: Nothing
Object family: `Date`

Sets the year value in the date object `dateObject`. The `year` value must be greater than 1900.

sin()
Syntax: `sin(val)`
Returns: The sine of argument `val`
Object family: `Math`

small()
Syntax: `stringObj.small()`
Returns: Nothing
Object family: `string`

Sets the string identified by `StringObj` in a small font using an HTML `<small>..</small>` container to encapsulate the string object.

sqrt()
Syntax: `sqrt(val)`
Returns: The square root of argument `val`
Object family: `Math`

sub()
Syntax: `StringObj.sub()`
Returns: Nothing
Object family: `string`

Causes the string object named `StringObj` to be set in a subscript font using a Netscape HTML `<sub>..</sub>` container to encapsulate the string.

submit()
Syntax: `submit()`
Returns: Nothing
Object family: `form`

Simulates the pressing of a submit button in an HTML `<form>..</form>` container. The HTML tag `<input type="submit">` is always provided in a form that sends its user input to a Web server for processing. JavaScript can intercept the pressing of this button using `submit()`.

substring()
Syntax: `StringObject.substring(start,length)`
Returns: The substring of string `StringObject`
Object family: `string`

The `substring()` method is used to extract substrings from a string object. The `start` argument specifies the index position of the string (starting at 0 for the beginning of the string, remember), whereas `length` specifies the number of characters after position `start` to be extracted. For example, if we had the statement:

```
aString = "http://www.gold.net/users/ag17/index.htm";
```

the substring statement:

```
theHost = aString.substring(7, aString.length);
```

would retrieve the characters from position 7 and onwards, i.e. the string of text `"www.gold.net/users/ag17/index.htm"`. If the `start` argument is greater than the `length` argument, JavaScript still returns the same substring, for example the expressions `aString.substring(0,4)` and `aString.substring(4,0)` both return the string `"http"`.

sup()
Syntax: `StringObj.sup()`
Returns: Nothing
Object family: `string`

Causes the string object named `StringObj` to be set in a superscript font using a Netscape HTML `<sup>..</sup>` container to encapsulate the string.

tan()
Syntax: `tan(val)`
Returns: The tangent of argument `val` (where `val` is specified in radians)
Object family: `Math`

toLowerCase()
Syntax: `StringObj.toLowerCase()`
Returns: Nothing
Object family: `string`

Converts the string object named `StringObj` to lower case.

toString()
Syntax: `DateObj.toString()`
Returns: Nothing
Object family: `Date`

Converts the date object `DateObj` to a string object.

toUpperCase()
Syntax: `StringObj.toUpperCase()`
Returns: Nothing
Object family: `string`

Converts the string object named `StringObj` to upper case.

tt()
Syntax: `stringObj.tt();`
Returns: Nothing
Object family: `string`

The `fixed()` method changes the string `stringObj` to a monospaced (fixed-pitch) font, as set in Netscape through its *Options/Preferences/Fonts* screen – the default being the `Courier` font. This is achieved by encapsulating the string in `<tt>..</tt>` tags (the HTML teletype tag).

unEscape()
Syntax: `unEscape(string)`
Returns: The ASCII character for a string, where `string` is either decimal or hexadecimal
Object family: Not applicable

The `unEscape()` method is used to return an ASCII character for the specified `string` value. The value of `string` can be of the form `"%nn"`, where `nn` is a hexadecimal number between 0 and 255, that is `00` to `FF` in hexadecimal notation. For example, the statement:

```
var asciiVal = unEscape("%26")
```

stores the value `"&"` in the variable `asciiVal`, since the hexadecimal value 26 is 38 in decimal, and 38 is the ASCII code for an ampersand (`&`).

write()
Syntax: `document.write(string);`
Returns: Nothing
Object family: `string`

The `document.write()` function writes a `string` of text to the browser without sending a line-feed code. The text string should ideally be HTML-formatted, i.e. contain the appropriate HTML tags.

Variables can also be concatenated (joined) into `string` so that they can be embedded within a string of text, for example:

```
document.write("The code for product " + productName +
               " is " + productCode);
```

Numeric values can also be concatenated by treating them as strings to begin with; JavaScript can perform numeric calculations on strings, remember, so specific casting (the changing of a variable's data type) is not actually required. If you need to join a string with a numeric value, the + signs can be changed to commas (`,`) for example:

```
var HoursInYear = 365 * 24;
document.write("Hours in a year = ", HoursInYear, ".");
```

`writeln()`
Syntax: `document.writeln(string);`
Returns: Nothing
Object family: `string`

This operates in the same way as `document.write()`, except that a line-feed code is generated automatically after the string. Again, the `string` argument should be HTML-formatted.

CHAPTER

6

Event programming in JavaScript

JavaScript provides the developer with a selection of *event-handling* attributes that are integrated into existing HTML tags. In this way, an event such as the clicking of a hyperlink or the submission of an HTML form can generate an event that can be caught by the JavaScript and then processed accordingly. In this chapter you will learn:

- How to write an event handler in JavaScript
- How to create *dynamic* HTML documents that are reflected in the Netscape browser using JavaScript's `write()` and `writeln()` methods
- How to validate HTML form fields and process form submissions locally
- How to attach JavaScript functions to user interface objects such as buttons and images

141

Event programming with JavaScript and HTML

Netscape 2.0 has introduced a number of new HTML tag attributes that are specifically for use with the JavaScript language. These new attributes work in conjunction with HTML objects such as form fields, radio buttons, checkboxes and hyperlinks.

JavaScript's main method of obtaining user input is by using an HTML form. Forms are containers for items such as text fields, text areas, selection lists and buttons, all of which can now have events attached to them to allow an HTML document to become fully interactive: JavaScript programs can interact with the user depending on the values that they enter into such fields. Field validation is a prime candidate for JavaScript's field events, for example. Other HTML tags that Netscape understands have also been modified; for example, there are new attributes that work with tags such as `<body>` to allow JavaScript statements to be invoked when a user arrives or leaves a certain hypertext page. The main types of event that JavaScript supports are *Click* events, *Focus* and *Blur* events, *MouseOver* events and *Select* events. These JavaScript events apply to HTML tags in the following ways:

- Click events: buttons, radio buttons, checkboxes, submit buttons, reset buttons and hyperlinks
- Focus, Blur and Change events: text fields, text areas and selections
- MouseOver event: hyperlinks
- Select events: text fields and text areas

If a JavaScript event applies to an HTML tag you can define an event handler for that tag. The event handler shares the name of the event, except that it is preceded by the string `"on"`. So, for example, the event handler for a *Change* event is `onChange` (the field change event). Table 6.1 contains a list of the event handlers and their invocation methods – the final column represents the actual event handler tag attribute.

TIP
It is also possible to mix event handler attributes, for example `onClick` and `onMouseOver` attributes could be mentioned in a single HTML tag to provide event handlers for both event types, e.g. an object that displays some text while the user is over a hyperlink and at the same time can invoke a JavaScript function when finally clicked (see the later examples).

TABLE **6.1** *Event handlers and their invocation methods*

Event name	Event occurs when:	Event handler
change event	User changes value of text, text area or select element	`onChange`
blur event	User removes input focus from form element	`onBlur`
click event	User clicks on form element or link	`onClick`
focus event	User gives form element input focus	`onFocus`
load event	User loads the page into Netscape	`onLoad`
mouseover event	User moves mouse pointer over a link or anchor	`onMouseOver`
select event	User selects form element's input field	`onSelect`
submit event	User submits a form	`onSubmit`
unload event	User exits the page	`onUnload`

Event-handling attributes

This section examines each of the above event-handling attributes in more detail, along with examples of their use in HTML documents. The tag objects that the event applies to are also given.

onBlur

Applies to:
- `<input type=text>`
- `<textarea>...</textarea>`

Description

The `onBlur` event attribute specifies the JavaScript code to execute when a field in an HTML form loses its *focus*, i.e. as soon as the user *leaves* the field with the `onBlur` attribute defined within it (either by clicking on another field or by trying to leave the current field using the `TAB` key). `onBlur` is particularly useful for field validation functions; for example:

```
<html>
<head>
<script language="JavaScript">
<!—
function ValidateAge(form) {
  if (form.value <= 18) {
    alert("Age must be greater than 18");
```

```
        // Reset the form value to zero:
        form.value = 0;
        // etc ...
    }
}
<!—>
</script>
</head>
<body>
<form name="blurForm">
Name: <input type="text" name="name" size=30>
Age : <input type="number" name="age"  size=5
   onBlur="ValidateAge(this.form.age)">
// etc ...
</form>
</body>
</html>
```

With this script, the function `ValidateAge()` is called when the user leaves the form field named `age`. In the example, `ValidateAge()` checks to see if the age is less than or equal to 18. If this is the case a warning is issued and the field is reset to a zero value. The `this.form.age` value refers to the current form (`this.form`) and the numeric `age` field. This notation should always be used in order to pass values to a JavaScript function. Once a value greater than 18 has been entered the user will be allowed to move freely between any other fields that exist within the same form.

OnChange
Applies to:
- `<select>..<option>..</select>`
- `<input type=radio>`
- `<textarea>...</textarea>`

Description
Triggers an event when the user changes the value of one of the HTML fields shown above. A field being modified for the first time does not count as a field change event. Only after a value has been entered and changed does the event become activated. The field must also lose *focus* to be activated, i.e. you must move to another field within an HTML form. As a more extensive JavaScript example, consider the script below:

```
<html>
<head>
<script language="JavaScript">
```

```
<!— start of script
function test() {
  alert("Value changed!");
}
<!— end of script —>
</script>
</head>
<body>
<h2>Example onChange form</h2><hr>
<form name="changeForm">
Name:<input type="text" size="30" name="name"
  onChange="test();"><p>
Age :<input type="number" size=3 name="age"><p>
</form>
</body>
</html>
```

This script is made up of a single JavaScript function called `test()` and an HTML form with two fields: `name` and `age`.

Whenever the field `name` has its valued changed by the user the JavaScript function `test()` is invoked. In order for Netscape to detect that the field has actually *changed*, focus must move out of the `name` field into another – in this case the `age` field. *Focus* is the term used for an object that is currently selected, i.e. active on the screen, and is commonly associated with windows and data fields. The JavaScript `alert()` method has been used to display a simple message when a change is made to the `name` field.

TIP

Because `onChange` events are triggered when the field loses focus, it is necessary to have more than one field for this to be possible, i.e. an HTML form with a single field clearly cannot lose focus to another field, since it doesn't exist (and hence the event cannot be triggered).

---

onClick

Applies to:
- `<a href>...</a>`
- `<input type=checkbox>`
- `<input type=radio>`
- `<input type=reset>`
- `<input type=submit>`

Description

The `onClick` handler specifies the JavaScript code to execute when an object such as a hyperlink, reset button or checkbox is clicked upon by the user. In the case of checkboxes and radio buttons, an `onClick` event is generated when an item is checked, i.e. enabled. The simplest way of using `onClick` is with a button created using the `<input type=button>` tag within a `<form>..</form>` container, for example:

```
<html>
<head>
<script language="JavaScript">
<!— start of script
function buttonA() {
   alert("You pressed Button A");
}
function buttonB() {
   alert("You pressed Button B");
}
<!— end of script —>
</script>
</head>
<body>
<h2>Example onClick form with two buttons</h2><hr>
<form name="buttonForm">
<input type="button" value="Button A"
onClick="buttonA()"><br>
<input type="button" value="Button B" onClick="buttonB()">
</form>
</body>
</html>
```

When the user clicks on a button the appropriate JavaScript function is called (either `buttonA()` or `buttonB()`, depending on which button is selected). The JavaScript `alert()` method has been used to display a simple message when a button is selected.

Here is a further example, this time using checkboxes and an `onClick` event handler within an HTML form:

```
<html>
<head>
<script language="JavaScript">
<!— start of script
```

```
function cb1() {
  alert("You clicked on checkbox 1");
}
function cb2() {
  alert("You clicked checkbox 2");
}
<!— end of script —>
</script>
</head>
<body>
<h2>Example onClick form with two checkboxes</h2><hr>
<form name="checkForm">
<input type="checkbox" onClick="cb1()">Item 1<br>
<input type="checkbox" onClick="cb2()">Item 2
</form>
</body>
</html>
```

The onClick event in the above program is invoked when both activating and deactivating a checkbox. In order to show a response for *only* those checkboxes that are enabled, it is necessary to use the **checked** property, a boolean property that returns a true value if a checkbox is enabled, i.e. selected. Here is a modified program to do just this:

```
<html>
<head>
<script language="JavaScript">
<!— start of script:
function msgcb1(f) {
  if (f.checked)
    alert("Checkbox 1 is checked");
}
function msgcb2(f) {
  if (f.checked)
    alert("Checkbox 2 is checked");
}
<!— end of script —>
</script>
</head>
<body>
<h2>Example onClick form with two checkboxes<hr></h2>
<form name="checkForm">
```

```
<input type="checkbox" name="cb1"
  onClick="msgcb1(form.cb1)">Item 1
<br>
<input type="checkbox" name="cb2"
  onClick="msgcb2(form.cb2)">Item 2
</form>
</body>
</html>
```

Notice how the two functions now pass arguments, namely `form.cb1` and `form.cb2` (from the two checkboxes), where `form` is the form property of the current form object. This argument is passed to the appropriate function, for example `msgcb1(f)`, as the `f` parameter, whereupon we check for `f.checked` (since `checked` is a property that returns a boolean, i.e. true or false, value). In effect we are therefore testing to see if `form.cb1.checked` is true. The two event handler functions will also be called when a checkbox is de-checked, although the `alert()` message will not appear.

It would have been better to use the `this` property to identify unambiguously the form that we are referring to in our `<input type>` tags, i.e. to use `this.form.cb1` instead of `form.cb1` etc. This is especially true if a document has more than one `<form>..</form>` container, which may often be the case. Remember that the `defaultChecked` property can also be used – this returns `true` if the `checked` attribute of the `<input type=checkbox>` tag has been selected by the user; for example:

```
<input type="checkbox" name="cb3" checked>
```

indicates that the checkbox named `cb3` is checked (i.e. selected) by default when the checkbox group first appears. `cb3.defaultChecked` will be `true` if this checkbox is left selected when we come to actually test each checkbox to see what value it holds.

Finally, consider the code below, which can also be used to check the status of a checkbox. This code differs in that we have not called a function with any arguments, but have instead specified the name of the checkbox to test within the event-handling function, in this case as `document.forms[0].cb1.checked` (the `forms` property is an array of forms that exist within the current HTML document):

```
<html>
<head>
<script language="JavaScript">
<!-- start of code:
function checkCB() {
```

```
     if (document.forms[0].cb1.checked) {
       alert("You have used JavaScript.");
     else
       alert("You have not used JavaScript.");
   }
   <!— end —>
   </script>
   </head>
   <body>
   <form>
   Have you used JavaScript before?
   <input type="checkbox" name="cb1"><br>
   <input type="button" value="Submit" onClick="checkCB()">
   </form>
   </body>
   </html>
```

In this case the checkCB() function is invoked by a button press using an onClick event. So, as you can see, it is possible to refer to form objects using a variety of notations, the easiest way being to specify a *fully qualified* field name, e.g. document.formname. fieldname. Alternatively, you can pass the name of the field(s) that you want to process to the event handler, although this does not improve performance. Remember that you can do away with the forms[n] property by naming your form with a name=formName attribute and then replacing forms[n] with formName.

TIP
It is also possible to make HTML hyperlinks JavaScript-aware. This is done by using the special javascript: URL prefix (this is also implemented as mocha: in Netscape 2.0N). For example, the hyperlink below invokes the JavaScript alert() function when the hyperlink 'Click me' is activated.

```
   <a href="javascript:alert('Hello')">Click me</a>
```

onFocus
Applies to:
   ■   <input type=text>

Description
The onFocus handler, as the name suggests, allows an event to be associated with a field that is given the *focus*. In Netscape a form field obtains the focus when either the

user clicks on the field with the mouse, or when the `TAB` key is used to move into the field. Selecting information within the field using the mouse by highlighting data is not considered to be a focus-gaining event.

onLoad

Applies to:
- `<body>...</body>`
- `<frameset>..<frame>..</frameset>`

Description

The `onLoad` attribute can be placed in the HTML `<body>` container to invoke a JavaScript function when Netscape has *finished* loading the current document. The event occurs when Netscape has completed loading the text of an HTML document into the current window or within the current *frameset document*. A frameset document is one in which the window is broken into separate regions, each of which can be loaded with a separate document, i.e. URL. Frames have been proposed for inclusion in the new HTML 3.0 standard, but remain a Netscape-enhanced HTML feature at the time of writing. Some of the existing HTML tags have been changed to include support for frames: for example, `<a href>` now has a `target` attribute to specify the exact window into which a URL (or other document) is loaded when a particular hyperlink is activated.

TIP

The `onLoad` event isn't of much use for writing text into documents, since the event is triggered *after* a document has been loaded. However, the event is useful for updating variables etc. after documents have been loaded.

See also the entry for `onUnLoad`, which allows an event to be associated with the unloading of a document.

onMouseOver

Applies to:
- `<a href>...</a>`

Description

This attribute allows a JavaScript statement to be activated when the user is positioned over an active hyperlink that uses the `onMouseOver` attribute. The status bar message appears after the user has moved over the hyperlink in question, and the message stays in the status bar until a new message replaces it. `onMouseOver` events are useful for altering status bar messages via the `window.status` property, although they could also be used to update text fields based upon the current hyperlink that the user is contemplating selecting etc. Remember that `<a href>` can encapsulate graphics and even complete Java applets (i.e. the *display area* of an applet via the `<applet>` container), so the target need not be a simple text-based hyperlink.

Consider the following document, which defines an `onMouseOver` event for a series of image-based hyperlinks. It is assumed, for the purposes of the example, that the user can see a series of *thumbnail* (i.e. small) still images and can magnify these using the appropriate hyperlink, which we assume contains a larger picture of the thumbnail image that the user was previously looking at. The `onMouseOver` events display messages about the pictures the user is going to see in more detail:

```
<html>
<head>
<script language="JavaScript">
<!— start of script
function msg1() {
  window.status="Magnified version of Saturn";
  return true;
}
function msg2() {
  window.status="Magnified version of Mars";
  return true;
}
function msg3() {
  window.status="Magnified version of Jupiter";
  return true;
}
<!— end of script —>
</script>
</head>
<body>
<h2>Please pick an image to see the planet in more
  detail:<hr></h2>

<a href="big_img1.gif" onMouseOver="msg1()">
<img border=1 src="small_img1.gif">
</a><br>
<a href="big_img2.gif" onMouseOver="msg2()">
<img border=1 src="small_img2.gif">
</a><br>
<a href="big_img3.gif" onMouseOver="msg3()">
```

```
<img border=1 src="small_img3.gif">
</a>
</body>
</html>
```

onSelect

Applies to:
- ■ `<input type=text>`
- ■ `<textarea>...</textarea>`

Description

The `onSelect` attribute triggers an event within a field when the text in that field is *selected* by the user. Selection is not selection in the form of clicking on the field, but rather selection of the text *within* the field via highlighting of the text using the mouse.

onSubmit

Applies to:
- ■ `<form>...</form>`

Description

The `onSubmit` event handler is used to validate an HTML form. By returning a `true` or `false` value from within a JavaScript function called by `onSubmit` it is possible to halt a form from being submitted. 'Submitted' in this case means the result of pressing an `<input type=submit>` button, which all forms that send data to a remote Web server have. Consider the following HTML/JavaScript example, which uses an HTML form with the `onSubmit` attribute to validate a text area field so that it is not left empty:

```
<html>
<head>
<script language="JavaScript">
<!— start of script
function validateForm(f) {
  if (f.value == "") {
    alert("Please provide some feedback");
    return false;
  }
  else
    // Let the form submit the data:
    return true;
}
<!— end of script —>
```

```
</script>
</head>
<body>
<h2>A sample form validation event handler<hr></h2>
<form name="myForm"
      method="post"

action="http://www.somehost.com/cgi-bin/process_form.pl"
      onSubmit="validateForm(myForm.feedback)"
>
Name: <input type="text" size=30 name="persons_name"><br>
Feedback:<br>
<textarea name="address" rows=5 cols=50></textarea><p>
<input type="submit" value="Submit data">
</form>
</body>
</html>
```

In the above HTML document, an `onSubmit` event handler has been used to stop the current form being submitted to a Web server until the text area field (`feedback`) has been submitted – notice the use of JavaScript `return` statements to return the appropriate `true` or `false` values (`true` to allow the form to be submitted and `false` to deny submission of the form).

TIP

In order to allow an HTML form to submit data on a remote Web server (as above) you have to learn some CGI-scripting skills. CGI, or Common Gateway Interface, is a popular standard that allows an HTML form to link into a script. A variety of languages are used to implement CGI scripts, including Perl (Practical Extraction and Report Language), C, UNIX shells such as `csh` and `ksh`, and many more besides. In the JavaScript example, shown above, the `action` attribute specifies the name of the script that will take the data from the current form and process it. *Processing* is a loose term, and could mean storing the data in a database for example. The `post` attribute of the `<form>` tag specifies a *transmission method* for the form; `"post"` is a method whereby the data from the form is sent in one large chunk and is received by the standard input stream by the script (the script is named as `process_form.pl` and is a Perl script in this case). `process_form.pl` could resemble the following:

```
#! /usr/bin/perl
```

```
require "cgi-lib.pl";
&ReadParse;
open(F,">>feedback.htm");
theName = $in{'persons_name'};
theFeedback = $in{'feedback'};
print F "<hr>Feedback from <b>$theName</b>.<hr>";
print F "<dl><dd>$theFeedback</dl>";
close(F);
```

which is a simple Perl script that uses a ubiquitous library known as `cgi-bin.pl` to extract the form field data into an array called `$in`. So, for example, the form field called **persons_name** is reflected as `$in{'persons_name'}` in the Perl script. The script writes the information that it receives into the file named `feedback.htm` (in fact it appends data to the file using the '>>' notation so that the file can *grow* over time as more entries are added by people). The file is written out with some basic HTML-formatting so that it can be marked up by a browser such as Netscape. So, for example, if we entered the form details:

Name: Joe Public
Feedback: JavaScript is great!

this would be written to the file as the following HTML-formatted paragraph:

```
<hr>Feedback from <b>Joe Public</b>.<hr>
JavaScript is great!
```

For more information on CGI scripting under Windows and DOS using some alternative scripting languages see my earlier book *The World-Wide Web, Mosaic and More* (McGraw-Hill 1994). My home page has details at the address: `http://www.gold.net/users/ag17/index.htm`. More information on Perl can be found at `http://www.perl.com` and via Netscape in USENET using the URL `news://comp.lang.perl`.

---

onUnLoad
Applies to:
■ `<body>...</body>`
■ `<frameset>..<frame>..</frameset>`

Description
This attribute works in the opposite way to `onLoad` in that a JavaScript function can be called when the user *leaves* the current document. This event handler attribute also works with Netscape frameset documents.

Button-based events

Buttons are useful to allow JavaScript functions to be activated manually by the user. The `onClick` attribute is designed specifically for button-based events, and can be placed on the screen in one of two ways:

- Using a form-based tag of the type:

```
<form ...>
<input type="button" .. onClick="function();">
...
</form>
```

- Using the `<img src>` tag (load image file) with the 'button' stored as an image file (in the GIF/JPEG formats); for example:

```
<img src="file.gif" onClick="functionName();">
```

where `functionName()` is the name of the function you want to call.

TIP

Specifying a function in an attribute such as `onClick` is beneficial, since multiple statements become too complex to place within a single HTML tag. If you want to attach multiple statements to a button event, place them in a JavaScript function and call that directly, as shown above.

The default button created using the `<input ... type="button">` is a small grey rectangular shaped area of the screen that can be clicked on by the user in order to activate a JavaScript statement – most conveniently a function to invoke a series of JavaScript statements. Such a button must be labelled with some descriptive text that identifies the button's purpose, and is done with the standard `value` attribute.

The `<img src>` tag has been modified in Netscape 2.0 to allow the inclusion of the `onClick` attribute to activate a JavaScript-based statement. This method has the advantage of not needing to be defined with a `<form>..</form>` container, and of course that the actual 'button' can be an image of any shape or size. For example, a form-based button script could be structured as:

```
<script language="JavaScript">
<!— start of script
function Button1() {
```

```
      alert("You pressed button 1");
      // Code for button 1...
   }
   function Button2() {
      alert("You pressed button 2");
      // Code for button 2...
   }
   <!-- end of script -->
   </script>
   <body>
   <form method="post">
   Please press a button:<p>
   <input type="button" value="Button 1" name="Button1"
      onClick="Button1();">
   <input type="button" value="Button 2" name="Button2"
      onClick="Button2();">
   </form>
   </body>
```

The end result of this script is that when the user clicks on a button an appropriate JavaScript function is called – either `Button1()` or `Button2()` , depending on the choice of the user.

Similarly, the same script could be written in more compact format using `<img src>` tags with the `onClick` attribute, for example:

```
<body>
<img src="button1.gif" onClick="Button1();">
<img src="button2.gif" onClick="Button2();">
...
</body>
```

where `button1.gif` and `button2.gif` are image files stored in the GIF format. These are the areas of the screen (i.e. 'buttons') that the user will have to press in order to activate the associated `onClick` event for that particular image. The semicolons after the functions are optional.

TIP

When should I use `<img src>` instead of `onClick`? Each situation has its advantages and disadvantages. Form-based buttons are useful when used in conjunction with user input fields in order to send values to a function for further processing, and 'standalone' buttons are useful when placed *ad hoc* in order to carry out miscellaneous tasks.

As a more extensive example, consider the JavaScript application below. This program implements a simple currency conversion application, whereby the user can enter an amount and have this changed to a number of different currencies according to a hypothetical exchange rate. The script updates a series of form fields to display its results back to the user, although you can of course create the table structure dynamically instead.

```
<!—JavaScript currency conversion application—>
<html>
<head>
<title>Currency convertor v1</title>
<script language="JavaScript">
<!— Hide script
// Variables:
var usd = 0;
var yen = 0;
var ff  = 0;
var gm  = 0;
var ecu = 0;

// Reset the currency values:
function ResetValues(form) {
  usd = 1.11;
  yen = 2.56;
  ff  = 7.55;
  gm  = 5.77;
  ecu = 6.00;
  form.pounds = 0;
}

// Calculate currencies and update form fields:
function Calc1(form, form2) {
  usd = (usd * form.value);
  form2.value = usd;
}
function Calc2(form, form2) {
  yen = (yen * form.value);
  form2.value = yen;
```

```
  }
  function Calc3(form, form2) {
    ff  = (ff  * form.value);
    form2.value = ff;
  }
  function Calc4(form, form2) {
    gm  = (gm  * form.value);
    form2.value = gm;
  }
  function Calc5(form, form2) {      // NB: Ecus are now known
    ecu = (ecu * form.value);        // as Euros!
    form2.value = ecu;
  }
  <!-- done hiding -->
  </script>
  </head>

  <body>
  <form method="post">
  Enter amount in pounds sterling:
  <input type="number" name="pounds" value=0><hr>
  <input type="button" value="Convert currency"
    onClick="ResetValues(this.form.pounds);
      Calc1(this.form.pounds, this.form.display1);
      Calc2(this.form.pounds, this.form.display2);
      Calc3(this.form.pounds, this.form.display3);
      Calc4(this.form.pounds, this.form.display4);
      Calc5(this.form.pounds, this.form.display5);
      ResetValues(this.form.pounds)">
  <p>
  <i>RESULTS:</i>
  <table width="33%" border=1>
  <tr>
    <td>
      <input type="number" name="display1" value=0> US $<br>
      <input type="number" name="display2" value=0> Yen<br>
      <input type="number" name="display3" value=0> FF<br>
      <input type="number" name="display4" value=0> DM<br>
      <input type="number" name="display5" value=0> ECU<br>
    </td>
  </tr>
  </table>
```

```
</form>
</body>
</html>
```

In the script the currency conversion amounts are *hard-coded* into the script as the variables usd (US Dollars), yen (Japanese Yen), ff (French Francs), gm (German Marks) and ecu (European Ecus (or Euros)). For the sake of the example it assumed that an amount in sterling is entered for purposes of the conversion (variable pounds). When the program starts these variables are initialized to zero and then a number of JavaScript functions are read into memory. The functions Calc1 to Calc5 carry out the actual conversions, which in this case are simple multiplication expressions, i.e. the number entered by the user, held in the form variable pounds, multiplied by the exchange amount. For example, in the case of US dollars, a statement of the form:

```
usd = (usd * form.value);
```

is used, where usd is the exchange rate for US dollars in this instance. The actual values passed to each function clearly change for each currency type, hence the five functions to handle five different currencies. The variable form.value represents the value passed from the <form ...> statement in the <body>..</body> container later on in the HTML file. The statement:

```
form2.value = usd;
```

simply updates the field passed to the argument form2.value, which becomes apparent when you see the <input> tag that controls the passing of arguments to the five currency conversion functions:

```
<input type="button" value="Convert currency"
  onClick="ResetValues(this.form.pounds);
    Calc1(this.form.pounds, this.form.display1);
    Calc2(this.form.pounds, this.form.display2);
    Calc3(this.form.pounds, this.form.display3);
    Calc4(this.form.pounds, this.form.display4);
    Calc5(this.form.pounds, this.form.display5);">
```

The button defined above uses the JavaScript onClick event attribute to call the five currency conversion functions (Calc1 to Calc5). The ResetValues() function is also called at the beginning and end to ensure that all variables are initialized and hold the correct values. In the code fragment above the Calc1 function is called with two arguments, namely this.forms.pounds (the amount the user wants to

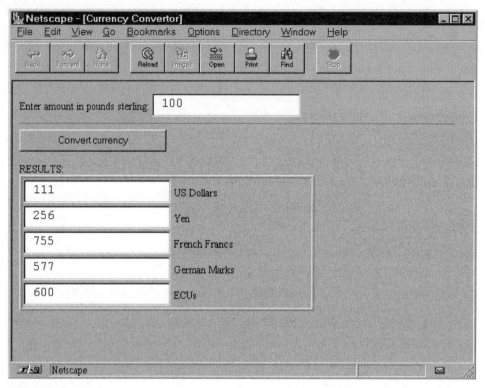

FIGURE 6.1 *The currency conversion application in action within Netscape 2.0.*

convert) and `this.form.display1`, so in fact `Calc1` is called with the values exactly as shown below – with both arguments substituted from the script above:

```
function Calc1(this.form.pounds, this.form.display1) {
   usd = (usd * this.form.pounds);
   this.form.display1 = usd;
}
```

which in turn carries out the currency conversion for US dollars (`usd * pounds`) and then updates the screen so that the results can be seen by the user (`display1 = usd`). This is done five times in total, for each currency. Notice how the `<form>..</form>` defined in the program uses `<input>` fields for the results, and how these are updated. Figure 6.1 illustrates the currency conversion program in action.

PART 2

Java

CHAPTER

7

A Java language primer

Java is an object-orientated language developed by Sun Microsystems, and which is now built into the popular Netscape Navigator 2.0 browser. In a nutshell Java brings 'executable content' to the World-Wide Web, allowing mini-programs known as *applets* to execute within a hypertext document. This is an important achievement, since Web pages are otherwise static repositories of data that do not leap out and interact with the user. The technology behind Java is also very interesting, since it wrestles with the 'client–server' model out of which the Web is born. The unusual thing about the compiled source code that comprises a Java applet is that it is stored in an 'architecture-neutral' byte-code format. The neutral format of a compiled applet allows a Java program to *migrate* anywhere on the Internet, irrespective of the operating system into which the applet is loaded.

In this chapter you will learn:

- The differences between and capabilities of Java *applets* and *applications*
- How to use Java classes and packages (via the `import` statement)
- How to develop Java programs from scratch: *editing, compilation* and *viewing*
- How to incorporate *executable* content within a hypertext document using the new `<applet>` tag
- How to pass parameters to Java applets using Java's `getParameter()` method
- How to program structure into a Java program using conditional statements and how to control program flow
- What the core programming elements are: arrays, variables and operators
- How to view applets using the JDK AppletViewer
- How to use the `JAVAC` applet compiler
- How to test your applets

Viewing the demonstration applets

Before starting, take a few moment to view the sample applets that accompany the Java Developer's Kit (JDK). This will give you some idea of the capabilities of Java as a programming language. A number of applets are provided in the `\JAVA\DEMO` directory that is installed along with the JDK. Each applet is stored in its own directory: for example, the game of *TicTacToe* (or *noughts and crosses*) can be found in the directory `\JAVA\DEMO\TicTacToe`. The source code for each applet is also provided, along with an HTML file to invoke it. In order to run a demonstration program you can use Sun's `appletviewer.exe` utility. For example, in order to run TicTacToe, simply change to the appropriate directory and then run the AppletViewer with the HTML file that is provided:

```
CD \JAVA\DEMO\TicTacToe
appletviewer example1.html
```

where `example1.html` loads the TicTacToe applet. Make sure that `\JAVA\BIN` is mentioned in your `PATH` statement in order to reference the AppletViewer or that you specify the fully qualified pathname. Some applets can be invoked with a variety of HTML files that alter the behaviour of the applet, so try each one out. AppletViewer can only run an applet if the HTML `<applet>` tag is mentioned within the file. Figure 7.1 shows the TicTacToe applet in action, as seen through the AppletViewer tool.

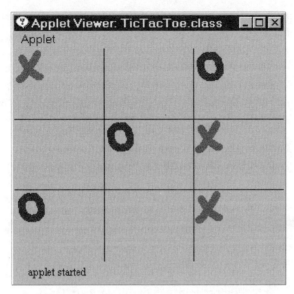

FIGURE 7.1 *The TicTacToe applet (in* `\JAVA\DEMO\TicTacToe`*).*

Developing Java programs

In order to develop programs in Java you will first need access to some basic tools, namely:

- ■ An ASCII editor (such as `WordPad` or DOS's `EDIT` – Java source code is always plain text)
- ■ The `JAVAC.EXE` and/or `JAVA.EXE` tools (applet/application compiler and application interpreter)
- ■ The Netscape 2.0 browser or AppletViewer tool (so that you can actually view your applet creations)

The steps necessary to create a working Java program are:

- ■ Write your Java program, and save it with a `.java` filename extension (e.g. `MyProgram.java`)
- ■ Compile the Java program (e.g. `MyProgram.java`) into a `.class` file (e.g. `MyProgram.class`) using the `JAVAC.EXE` compiler. The class file is an architecture-neutral file that is a *tokenized* 'byte-code' version of your program. It can now be loaded and run by *any* Java-aware browser on the Internet

■ For an *applet*: Build an HTML file that references the `.class` file in an `<applet>` tag (for example: `<applet code="MyProgram.class">`) and then load the HTML file into Netscape 2.0 in order to run the applet. For a Java *application*, run the `.class` file through the Java interpreter `JAVA.EXE` (see below for more details on *applets* vs. *applications*)

■ View the applet via AppletViewer or by using Netscape 2.0, or the application from the command line using `JAVA.EXE` (described later)

The last two steps mentioned above will clearly be repeated as you modify and test your Java program. `JAVA.EXE` and `JAVAC.EXE` are part of the Java Developer's Kit.

TIP
A `.class` file for a particular Java applet is loaded using the HTML `<applet code...>` tag. Each class file is the compiled version of a `.java` source code program. All of the standard Java classes are kept in the file `CLASSES.ZIP`.

TIP
All of the Java source code is contained in the file `SRC.ZIP`, which you can unzip (using a 32-bit unzip utility, such as WinZip) and examine using an ASCII editor.

Developing Java programs: applets *vs.* applications

With Java it is important to distinguish between an *applet* and an *application*. Both of these terms relate to a Java source code program, although they refer to a different environment in which the program actually runs. Java *applets* execute within the browser, i.e. Netscape 2.0, while Java *applications* run outside the browser environment, perhaps from a DOS shell. In the case of the latter, the Java *interpreter* – `JAVA.EXE` – is used to run Java application programs. When you decide whether or not to write an *applet* or an *application* you will first need to ascertain whether you need to view the applet within the browser or outside it.

TIP
Applets and applications can use all of the same graphical functions, although applications require slightly more effort since you have to recreate the browser environment to some extent (e.g. create a window area).

Developing Java *applications* is a slightly quicker process, since with an *applet* you need to create an HTML file, load it from within Netscape and then view the results. The only main limitation of using a Java application, as opposed to an applet, is the fact that the program runs outside the browser environment. When a Java program runs outside the browser environment extra effort has to be made in order to allow the program to use graphical features (e.g. you will have to create a window in order to display an image), whereas an *applet* could draw straight into the browser area.

TIP
Sun provide an *applet viewing* tool called `appletviewer.exe` for Windows 95. It resides in the `\JAVA\BIN` directory, by default. Run it with an HTML file that has the `<applet>` tag that references your applet.

Class files are not *executable programs* in the true sense of the word; that is to say you cannot run them as you would a normal `.EXE` file. Class files are 'machine-neutral' programs that can only be recognized by the Java run-time software. Class files are generated for both Java *applets* and *applications*.

TIP
`JAVAC.EXE` is the Java compiler that is used to compile `.java` source code files (applets and applications) into `.class` (*architecture-neutral*) files. It is the `.class` file that is loaded from within your HTML File. A `.class` file requires a Java-capable browser (*run-time*) in order to function properly, such as Netscape 2.0.

So, how can one actually distinguish between an *applet* and an *application* if one arrives in front of you to examine? Well, there is always one tell-tale sign: Java *applications* can be recognized by the fact that they have a `main()` method declared within them. C programmers will be familiar with the `main()` *function*, since it is also used in their programming language as the main entry point to a program. The first instructions to be executed within a Java application are contained within `main()`. When you run the Java interpreter (`JAVA.EXE`) with a Java application, `JAVA.EXE` searches for `main()` and then executes the instructions contained within its scope. Applets, on the other hand, do not need a `main()` method; their entry point is defined by the *initialize* method, `init()`. The Java run-time built into Netscape therefore seeks out `init()` and executes the instructions thereafter. So now you know the essential differences between applets and applications.

TIP
Applications always have a static `main()` method (static indicates that the `main()` method is the only instance of this method, and is therefore the main entry-point for the program). Applets have an `init()` or `start()` method (and sometimes may have a `main()` method defined also, although this will not be the main entry-point for the program). Applets run *within* the browser; applications run *externally* through `JAVA.EXE`.

For example, here is a simple Java *application* (`TestProgram1`) that prints out a greeting message:

```
class TestProgram1 {
  public static void main(String args[]) {
    System.out.println("This is a java application.");
  }
}
```

Compile the program using `JAVAC.EXE` and then run with `JAVA.EXE` (from a DOS shell). For example:

```
javac TestProgram1.java
java TestProgram1
```

TIP
In order to run a Java application first compile your program with `JAVAC.EXE` and then run the `.class` file that is generated with `JAVA.EXE` (the Java interpreter). Note: do *not* include the `.class` extension when running applications or a run-time error will occur.

Re-compile your applet every time you make a change to it so that you generate a new `.class` file for it.

The same program written as an applet would be slightly more complex, since we have to operate within the Web browser's environment. Consider the program below, `TestProgram2` , which performs the same task.

```java
import java.awt.*;
class TestProgram2 extends java.applet.Applet {
  public void init() {
    resize(100,150);
  }
  public void paint(Graphics g) {
    g.drawString("This is a Java applet", 10, 10, this);
  }
}
```

Notice how we are now using `drawString()` instead of `System.out.println()` to display some text. `drawString()` is a method found in the Awt (Abstract Window Toolkit) that allows a string of text to be drawn at a specific x, y pixel coordinate within the applet's display area. The display area is set using the `resize()` method, which sets the number of rows and columns (measured in pixels) of the applet when it appears within the Web browser (alternatively, if you are using the AppletViewer tool this will dictate the final size of the AppletViewer's main window). The `paint()` method is called automatically and specifies the statements that will *paint* or *draw* information into the applet. Needless to say, you will learn all about Awt later on in this book. In order to run this program you should create an HTML file that uses the `<applet>` tag in order to reference and run the applet. This simple task is discussed later in the chapter.

TIP

Applets and applications can in fact use *all* of the same graphical features. Applications need slightly more programming effort to complete, since you must effectively recreate the browser environment in the program (e.g. by creating a window). The only core difference between applets and applications is that applications will send their output to a region outside the browser environment (i.e. to an autonomous window), and also that applets are called from an HTML file using the `<applet>` tag (see the next section); applications are run directly from the command line.

Incorporating an applet into an HTML document

The whole purpose of an applet is that it can be executed *within* an existing HTML hypertext document. The term *executable content* is derived from this behaviour. In order to include an applet within an HTML file, Netscape has introduced a new HTML tag called `<applet>`. The `<applet>` tag is known as a *container* tag, that is to say that a closing tag, `</applet>`, must also be specified. The full syntax for the `<applet>` tag is as follows (those parts of the syntax enclosed in `[` and `]` brackets are optional attributes):

```
<applet
  code="File.class"
  [ codebase="ClassDirectory"]
  [ width=w ]
  [ height=h ]
  [ vspace=vs ]
  [ hspace=hs ]
  [ alt=text ]
  [ name=appletName]
  [ align=left|right|top|middle|baseline|bottom ]
>
[ <param name=ParamName value=ParamValue> ]
[ HTMLText ... ]
</applet>
```

where `code` specifies the name of a `.class` file to load, `codebase` specifies a directory in which the class(es) exist, `width` is the width of the applet in pixels and `height` is the height of the applet in pixels. The use of quotation marks (`"`) in arguments is optional. The new `<param>` tag specifies a parameter name (`ParamName`) and value (`ParamValue`) that can be passed to the applet from within the HTML file. Multiple `<param>` tags can be specified. `HTMLText` is the text displayed verbatim to people who do not have a Java-aware browser, and should ideally be HTML-formatted, and can be as long as the user requires. The `ALT` attribute allows some alternative text to be displayed for those browsers that understand the `<applet>` tag, but which cannot run applets (a slightly contradictory attribute it seems). The JDK 1.0b2 also introduced the `ALIGN` attribute, which works along the same lines as `<IMG ALIGN=... SRC>` to align the applet on the page. The `VSPACE` and `HSPACE` attributes specify the vertical and horizontal spacing that is to be used around the applet's display area (both are measured in pixels).

TIP
With Netscape 2.0 the WIDTH and HEIGHT attributes will define the size of the applet when viewed in the browser. It seems that an applet viewed through Netscape 2.0 cannot extend beyond this region, even when it is possible for applets to re-size themselves. Ensure that your applet has the correct dimensions, i.e. that any graphical output does not exceed the boundary set by the <applet> tag. Note that the AppletViewer utility *must* be used on an HTML file that has an <applet> tag with the CODE, WIDTH and HEIGHT attributes specified within it.

Figure 7.2 illustrates how the WIDTH and HEIGHT attributes define an applet's display area.

For example, we could have an applet tag defined as:

```
<applet code="MyApplet.class"
  codebase="CLASSES"
  width=150
  height=150>
<hr>To view this applet you will need a Java-aware
  browser!<p>
<img src="scrndump.gif"><hr>
</applet>
```

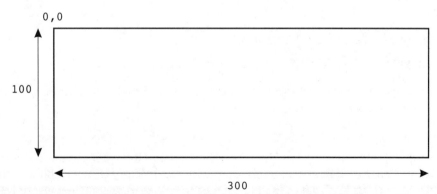

FIGURE **7.2** *The applet display area.*

which calls the applet named `MyApplet.class`. The text *'To view this applet you will need a Java-aware browser!'* will appear along with an image (the `<img src...>` tag) instead of the applet if the user accessed this page using a non-Java-aware browser. Some applications like to display a static image taken from the applet to convey to the user what they would be seeing, as in the example. The applet, when running, will occupy a square on the browser screen measuring 150×150 pixels. It is up to the applet to ensure that it does not draw outside the bounds of its allotted area (applets can set their size internally and the `width/height` attributes are optional). It is bad practice to include an applet within a hypertext page and then not to provide some alternative text for those people without a Java-aware browser. The `<applet>` tag will doubtless become part of standard HTML specification in the future now that more browsers are starting to incorporate the Java technology. The `codebase` attribute in the example specifies that the `MyApplet.class` file exists in a subdirectory called `CLASSES` (relative to the directory in which the HTML file is stored).

TIP

Ensure that you use `<applet>` and `</applet>` and that you provide some text inside this container for people who are not using Netscape 2.0 or HotJava. Perhaps you should consider asking the user to upgrade! If an applet displays an image animation you may also consider providing just a static image (using the HTML `<img src>` tag) for those people who do not yet have a 'Java-aware' browser, or perhaps a link to an animation-formatted file (e.g. MPEG) if available.

Example `<applet>` tags in use

Consider this example first:

```
<applet code="MyApplet.class" codebase="myclasses">
Applet would appear here!
</applet>
```

In this HTML extract, the `codebase` attribute points to the `myclasses` directory, which is assumed to exist as a subdirectory of the directory from which the current HTML file was loaded. For example, if the above tags were contained in the HTML file `C:\Applets\Demo_Applet.html`, Netscape would look in the directory `C:\Applets\myclasses` for the file `MyApplet.class` .

TIP
You can also used the HTML `<applet>` tag shown above for use with *local* applets (e.g for testing purposes on your own computer before moving them to a Web server).

Some applets may of course exist elsewhere on the Internet, and not on the same site as the HTML file that references them. In such cases the `codebase` attribute is used with an appropriate URL that specifies the location of the applet's class file, for example:

```
<applet code="RemoteApplet.class"
   codebase="http://www.somehost.com/appletdir/classes/">
A sample applet.
</applet>
```

which calls the applet `RemoteApplet.class` that exists on the Internet host `www.somehost.com` in the directory `/appletdir/classes/`. Netscape then uses the HyperText Transfer Protocol (HTTP) to download the applet to your computer, whereupon the Java run-time built into Netscape runs the file.

TIP
When you come to upload your applets to a Web server (via FTP), make sure that the HTML file that points to them has a `codebase` attribute. You can omit the `codebase` attribute if the `.class` file for an applet is located in the *same* directory as the HTML file that invokes it, i.e. the HTML file with the `<applet>` tag within it. It is better, however, to separate your class files and Java source code files if possible.

TIP
The AppletViewer tool can be invoked with a URL (such as `http://hostname`) in order to view a remote applet. You will need to be connected to the Internet in order to download the applet, of course. AppletViewer experiences a slight delay when loading and viewing an applet (typically up to a minute on an ordinary 486-based PC).

Picking up parameters using `getParameter()`

Applets can pick up parameters sent to them from the HTML from which they were invoked using the `<param>` tag. The `getParameter()` method facilitates this. For example, here is a segment of code that prints the contents of the PERSON parameter that is sent to it:

```
class myApplet extends java.applet.Applet {
...
  public start() {
    String personParam = getParameter("PERSON");
    ...
  }
...
}
```

In this code fragment, the variable `personParam` is a string that stores the contents of `getParameter()`. Notice how the argument `"PERSON"` has been supplied so that the parameter named PERSON is obtained. In order for this statement to work, the HTML file that invoked the complete applet would need a tag such as:

```
<applet code=myApplet codebase=classes>
<param name=PERSON value=Jason>
</applet>
```

The value of the PERSON parameter is `"Jason"` in this case. Note that the case of the parameter name does not matter.

TIP

HTML-based parameters are an extremely useful feature since they allow values to be passed to an applet without the need to recompile the applet. For example, an image animation can be passed the name of a number of static image files using `<param>` tags, rather than *hard-coding* the names of the images into the program – the latter would require the program to be recompiled again.

Using multiple applets within a single HTML file

An HTML file can have as many `<applet>` tags as you require. Large and complex applets can take as much as 3–5 minutes to load, depending on the speed of your computer and the time taken to download the applet and any images, sounds or other files that it needs to function. Some applets may refer to other classes, and these will also have to be downloaded and executed.

Compiling a `.java` file using `JAVAC`

Java source code applets are themselves identified by the filename extension `.java` and must be compiled into a `.class` file using `JAVAC.EXE`, the applet compiler. `JAVAC.EXE` resides in the `\JAVA\BIN` directory by default. During compilation of your applet, any errors that occur will be shown to you on the screen, along with their line numbers and a brief description of the error. After successful compilation one or more `.class` files will then be generated (depending on the number of classes actually defined in your Java program). An `<applet>` tag within an HTML file then references the applet's class file that you want to invoke. When you load the HTML file using Netscape the class file referenced in the `<applet>` tag will then be loaded. Any Web browser other than HotJava or Netscape 2.0 will not be able to see any applets that are embedded within the current HTML file. In order to compile a Java program under Windows 95 you can do one of the following:

- Use the *Run* option to call `JAVAC.EXE` directly with the applet you want to compile
- Run `JAVAC` on your `.java` source code file from within a DOS shell.

You could even 'associate' a `.java` file with the `JAVAC.EXE` compiler and then double-click on a `.java` file from within the Windows 95 Explorer in order to launch the compiler on that file, albeit that this is a much more lengthy and complicated alternative that is not really recommended.

Running `JAVAC` using the Windows 95 *Run* option

In order to do this you should first of all click on the **Start** button and then select *Run*. You can then enter the command you require, for example:

```
C:\JAVA\BIN\JAVAC C:\DEMO\CLASSES\MyApplet.java
```

which in turn would attempt to compile the Java applet named `MyApplet.java`. As soon as the command is entered, `JAVAC` will be executed. Any errors and other messages will also be shown in this window as they are encountered, although you will have a hard time seeing them, because as soon as `JAVAC` finishes the window in which `JAVAC` was running will be closed. It is therefore better to use a DOS shell to execute `JAVAC.EXE`, as described in the next section. By modifying your DOS `PATH` statement (in the configuration file `AUTOEXEC.BAT`) so that `\JAVA\BIN` is included, you can then run `JAVAC.EXE` without the hassle of changing directories first, i.e. you could simply type

```
JAVAC C:\DEMO\CLASSES\MyApplet.java
```

(the `.EXE` extension can be omitted when running such files).

Running `JAVAC` from within a DOS shell window

By far the easiest way to run the Java compiler on a program is from within a Windows 95 DOS shell. The standard DOS command interpreter `COMMAND.COM` can be run within a window, allowing you to access all of the Java utilities that exist within the `\HOTJAVA\BIN` (*binaries*) directory. You can also launch applets in this way.

In order to use a DOS shell within its own window, simply create a shortcut to `\COMMAND.COM`; Windows 95 will then provide an icon you can use to launch the DOS shell. Do this by clicking once on the desktop with the right mouse button, and select *New* followed by *Shortcut*. Type `COMMAND.COM` in the dialog box and give the shortcut a name. Then, by clicking once with the right mouse button on the newly created icon, choose *Properties* and then *Screen* and select the *Windowed* option for the program.

TIP

Using `JAVAC` from the DOS prompt is the most effective method for applet development, since you can see any errors that appear during compilation. Some DOS shells (such as Norton DOS) have additional tools that allow the output of a program, such as `JAVAC`, to be *piped* into a buffer in order that they can be read if the output would otherwise scroll off the screen very quickly. Examine the filter and piping tools on your system to see if you can use them.

Viewing your applets using the AppletViewer

The `appletviewer.exe` tool can be used to load an applet that is referenced via an HTML file. For example if we had the HTML file:

```
<applet code="MyApplet.class" codebase="classes">
A sample applet.
</applet>
```

and it was named `test.html` we could use the command (from a DOS shell window, or via the *Start/Run* option in Windows 95):

```
appletviewer test.html
```

which would expect **MyApplet.class** to reside in the subdirectory **classes** that is directly below the directory in which the **test.html** file resides.

TIP

The AppletViewer tool has an annoying copyright window that appears whenever it is loaded. In order to remove this notice simply create the directory **.hotjava** inside the **\JAVA** directory, for example using the DOS commands shown here:

```
CD \JAVA
MD .hotjava
```

As soon as you press the *Accept* button this will be the last time that the copyright notice will be displayed.

TIP

If you click on the *Applet* menu within the AppletViewer you can select options that control the applet, e.g. you can restart the applet or shut it down.

Viewing your applets using a Windows 95 shortcut

Shortcuts are new to Windows 95. Basically, they are icons on the desktop that allow programs to be invoked. You can use a shortcut to invoke a Java applet using the AppletViewer by following these steps:

- Click on the desktop using the right mouse button. Select *New* and then click on *Shortcut*;
- Enter as a command line:

  ```
  c:\java\bin\appletviewer.exe test.html
  ```

  where **test.html** is the HTML file that invokes your applet in this case.
- Now click on the *Next* button and provide a name for the shortcut. Enter *Test Applet* and then click on *Finish*. Windows 95 now creates an icon for the shortcut that resembles that shown in Figure 7.3.

FIGURE 7.3 *A Windows 95 shortcut.*

Press the right button while on the new shortcut icon, and a small menu pops up. Select *Properties* and then carry out the following instructions:

- Place the name of the directory in which `test.html` exists in the *Start In:* field, e.g. `c:\demo`
- Select the *Run minimized* option in the *Run* field
- Optionally, change the shortcut icon (if you require)
- Click on *OK* to finish.

You can now click on the icon to start the AppletViewer with the HTML file `test.html`. Clearly, you will have to ensure that this file starts the correct applet.

TIP

You can use applet shortcuts to allow easy access to your Java applets without fiddling with the command line. *Applications* can also be started in this way, by replacing `appletviewer.exe` with `JAVAC.EXE`, the Java interpreter, and replacing the HTML file with the name of a `.class` file to invoke. Ensure that `JAVAC.EXE` can find the application by starting the shortcut in the directory in which the program resides. Another good 'hack' to get the Windows 95 Explorer program to launch an applet via an HTML file can be found at the World-Wide Web site `http://www.io.org/win95hack.txt`. This workaround allows HTML files to be associated with the AppletViewer tool, and uses a batch file and a Java application to fix a bug that stops Explorer working with Windows 95's longer filenames. Explorer is similar to Windows 3.x's File Manager, albeit an enhanced 32-bit version.

The Java language

This section examines the nuts and bolts of the Java language.

Comments

Comments are pieces of descriptive text that are used to annotate parts of a Java program. Java supports comments that span one or more lines. The simplest form of comment is //, which can only span a single line, for example:

```
// This is a Java comment on a single line
```

Comments that span multiple lines are based upon the C and C++ languages, where /* is used to start the comment and */ is used to end it, for example:

```
/*
This is a Java comment spanning
four lines
*/
```

Operators

Java has a number of operators that can be used within expressions. We have seen a few already, for example the equality operator '=='. Table 7.1 lists the most common operators used within Java, along with examples and return values.

The later sections on variables and identifiers and flow of control within a Java program illustrate how these operators can be used.

Variables and identifiers

Identifiers are the names that identify a variable. Variables are used to store values within a Java program. In Java an identifier must begin with a letter (`a..z`, `A..Z`), a dollar ($) or an underscore (_) character, and are case-sensitive. Examples of valid

TABLE **7.1** *Operators within Java*

Operator	Description	Example	Returns
==	Equality	a == b	true|false
+	Addition (increment by 1)	num_var ++	num_var+1
—	Subtraction (decrement by 1)	num_var —	num_var=-1
+=	Addition	a += b	a = a+b
>=	Greater than or equal to	a >= b	true|false
<=	Less than or equal to	a <= b	true|false
!=	Not equal to	a != b	true|false
=	Assignment	num_var = 100	num_var

identifiers are `_temp`, `UnitValue` and `$noHits`. Variables are created under Java according to their *data type*. A variety of common data types are supported, including:

- Integer: a whole number, e.g. `0`, `-1`, `68`
- Boolean: a logical value accepting only the special values `true` or `false`
- String: one or more alphanumeric characters enclosed in quotes, e.g. `"Java"`, `"2.0J"`
- Floating point: a number with a fractional part, e.g. `2.71828`.

TIP

Variables in Java are *case-sensitive*. Referring to the variable `CurrentYear` that has previously been created as `currentYear` will result in a compilation error (and vice versa).

In addition, Java supports multi-dimensional variables such as *arrays*, and single characters that conform to the *UniCode* character set (see `http://www.unicode.com`) are also supported.

TIP

For more details on the UniCode character set see `http://www.unicode.com`, which is the main Web site for this particular character-encoding standard.

Creating a variable requires use of the assignment operator (`=`) in conjunction with a statement that declares the data type of the variable being created. A variable can be created with or without an initial value. The variable declaration statements in Java are `int` (create an integer); `float` (create a 32-bit single-precision number); `boolean` (create a `true`/`false` value); `char` (create a UniCode character variable) and `String` (to create an alphanumeric string variable). Here are some examples of some Java variables being created – notice the semicolon (`;`) which must be used to terminate a Java statement.

```
// Create an integer variable and initialize it:
int my_age = 28;

// Create a floating point variable and initialize it:
float e = 2.71828;
```

```
// Define a string;
String Full_Name;

// Create a character variable and initialize it:
char asterisk = "*";

// Create a boolean variable and initialize it:
boolean InCredit = true;
```

TIP

It is probably best to initialize a variable with a value when you actually create it in order to save confusion later. Remember that variables cannot have spaces in them and must be prefixed with a statement that identifies the data type of the variable (e.g. `String` for a character string). An identifier and a variable differ in that the identifier is the literal *name* of the variable. Many people use the terms interchangeably. Also, don't confuse the *assignment* operator (=) with the *equality* operator, which uses two equals signs (==).

Arrays

Arrays are variables that can contain multiple values. Multi-dimensional arrays can only be implemented using an 'array of arrays'. Arrays are created using the **new** statement in the following way:

```
int days[] = new int[30];
```

which creates an array of `int`egers (whole numbers) called **days** that can contain 31 values – Java arrays start at position 0, note. Values are assigned to an array according to the position required, for example:

```
days[7] = 24;
```

would assign the integer value **24** to the seventh array position. In order to access each value in an array one simply specifies the position required, so for example we could assign the value of the 10th element in our array to the variable **counter** using the Java statement:

```
int counter = days[10];
```

Arrays for most data-types can be created. For example we could have an array of strings coded as:

```
// Create an array of seven null strings:
String dayNames[] = new String[6];
// Fill up the array:
dayNames[0] = "Monday";
dayNames[1] = "Tuesday";
dayNames[2] = "Wednesday";
dayNames[3] = "Thursday";
dayNames[4] = "Friday";
dayNames[5] = "Saturday";
dayNames[6] = "Sunday";
```

TIP
The **new** statement must be used in order to create a new array object. Remember that arrays start at position zero (0) in Java, and not 1 as in some other programming languages. The **new** statement is used to create a variety of objects, arrays being one such example.

Flow of control

The flow of control within an applet can be controlled using a number of control statements, each of which is now examined.

```
if (condition)
   statement(s);
else
   statement(s);
```

The **if** statement is the most common control statement in Java. It allows a condition to be evaluated, and if held true allows the execution of an appropriate code-block; for example:

```
if (label == "Button1") {
System.out.println("You pressed button 1");
...
}
```

tests to see if the variable **label** equals the string **"Button1"**, and if so executes the two statements within the code-block immediately following it. This example could be extended further to include an `else` statement in order to provide an alternative code-block in the case that the condition did not hold true, for example:

```
if (label == "Button1") {
System.out.println("You pressed button 1");
...
} else
if (label == "Button2") {
System.out.println("You pressed button 2");
...
}
```

```
switch (variable) {
  case value: statement(s);
  default: statement(s);
}
```

The `switch` statement allows multiple values to be tested. The `case` statement allows each value to be tested, triggering a code-block when this value is matched, while `default:` allows a statement or code-block to be executed when none of the `case` statements is triggered. Consider the following Java application:

```
// TestSwitch.java:
class TestSwitch {
  public static void main(String args[]) {
    int letter = System.in.read();
    switch (letter) {
      case 'a' : {
        System.out.println("You pressed: a.");
        break;
      }
      case 'b' : {
        System.out.println("You pressed: b.");
        break;
      }
      // etc...
      default:
        System.out.println("A or B not pressed.");
    }
  }
}
```

TIP

The `switch` statement will evaluate every `case` statement unless you use a `break` to leave the scope of the `switch`. In the above example, leaving out the `break` statements would result in *all* the `case` and `default` statements evaluating to `true` and thus the code-blocks for these would be executed. The `default` statement has no `break`, since it is the last item in the `switch` statement.

In the example Java application shown above the `System.in.read()` method is used to read data from the *standard input*, i.e. from the keyboard. Remember that this program is an application and should run from the command-line (e.g. from within a DOS shell). After pressing a key and hitting ENTER, the program tells the user which key was selected. Only the letters 'a' and 'b' are detected in the program, otherwise the message *A or B not pressed* is displayed instead.

TIP

The `switch` statement can be confusing since it does not allow *expressions* to be evaluated. For example, the statement `switch (letter == "a")` is invalid. This form of expression is used with the `if..else` statement.

Classes

A *class* is essentially a collection of Java statements encapsulated within a `class` definition statement. All classes are derived from the super-class `java.applet.Applet`; that is to say they are an *extension* of that class, and hence the `extends` keyword is used along with the class that they are *derived* from. In fact, the `extends` keyword is optional because the default applet class is always `java.applet.Applet`. For example, we would write an applet called `TestApplet.java`, defined as:

```
class TestApplet extends java.applet.Applet {
...
}
```

All Java statements (`...`) must be encapsulated within a `class` definition; statements cannot appear outside this definition, with the exception of *comments* and `import` statements (discussed below).

TIP
The *scope* of a class is indicated by the { and } brackets. The **extends** keyword can be omitted if you wish, since `java.applet.Applet` is the super-class, although it has been included for completeness at this early stage of our treatment of the Java language.

Importing packages

All of Java's standard capabilities are included within class files that are themselves written in the Java language. The methods required for tasks such as displaying graphics and playing audio files must be *imported* from an existing class file that carries out such tasks. There are a number of standard classes that handle these functions. For example, the class `java.applet.AudioClip` has the necessary methods (discussed next) to play audio files. The `AudioClip` class has functions such as `java.applet.AudioClip()` and `play()`, which load and play the audio file required, and in order to access such functions the class that contains them must first be loaded – in this case using the Java **import** statement:

```
import java.applet.AudioClip;
```

TIP
Groups of related classes are known as *packages* in Java. The **package** statement within each such file identifies this to be the case.

Place your **import** statements at the very top of your Java programs (just as C programmers use **#include** statements to load various libraries, for example). If a method is called without loading the appropriate class in which it is defined a compilation error will occur.

And now for another caveat. Some Java methods do not need an associated **import** statement, for example the function `System.out.println()`, which is derived from the `System` class. This class is always available throughout the duration of a program's lifetime. The `System` class is used for general-purpose functions, such as returning the current date and time. More information on the `System` class appears later on.

TIP

Once a package has been loaded with the `import` statement, all of the variables and methods within that package become available to the applet.

Classes can also be loaded using a *wildcarded* expression. Take the case of `java.applet.AudioClip()`, shown earlier, which loads Java's audio-playing package. In this case we are loading just a single file, although the `import` statement:

```
import java.awt.*;
```

uses the asterisk wildcard character (∗) to specify that we should load everything that makes up the `java.awt` *package*, i.e. multiple classes. If you can avoid using wildcarded import statements, do so. They can increase the size of your compiled classes and can slow down program execution.

TIP

The *dotted* notation of the classes imported with the `import` statement is based upon the *location* of the class. For example the `import` statement:

```
import java.applet.Applet;
```

is in fact loading the file `\java\classes\java\applet\Applet.class`. Now you can see why wildcarded `import` statements are allowed as a shorthand notation. For example:

```
import java.awt.*;
```

loads every `.class` file that exists in the `\java\classes\java\awt` directory. It is not wise to load multiple classes when you can specify them individually, since the compiled version of your program will be larger and may also take slightly longer to load and execute.

Methods

A *method* is either a function or procedure contained within a class definition. Functions and procedures are terms used heavily in a variety of other programming languages. They are used to perform just about every task and operation within your program. Methods have the general syntax:

```
returnType methodName(param-1, ... param-n) {
```

```
... Java statements ...
  }
```

where `returnType` is the data type that is returned by the method, e.g. `int` for integer (if you want to return a value from the method, rather like a conventional *function*), or `void` for a method that returns no value (like a conventional *procedure*). Examples of standard Java methods include `init()` and `start()`, which will be executed automatically if defined by the user. These methods do not return values as such, so they are always defined as `void` methods.

The `methodName` keyword is the name of the method, and `param-1 ... param-n` is a list of optional parameters that can be passed to the method. Each parameter must be paired, and consists of a data type and argument name. For example, we could create a method called `WriteMsg` that displays some text on the standard output using Java's `System.out.println` function:

```
public void WriteMsg(String msg) {
System.out.println(msg);
  }
```

The above example uses the `System.out.println` to display some text passed to the method through the single argument `msg`. The argument `msg` must be a string of text in this instance, hence the `String` definition inside `WriteMsg`'s method-definition. `System.out.println` is a standard Java function that is used to display text on the standard output device. Output from this function can only be seen if viewed though Netscape's *Java Window* option, or if the function is defined within a Java application and run through the Java interpreter (`JAVA.EXE`) from the DOS prompt. In our example, the method could be called in the following way:

```
WriteMsg("Hello World!");
```

which passes the string `"Hello World!"` to the method `WriteMsg`. Methods that return values do so with the `return` statement as the last line, along with the value (or expression) to return. Here is a complete Java applet with this code used within it:

```
import java.applet.Applet;
public class TestProgram extends Applet {
  public void init() {
    WriteMsg("Hello World!");
  }
  public void WriteMsg(String msg) {
    System.out.println(msg);
  }
}
```

As another example take the method below, which calculates the number of hours passed during a person's lifetime:

```
// Simple method to calculate hours in a lifetime:
int HoursInLife(int years) {
   int result = (365 * 24) * years;
   return result;
}
```

This method returns an integer (i.e. a whole number (`int`)) and takes as an argument another integer called **years** that represents the age of the person. The variable result (also an integer) then calculates a result based upon this value – in this case a simple multiplication expression. The variable **result** stores this value, and this is returned from the method accordingly. In order to call the method with a value of 30 years we could have a statement such as:

```
int CalcAge = HoursInLife(30);
```

which deposits the final result in the integer variable **CalcAge**. (Enough of this method; the figures are starting to worry me slightly!)

Defining local variables

Variables created within the scope of a method must first be initialized with a value, otherwise a compiler error will occur. Finally, be sure not to conflict any variable names created within a method with those mentioned as arguments to the method. Such instances will cause a run-time error to occur.

What are void methods?

In many instances a method will return a value, although not if the method defined is defined as `void`. If a method does not return a value, the method is probably carrying out some tasks that do not involve calculation – perhaps it is just writing some text to the screen. Many of the standard methods such as `init()` and `Paint()` do not return values and must therefore be defined as `void` methods. Java requires that a method must specify a return value or otherwise be defined as `void`.

TIP

Methods defined with the `void` keyword to do not return a value. Any other method is expected to return a value. The `return` statement is used to return values from a method.

Writing a complete Java applet

A Java applet (or *program*) consists of one or more 'units' known as *compilation units*. A compilation unit can contain any valid Java programming statement, including comments and white space. There is no fixed layout for Java programs, so you can indent your code as required – in fact this makes sense to aid the readability of your programs. Consider the example applet below, which implements the ubiquitous 'Hello World' program, and which we can quickly follow line-by-line:

```java
// The 'Hello World' Program
import java.awt.Graphics;
public class HelloWorld extends java.applet.Applet {
  public void init() {
    resize(150,25);
  }
  public void paint(Graphics g) {
    g.drawString("Hello World!", 50, 25);
  }
}
```

The applet in the example above starts with a comment line. Comments in Java are created using the `//` notation, and allow you to insert annotations that describe the workings of your Java programs, for example:

```
// The 'Hello World' Program
```

Comment lines are ignored by the Java compiler. The second line contains an `import` statement, and you will find that all Java applets contain one or more such statements.

Import statements always appear at the very top of your Java program. They allow the features of another pre-written Java *class* known as a *package* to be incorporated into the current applet. These packages act rather like libraries of pre-written code that you can pull into your applets as and when needed. C programmers will be familiar with the `#include` statement to include various header files for example; Java's `import` function is similar to this in concept. Java comes with a number of packages to handle just about everything from drawing shapes to playing audio files, and you will learn more about such classes later on in the book when we will use them in various applet examples. For example, the Java statement:

```
import java.awt.Graphics;
```

would load the `java.awt.Graphics` class into the current namespace. The *namespace* is a term used to describe the environment in which an executing program is placed – referring to all of the items that make up the application, i.e. its variables and classes etc. In this context `awt` stands for *Abstract Window Toolkit*, the Java package that allows you to incorporate graphical components, such as menus, windows and pick lists, into your applet. You will learn more about Awt in Chapter 8. For example, the `drawString()` method in our program is contained within Awt, and thus the Awt package containing this method must be imported in order to make use of it.

Applets import a variety of packages to allow them to use certain functions. After all, you wouldn't go to all the bother of writing a Java program to play an audio file when a package exists with a class that performs this very task (`java.applet.AudioClip` in this particular case).

TIP

More can be found on the Awt package and associated classes in Chapter 8, including information about designing your own graphical user interfaces (GUIs) in Java.

Defining a new Java class

The next significant line in our program contains a **class** statement:

```
class HelloWorld extends java.applet.Applet {
```

The **class** statement is used to create a new Java class, in this instance the class named **HelloWorld**. When compiled, this applet will create a file called **HelloWorld.class**. The **class** statement therefore determines the name of the **.class** file that is eventually generated by the Java compiler. You should also try to ensure that the name of your **.java** applet is the same as that mentioned in the **class** statement definition, e.g. **HelloWorld.java** in this context.

As mentioned earlier, every applet is in fact a *subclass* from the super-class **java.applet.Applet**. In other words, **java.applet.Applet** is the *base class* for all applets. The format:

```
class ClassName extends java.applet.Applet {
   ...
}
```

should therefore be used for all of your future Java applets, where **ClassName** is the name of your applet. It is also possible to abbreviate the class name specified after the **extends** keyword. For example '**java.applet.Applet**' (a *fully qualified* class name) and '**Applet**' (a *partially qualified* class name) are synonymous with one another, as is the case with all other Java classes. So, for example, you could have the statement:

```
class ClassName extends Applet {
   ...
}
```

which is the same as the previous example. Java would assume you were in fact referring to the file named **java.applet.Applet.class** (which resides in the directory **\JAVA\CLASSES\JAVA\APPLET**).

TIP
If you specify your main class statement as an extension of just '**Applet**' instead of '**java.applet.Applet**' you must specify the **import** statement:

```
import java.applet.Applet;
```

at the very top of your program so that 'Applet' can be expanded to `java.applet.Applet`. As a rule of thumb, always use *fully qualified* class names if possible.

TIP

The name of your main applet class should be the same as the `.java` source code filename. For example, an applet defined with:

```
class GUIapplet extends Applet { ... }
```

requires that the current filename is named as `GUIapplet.java`.

What about multiple class definitions?

A single `.java` source code file can contain more than one class definition; indeed this will be the case with many of Java programs that you write. If an applet contains more than one `class` statement the compilation process for that applet will simply result in multiple `.class` files being generated. The `extends` keyword must be used in the main `class` statement to indicate that your applet is derived from the super-class `java.applet.Applet`, i.e. that your program is an applet that runs inside the Netscape environment. The code for all classes that you define is enclosed in { and } brackets, known as a *code-block*. Notice the indentation used in the earlier example in order to indicate the statements that actually make up the entire `class` definition. Indentation is useful for readability purposes (one tab per statement level is commonly used).

Applet initialization

When an applet initially starts it must do so at an unambiguous point within the program. This point is set by a method known as `init()`. All applets undergo a series of *milestones* during their lifetime, i.e. while they are executing. The first such milestone is `init()`, the *initialization* method, and is commonly used to prepare the applet's environment. Looking quickly back to the current program listing we can see the following code:

```
public void init() {
  resize(150,25);
}
```

From this we can see that the `init()` method is defined and its scope is indicated with the { and } brackets. The `resize(width,height)` function is defined in the `java.awt.Graphics` class that was `import`ed at the beginning of the applet. It is used to set the dimensions of the applet as it will appear when viewed with Netscape 2.0 or any other browser with Java capability (see the tip below regarding this, however). The `width` and `height` arguments are measured in screen pixels.

TIP
The *milestones* in an applet's life are: `init()`, `start()`, `stop()` and finally `destroy()`, in that order. You do not have to use all of these methods, with the exception of `init()`. It is essential that the applet knows where to begin execution, so `init()` must be defined within an *applet*. Java *applications* use the `main()` method as an 'entry-point'.

TIP
The `public` definition ensures that methods such as `init()` are accessible to the entire applet, and is compulsory within Java. The additional `void` statement states that the `init()` method returns no value, as is the case with `start()` and `stop()` etc.

Displaying information within an applet

In order to make an applet display some information in the browser's window the `Paint()` method must be used. All of the applets that you come to examine will have such a method defined, since they output a mixture of textual and graphical information. For example, our program has the following `Paint()` method:

```
public void paint(Graphics g) {
   g.drawString("Hello World!", 50, 25);
 }
```

The `Paint()` method must be called with the compulsory `Graphics` argument along with an object that refers to it. The object that refers to the `Graphics` argument in this instance is called `g`, although this can of course be changed to any other suitable identifier. The `Graphics` argument relates to the Awt class called `java.awt.Graphics` that was imported at the start of the example program. Hence the statement:

```
g.drawString("Hello World!", 50, 25);
```

is using the Awt-based function **drawString(string, x, y)** by referring to the **Graphics** class in which it is contained, using the object **g** to access the class. **drawString()** is an Awt-based function that draws some text on the screen at an **x,y** pixel coordinate relative to the applet's dimensions. Any other graphical function in Awt could now be called in this way. The result of this applet is to draw the string *"Hello World!"* in the Netscape browser's screen. **drawString()** is the principal Java function used to display text strings within an applet.

In summary, all of your applets should undergo the following order of tasks:

- Import the necessary classes, e.g. **java.awt.Graphics** for graphical functions
- Define your class (**MyClassName**) using a **class** statement of the form:

  ```
  public class MyClassName extends java.applet.Applet {
      ...
  }
  ```

- Add an **init()** method and use **resize(x,y)** to define the applet's dimensions
- Add a **Paint(Graphics obj)** method to draw into the applet's space

After writing the applet you must compile it using the **JAVAC.EXE** compiler, as shown earlier. After successful compilation you should end up with a file called **HelloWorld.class** that you can now reference in an HTML document using the **<applet>** tag. In this context your HTML file could resemble the following:

```
<html>
<head>
<title>Hello World!</title>
</head>
<body>
<applet code="HelloWorld.class" codebase="classes">
<hr>The 'Hello World!' applet would normally appear
  here<hr>
</applet>
</body>
</html>
```

Create the above file and then load it into Netscape, ensuring that the **.class** file can be located by the Netscape program. If your classes exist in another directory, rather than the same directory as the HTML file referencing it, use the **codebase** attribute to specify the exact directory location relative to the current directory.

TIP
The quotes around the **code** and **codebase** arguments are optional.

CHAPTER

8

The Abstract Window Toolkit (Awt)

In this chapter you will learn:

- How Awt is used to create graphical user interfaces
- All about Awt basics: the canvas, panels and frames (windows)
- All about programming Awt's GUI components, such as buttons, frames, selection lists, checkboxes, text fields, text areas, radio buttons and scroll bars
- How to obtain user input within a Java program
- How to write an event handler to process button presses etc.
- How to manipulate colour and change fonts

196

Awt basics

One of the most important features that Java offers the Web developer is *Awt*, the Abstract Window Toolkit. Awt is essentially a collection of graphical functions and procedures that are grouped into a file known as a *package*. A package is a compilation unit, a Java source code file made up of methods and other statements. Classes that are related to one another are grouped together into units known as packages. In order to use the facilities of Awt, an `import` statement of the form below is required:

```
import java.awt.*;
```

which loads all of the classes associated with the Awt package, essentially loading the complete Awt package.

TIP
All of the source code examples in this chapter are on-line for you to access and download. Visit the *Essential Internet Home Page*, currently located on the Net at the following URL (and look out for the '*Java Book Support*' hyperlink, which links to McGraw-Hill's Web server):

```
http://www.gold.net/users/ag17/index.htm
```

Alternatively, visit McGraw-Hill's server, which is located on the Net at:

```
http://www.mcgraw-hill.co.uk
```

It is important to remember that Awt is made up of a variety of different packages for many different types of graphical function. In order to gain access to every Awt method it is easier to import every class that makes up the entire Awt package, as the import statement above does. As you become a more confident Java programmer, you will know which classes you require and can import these separately instead. This is advisable, since wildcarded import statements, such as that above, are wasteful; they increase the size of the final `.class` file and they can slow execution speed. Appendix C lists the most frequently used classes that make up the Awt package.

TIP
Netscape 2.0 has the Awt package built into a library that resides in the directory called `\NETSCAPE\PROGRAM\JAVA\BIN` (assuming that the

directory named \NETSCAPE houses the Netscape 2.0 program and associated libraries). The Awt library is stored as a Windows DLL file named AWT3220.DLL, and is roughly a quarter of a megabyte in size. It is based upon the JDK beta 2 version of Awt, which has changed significantly from the first alpha-release of Java.

The look and feel of user interface objects provided by Awt are taken from the underlying operating system (Windows 95 in this case), so you can expect all of the user interface features that you create to resemble those already found in Windows 95.

TIP

The AppletViewer tool has been used to view many of the examples in this chapter. You can think of the AppletViewer as Netscape's main document display area, in that the components you create will appear in much the same way, albeit that you can of course combine HTML and applets together into one document within Netscape. AppletViewer is really a convenience tool which is useful during program development to see your applets as they are constructed. Eventually, you will want to view applets through a fully fledged Web browser such as Netscape.

TIP

The appletviewer.exe tool resides in the \JAVA\BIN directory after installing the Java Developer's Kit (JDK). When using this utility ensure that you invoke it with the name of an HTML file (not a Java source code file), i.e. a file with an <applet> tag within it. Once you have done this, click on the *Accept* button, which acknowledges the copyright notice, and the applet should start. If your <applet> tag uses the codebase attribute to specify a directory for your classes, make sure that it exists below the directory from which you are calling appletviewer.exe. You can also use Netscape.

User interface components

A number of components are used when designing user interfaces, and these are discussed in greater detail within this section. Many of the examples are complete applets and can be run autonomously using the AppletViewer or Netscape 2.0 browser.

The canvas

The *canvas* is an area in which you can draw in an *ad hoc* manner. It is essentially a drawing surface that can be used with a variety of Awt's drawing functions. It is also a class in its own right, and any method that wishes to use the canvas must inherit from this class, for example:

```
// Define a new class to access the canvas:
class MyCanvas extends Canvas {
  void paint(Graphics g) {
    ...
  }
}
```

In this instance `MyCanvas` is derived from the `Canvas` class. The `paint()` method can then be used to house the Awt statements that you need to use for drawing, e.g. `drawString()` or `drawLine()`. Appendix C documents many of the Awt functions in more detail.

Frames

Frames are windows in their own right. When created they appear on the screen and can be moved, minimized and even have menus and objects (such as those mentioned above) attached to them. Frames are useful for presenting menus and pick lists. In a nutshell, frames are windows that hold components. In order to create a frame you can use the `Frame()` constructor. Consider the `MyFrame1` applet below, for example:

```
// Create a simple frame:
import java.awt.*;
import java.applet.Applet;
public class MyFrame1 extends Applet {
  Frame f;
  public void start(){
    f = new Frame("Sample Frame");
    f.show();
  }
}
```

TIP

A Java *application* must create a frame in order to display graphical information (effectively simulating the browser environment).

The frame in our example is created in the true *minimalist* style. It has no clickable regions other than the normal Windows 95 controls to allow the frame to be minimized and maximized etc. (the window cannot be closed at this stage either; this is discussed later). The frame will also have no size; *drag* a corner to re-size it. Windows 95 will also supply a button for the window in the taskbar, the name of which is taken from the string that is passed to **Frame()** – 'Sample Frame' in this instance, as shown in Figure 8.1.

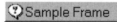

FIGURE 8.1 *The Windows 95 button for our Java frame.*

TIP

Frames, and the components you place within them, are created in memory and are *only* made visible when you issue the **show()** method (see examples).

In order to alter the dimensions of your frame you need to use the **resize()** function with the name of the frame you want to resize, as shown in a modified version of the previous applet:

```
// Applet to create a 200x200 (rows x cols) pixel frame:
import java.awt.*;
import java.applet.Applet;
public class MyFrame2 extends java.applet.Applet {
  Frame f;
  public void start() {
    f = new Frame("Sample Frame");
    f.resize(200,200); /* 200 by 200 pixels */
    f.show();
  }
}
```

In this applet the `resize()` function has been used to create a square frame which is 200×200 pixels in size. You should ensure that your frames are large enough to show any components that may exist with them, otherwise the user will have to resize them manually. We will return to the topic of frames and their subcomponents later in this chapter.

Creating buttons

A *button* is a region of the screen that can be clicked on by the user. Buttons are a fundamental user interface component found in every Windows-based application, and are created using the `Button()` constructor. Buttons are *added* to an applet using the `add()` method. The program below places two buttons on the screen in their *default* layout, that is to say that the buttons are not placed within a frame or other container:

```
// Applet to display some default buttons:
import java.awt.*;
import java.applet.*;
public class MyButtons1 extends java.applet.Applet {
  public void init() {
    add(new Button("Button 1"));
    add(new Button("Button 2"));
    showStatus("Some default layout buttons");
  }
}
```

When this program is compiled the class `MyButtons.class` will be generated. This applet will place two buttons side-by-side on the browser's screen. The buttons will be labelled 'Button 1' and 'Button 2', respectively. While the user will be able to click on the buttons, they will not carry out any actions. Figure 8.2 illustrates how the buttons look when viewed through the AppletViewer utility.

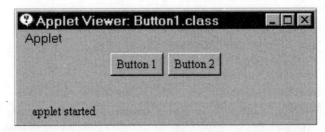

FIGURE 8.2 *Our default buttons as viewed through the AppletViewer.*

TIP

You can use the `showStatus()` function to provide users with some instructions about the buttons they are presented with. For example, with *Yes/No* buttons you could have the message:

```
showStatus("Are you sure?");
```

The resulting message will be displayed in Netscape's status bar at the bottom of the window (as well as in the AppletViewer tool).

In order to handle the pressing of a button, or indeed any other selectable object, an event-handling method must also be written (described after our discussion about buttons).

Using alternative button layouts

Buttons can also be laid out according to a number of pre-specified styles. The Awt `setLayout()` method should be used for this purpose. For example, the Java applet shown below uses the `setLayout()` to allow us to specify the positioning of each button using a 'compass-style' layout pattern:

```
// Applet to display some BorderLayout buttons:
import java.awt.*;
import java.applet.*;
public class MyButtons2 extends java.applet.Applet {
  public void init() {
    resize(200, 200);
  }
  public void start() {
    setLayout(new BorderLayout());
    add("West",   new Button(" W "));
    add("East",   new Button(" E "));
    add("South",  new Button(" S "));
    add("North",  new Button(" N "));
    add("Center", new Button(" C "));
    showStatus("Some BorderLayout buttons");
  }
}
```

Figure 8.3 illustrates how the `BorderLayout` buttons look when viewed through the AppletViewer utility. The buttons themselves are laid out to occupy the

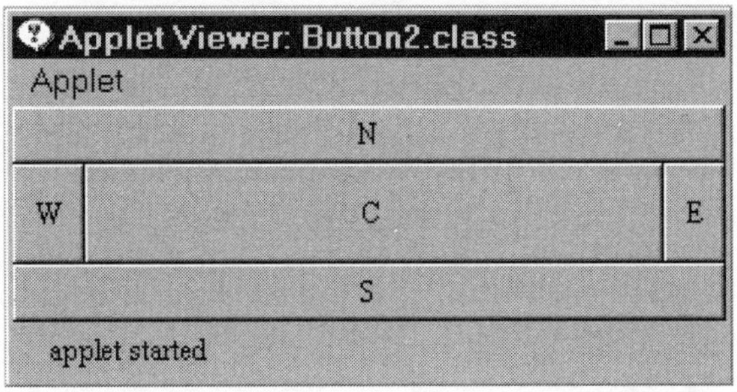

FIGURE 8.3 *The BorderLayout buttons as viewed through the AppletViewer.*

dimensions of the applet. In order to make the buttons occupy a certain area they should be placed within a *panel*, as described later.

Another layout style is provided by the Awt `GridLayout()` method. When used in conjunction with the `setLayout()` method it can be used as follows:

```
// Applet to display some GridLayout buttons:
import java.awt.*;
import java.applet.*;
public class MyButtons3 extends java.applet.Applet {
  public void init() {
    resize(300,200);
  }
  public void start() {
    setLayout(new GridLayout(15,15));
    add(new Button("Button 1"));
    add(new Button("Button 2"));
    add(new Button("Button 3"));
    add(new Button("Button 4"));
    showStatus("Some GridLayout buttons");
  }
}
```

(see Figure 8.4). The `GridLayout(rows,cols)` method accepts two integer parameters, `rows` and `cols`, which represent the number of rows and columns to use as a layout matrix.

Finally, there is a `FlowLayout()` method in Awt that allows buttons to flow in a certain direction. For example, we could have the program:

```
import java.awt.*;
```

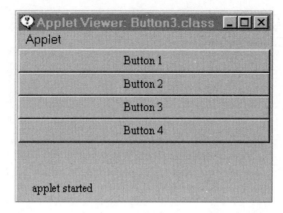

FIGURE 8.4 *A `GridLayout` button scheme as seen though the AppletViewer.*

```
import java.applet.*;
public class BtnFlowLayout extends java.applet.Applet {
  public void init() {
    resize(100,300);
  }
  public void start() {
    setLayout(new FlowLayout(FlowLayout.LEFT));
    add(new Button("Button 1"));
    add(new Button("Button 2"));
    add(new Button("Button 3"));
    add(new Button("Button 4"));
    showStatus("Some FlowLayout buttons");
  }
}
```

The `FlowLayout()` method is used to lay out buttons in a panel. It will arrange each button left-to-right until no further buttons fit on the same line in relation to the dimensions of the applet. In our applet the buttons are aligned from the left, hence the use of `FlowLayout(FlowLayout.LEFT)`. Figure 8.5 illustrates some `FlowLayout` buttons viewed using the AppletViewer tool.

TIP
The exact layout of your buttons will ultimately depend on the applet's width and height. The `<applet>` attributes `WIDTH` and `HEIGHT` control these values. If an applet is not allocated enough space in which to draw a

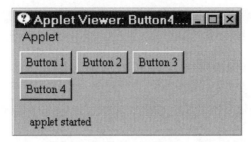

FIGURE **8.5** *A series of* `FlowLayout` *(left-aligned) buttons.*

button or other user interface component the component(s) that cannot fit
will either be squashed within the applet's pre-allocated dimensions
(notably *text areas* – to be discussed) or wrapped onto the next line (as with
buttons – see Figure 8.5).

Panels

Panels are containers for user interface components. A container groups items such as
canvases, buttons and other objects together into different *regions* of the applet. A
panel is not an area into which you can draw freely, like a *canvas* for example – it is
merely an area that other components can be laid out within.

TIP
An application would create a frame and then place panels within this. An
applet could create one or more panels without the need for a frame, since
the browser's display area would be available for such purposes.

In order to define a panel *within* a frame (i.e. a separate window) you should
create a new class that *inherits* its characteristics from the **Frame** class. For example,
we could define a class, **MyWindow**, within the incomplete applet structure shown
below:

```
// Main applet class declaration:
public class MyFrame2 extends java.applet.Applet {
   // Declare a frame, and reference using object 'f':
   Frame f;
   ...
```

```
public void init() {
  f = new MyWindow("Sample Frame");
  ...
}
}

// Class to handle what goes inside our frame:
public void class MyWindow extends Frame
  // This is the MyWindow classes constructor:
  MyWindow(String title) {
    super("Sample Frame");
    // Statements that add things to the frame:
  }
  ...
}
```

You then need to specify a *constructor*, which is named after the class in which it resides.

TIP

A *constructor* is a specialized method that exists within a class. Constructors always take the same name as the class that they are defined within, but do not themselves return any value, i.e. they are implied as being void (although a `void` declaration is not required).

Constructors are invoked when the new operator is used, so for example the Java statement:

```
f = new MyWindow("Sample Frame");
```

creates a new frame using the code situated in the `MyWindow` class. The frame is named 'Sample Name'. When `MyWindow` is invoked, a `super()` statement is then used in order to allow the class to access the parent class's constructor, which in this case is the frame we have created (labelled 'Sample Frame' in the program). If we did not use `super()` all of the components we created would be drawn into the browser (or AppletViewer) rather than into the frame. Here is the applet in its entirety:

```
// Display a frame and place some buttons within it:
import java.awt.*;
import java.applet.Applet;
```

```
public class MyFrame2 extends Applet {
  Frame f;
  public void init() {
    // Create a frame:
    f = new MyWindow("Sample Frame");
    // Size and show the frame:
    f.resize(350,150);
    f.show();
  }
}

public void class MyWindow extends Frame {
  MyWindow(String title) {
    super("Sample Frame");
    // Create some panels in the frame:
    setLayout(new BorderLayout());
    Panel topPanel = new Panel();
    Panel botPanel = new Panel();
    add("North", topPanel);
    add("South", botPanel);

    // Add some buttons the panels:
    topPanel.add(new Button("Button 1"));
    topPanel.add(new Button("Button 2"));
    botPanel.add(new Button("Button 3"));
  }
}
```

From the code listing we can see that our frame has two panels, `topPanel` and `botPanel` respectively. The layout of the panels is based upon the compass-style layout provided by the `setLayout(new BorderLayout())` statement that has been used in earlier examples. Once the panels are created they are stacked on top of one another, i.e. in the *north* and *south* positions. The buttons are then placed into the panel: two in the top panel and one in the bottom panel. Control then passes back to the `init()` function, where the frame is sized using `resize()` and then made visible using `show()`.

Writing an event handler using `handleEvent()`

In order to allow the user to click on a button or other UI object, an *event handler* must be written. Java provides the `handleEvent()` method for this purpose. We'll cover event handlers here, since you now have a good knowledge of how button components are constructed within the Java environment. The `handleEvent()` method returns a boolean value, i.e. `true` or `false`. Take the event handler shown below, for example. This method uses the Java `switch()` method to test the value of an event generated by the user.

TIP

If you need to find out more about Java events, take a look at the source code for the `Event.class` file that resides in the file `SRC.ZIP` that accompanies the JDK. You will need to unzip the file with a tool such as WinZip. See `http://www.winzip.com` for more details.

Examples of events in `Event.class` are `MOUSE_EVENT`, which deals with mouse events (e.g. specific movements), `WINDOW_DESTROY`, called when the current window is shut down by the user, and `ACTION_EVENT`, which handles events such as button clicks. By *catching* these events you can process the actions of the user in relation to objects such as buttons and other user interface components. The skeletal Java code below illustrates a simple way of dealing with the `ACTION_EVENT` event. This code just demonstrates how button clicks can be processed at this stage.

```java
// Some buttons and an event handler:
import java.awt.*;
import java.applet.*;
public class test extends java.applet.Applet {
  public void init() {
    resize(100,300);
  }
  public void start() {
    setLayout(new FlowLayout(FlowLayout.LEFT));
    add(new Button("Button 1"));
    add(new Button("Button 2"));
    add(new Button("Button 3"));
  }
  public boolean handleEvent(Event evt) {
    switch(evt.id) {
      case(Event.ACTION_EVENT) : {
        //
        // Just print the object that
        // triggered the event ...
        //
        System.out.println(evt.arg);
```

```
        return true;
    }

    default: {
      System.out.println("Mouse movement");
      return true;
    }
  }
  }
}
```

In this applet the `handleEvent()` method awaits *action events* using the `ACTION_EVENT` event type. Events in this class include button-presses as well as mouse movement. When an `ACTION_EVENT` event is detected the program prints out the event argument, i.e. the *label* of the object that created the event. The labels in this case are provided via three buttons created earlier in the program within the `start()` method. The `switch()` statement has a *default code-block* (named, not surprisingly `default:`), which is executed when an event is generated that exists in an earlier `case` statement. Moving the mouse causes an event (`MOUSE_EVENT`), although `default:` will pick this up in the program, in which case the program prints *'Mouse Movement'* on the standard output. If you are using Netscape to view such messages, enable the *Java Console* feature. If a button is clicked upon, the button's label is printed, e.g. *'Button 1'*.

The event handler below is an extended version of the previous one and allows specific buttons to be assigned code-blocks. This is done by testing for specific values stored within the `evt.arg` variable as follows:

```
// Event handler for button events:
public boolean handleEvent(Event evt) {
  switch(evt.id) {
    case Event.ACTION_EVENT: {
      if (evt.arg == "Button1 ") {
        System.out.println("1");
      } else
      if (evt.arg == "Button 2") {
        System.out.println("2");
      } else
      if (evt.arg == "Button 3") {
        System.out.println("3");
      } else
      return false;
    }
```

```
    default:
       return false;
   }
}
```

Here is a complete applet with the buttons and event handler all in place:

```
// A button event handler:
import java.awt.*;
import java.applet.*;
public class test extends java.applet.Applet {
  public void init() {
    resize(100,300);
  }
  public void start() {
    setLayout(new FlowLayout(FlowLayout.LEFT));
    add(new Button("Button 1"));
    add(new Button("Button 2"));
    add(new Button("Button 3"));
  }

  public boolean handleEvent(Event evt) {
    switch(evt.id) {
      case(Event.ACTION_EVENT) : {
        if (evt.arg == "Button 1") {
          // Code for label 1:
          System.out.println("Button 1");
          return true;
        } else
        if (evt.arg == "Button 2") {
          // Code for label 2:
          System.out.println("Button 2");
          return true;
        } else
        if (evt.arg == "Button 3") {
          // Code for label 3:
          System.out.println("Button 3");
          return true;
        } else
        return false;
      }
```

```
    default:
      return false;
  }
 }
}
```

TIP

Java provides another way of catching events – by using the `action()` method (as described below). You can use `handleEvent()` and `action()` interchangeably, although both have a slightly different coding scheme.

Writing an event handler using `action()`

Besides `handleEvent()`, Java also provides the `action()` method for event handling. To use this new type of event handler, simply construct a method within your class as follows:

```
public boolean action(Event evt, Object arg) {
   if ("objLabel".equals(arg)) {
      // Code for user selecting UI-object with the
      // label 'objLabel'
      return true;
   } else
   return false;
}
```

In this piece of code, the statement:

```
if ("objLabel".equals(arg)) {
   ...
}
```

is defining a code-block (**. . .**) that will be executed when the user selects an object with the label `"objLabel"`. The `equals()` method is one of Java's equality testing mechanisms, and works for values with the `Object` data type (rather than literal strings using the `==` operator). If you want to use the `==` operator with `arg` you must *cast* (change the data type of) `arg` to a string, which can be done with the method below for example:

```
public boolean action(Event evt, Object arg) {
  String label = (String)arg;
  if (label == "objLabel") {
    // Code for user selecting UI-object with the
    // label 'objLabel'
    return true;
  } else
  return false;
}
```

where (**String**) is the new data type we want to change **arg** to. We'll return to the **action()** method in later examples.

TIP

When writing an event handler for an applet that is ready to ship, always place some code in your event handler for the **WINDOW_DESTROY** event. This event is called when the user shuts down the applet by clicking on the button in the top right-hand corner of a window. Windows 95 supplies this button automatically for every newly created window. The **exit()** method, which is part of the **System** class, can be used to close down the applet, as shown below:

```
...
case Event.WINDOW_DESTROY): {
  // Exit the applet at this point!
  System.exit(0);
}
```

You can of course attach **exit()** calls to a component such as buttons and menu items.

Creating pull-down menus and submenus

A pull-down menu is a user interface component found in just about every Windows-based application. Menus can also be *nested* within each other, allowing *submenus* to be created. In Java, a pull-down menu is created using the **MenuBar()** and **MenuItem()** methods. Consider the following Java code extract:

```
...
// Step 1: Create a menu bar:
MenuBar mybar = new MenuBar();
```

```
// Step 2: Create a new menu within the menu bar:
Menu m = new Menu("Help");
// Step 3: Add an option to the menu and name it:
m.add(new MenuItem("Menu item 1"));

// Add the new option to the menu bar and enable it:
mybar.add(m);
setMenuBar(mybar);
```

This code uses `MenuBar()` to create a new menu bar called `mybar`. Once a menu
bar has been created, individual menus can be added using `Menu()`, and options
can be added using `MenuItem()`. The `add()` method adds the menu to the menu
bar, and then finally `SetMenuBar()` places the entire menu bar into the frame. For
example, here is an extended version of our previous applet which creates a frame
with some panels. In this modified example the applet now has a pull-down *Help*
menu with a list of options using the Java code shown above:

```
import java.awt.*;
import java.applet.Applet;
public class MyFrame3 extends java.applet.Applet {
  Frame f;
  public void init() {
    // Create a frame with some buttons and a menu:
    f = new MyWindow("Sample Frame");
    // Size and show the frame:
    f.resize(350,100);
    f.show();
  }
}

class MyWindow extends Frame {
  MyWindow(String title) {
    super("Sample Frame");
    // Create some panels in the frame:
    setLayout(new BorderLayout());
    Panel myPanel = new Panel();
    add("Center", myPanel);

    // Add some buttons to the panel:
    myPanel.add(new Button("Yahoo"));
    myPanel.add(new Button("InfoSeek"));
    myPanel.add(new Button("WebCrawler"));
```

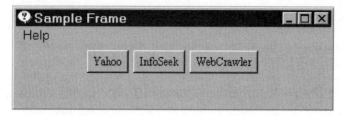

FIGURE 8.6 *The frame, buttons and Help menu from the example.*

```
// *** Create a menu bar and options ***
MenuBar mybar = new MenuBar();
Menu m = new Menu("Help");
m.add(new MenuItem("Menu item 1"));
m.add(new MenuItem("-"));
m.add(new MenuItem("Menu item 2"));
m.add(new MenuItem("Menu item 3"));
mybar.add(m);
setMenuBar(mybar);
        }
    }
```

Figure 8.6 illustrates the frame as it appears on screen. Notice the new menu bar and the *Help* option, which can be selected by the user. Figure 8.7 shows the menu as it appears when selected.

TIP
You must create a frame in order to use pull-down menu components (it is not possible to add a menu to the Netscape browser's existing menus either – nice thought though!). If you need to add a *separator* within a menu list (a vertical bar to separate different categories of menu options) use a single hyphen ("-") as an argument to `MenuItem()`, as shown in Figure 8.7.

TIP
You can use the **ALT** key to invoke a menu. For example, a menu called *Help* can be invoked with the keystroke **ALT-H** (as in Figure 8.6 for example), where 'H' is the first letter of the menu name.

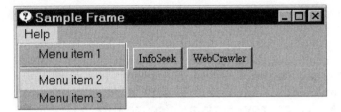

FIGURE 8.7 *The menu in our example (option 2 selected).*

Writing an event handler for multiple UI components

In order to write an event handler for multiple interface components (e.g. buttons and menu bars), simply extend your event handler to include the new objects. For example, consider the applet below, which creates a frame containing a menu bar and three buttons. The event handler `handleEvent()` checks each event name (stored in the variable `arg`) to see what value it contains. If this value matches a label given to one of the UI components, such as a button, a code-block is executed accordingly. For the sake of the example, our applet just outputs the name of the object that the user has selected; you will of course add your own code in such instances. Here is the applet:

```java
// Buttons, menus and an event handler:
import java.awt.*;
import java.applet.Applet;

public class MyFrame4 extends java.applet.Applet {
  Frame f;
  public void init() {
    // Create a frame with some buttons and a menu:
    f = new MyWindow("Sample Frame");
    // Size and show the frame:
    f.resize(350,100);
    f.show();
  }
}

class MyWindow extends Frame {
  MyWindow(String title) {
    super("Sample Frame");
    // Create some panels in the frame:
    setLayout(new BorderLayout());
```

```java
    Panel myPanel = new Panel();
    add("Center", myPanel);

    // Add some buttons to the panel:
    myPanel.add(new Button("Yahoo"));
    myPanel.add(new Button("InfoSeek"));
    myPanel.add(new Button("WebCrawler"));

    // Create a menu bar and options:
    MenuBar mybar = new MenuBar();
    Menu m = new Menu("Help");
    m.add(new MenuItem("Menu Item 1"));
    m.add(new MenuItem("-"));
    m.add(new MenuItem("Menu Item 2"));
    m.add(new MenuItem("Menu Item 3"));
    mybar.add(m);
    setMenuBar(mybar);
}

// Event handler for menu-selections and buttons:
public boolean handleEvent(Event menEvt) {
  switch(menEvt.id) {
    case Event.ACTION_EVENT: {
      if (menEvt.arg == "Menu Item 1") {
        System.out.println("Menu 1");
        return true;
      } else
      if (menEvt.arg == "Menu Item 2") {
        System.out.println("Menu 2");
        return true;
      } else
      if (menEvt.arg == "Menu Item 3") {
        System.out.println("Menu 3");
        return true;
      } else
      if (menEvt.arg == "Yahoo") {
        System.out.println("Yahoo");
        return true;
      } else
      if (menEvt.arg == "InfoSeek") {
        System.out.println("InfoSeek");
        return true;
```

```
      } else
      if (menEvt.arg == "WebCrawler") {
        System.out.println("WebCrawler");
        return true;
      } else
      return false;
    }

  default:
    return false;
    }
  }
}
```

TIP
When comparing labels in an event handler be sure to use the *exact* case of
each label. For example, an object with the label `"WebCrawler"` is *not*
the same as `"Webcrawler"`.

Creating text areas and text fields

A *text area* is an area of the screen into which text can be freely input by the user. A
text field is similar to a normal HTML form field, and allows small strings of text (on a
single line) to be entered by the user. The `TextArea()` and `TextField()`
methods are used for this purpose and are the two main ways of allowing textual
input by the user. Both text areas and text fields should be drawn into a *panel* region
(along perhaps with other user interface components). Consider the following applet:

```
// Create a text area to allow some user input:
import java.awt.*;
import java.applet.Applet;

public class textarea extends java.applet.Applet {
  public void init() {
  Panel mainPanel = new Panel();
  setLayout(new BorderLayout());
  add("Center", mainPanel);
  mainPanel.add(new TextArea("TextArea", 5, 20));
  }
}
```

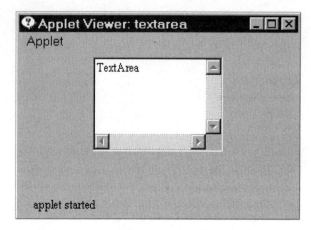

FIGURE 8.8 *The text area in our example as viewed through the AppletViewer.*

This applet draws a `TextArea()` field into a single panel (`mainPanel`). `TextArea()` is called with three arguments in the example, namely: (i) a string to initially place within the text area; (ii) the *width* of the text area; and (iii) the *height* of the text area. All text area dimensions are measured using individual characters. The applet in our example creates a text area that is 20 characters in width and 5 characters in height. Scroll bars are added to the text area automatically. Figure 8.8 illustrates the text area created in our example applet.

Text fields are created in much the same way. Consider the applet below, which has two text fields:

```
// Create text field to allow user input:
import java.awt.*;
import java.applet.Applet;

public class tarea2 extends java.applet.Applet {
  public void init() {
    Panel Panel1 = new Panel();
    Panel Panel2 = new Panel();
    add("Center", Panel1);
    add("South",  Panel2);
    Panel2.setLayout(new GridLayout(2,1));
    Panel1.add(new TextArea("TextArea", 5, 50));
    Panel2.add(new TextField("TextField 1", 15));
    Panel2.add(new TextField("TextField 2", 15));
  }
}
```

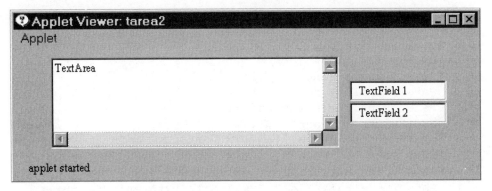

FIGURE 8.9 *Our applet as seen through the AppletViewer utility.*

This applet defines two panels (`Panel1` and `Panel2`) which are situated on top of one another. The first panel has a single text area field placed within it, while the second has a grid layout consisting of two text fields. Because the second panel has a grid layout, each component placed within this panel will be fitted according to an area that has two rows and one column. The two text fields that are added to this panel are therefore placed on top of one another. Each text field is created using `TextField()`, which in the example is specified with two arguments: (i) a string of default text to be placed within the field and (ii) the width of the field, in characters.

Figure 8.9 illustrates how the applet in this example looks when seen through the AppletViewer utility. Ensure that you have assigned appropriate `WIDTH` and `HEIGHT` values to the `<applet>` tag that loads this program, so that each of the elements is visible (the AppletViewer tool requires that these attributes are specified in order for it to run the applet).

In order to store the values entered by the user you will have to define a variable and then assign it the value of the text field or text area in question (both are held as character strings).

The extended applet below accepts input from the user via three fields and then outputs the current values entered whenever the user clicks on the button provided:

```
// User-input manipulation applet:
import java.awt.*;
import java.applet.Applet;

public class tarea3 extends java.applet.Applet {
  TextField fld1;
```

```
    TextField fld2;
    TextArea  ta1;

public void init() {
   Panel Panel1 = new Panel();
   Panel Panel2 = new Panel();
   Panel Panel3 = new Panel();
   add("North",  Panel1);
   add("Center", Panel2);
   add("South",  Panel3);
   Panel1.add(new Button("See values"));
   Panel2.add(ta1  = new TextArea("TextArea", 5, 50));
   Panel3.add(fld1 = new TextField("TextField 1", 15));
   Panel3.add(fld2 = new TextField("TextField 2", 15));
}

public boolean action(Event evt, Object arg) {
   String label = (String)arg;
   if (label == "See values") {
     System.out.println("TextArea     : "
       + ta1.getText());
     System.out.println("");
     System.out.println("TextField 1 : "
       + fld1.getText());
     System.out.println("");
     System.out.println("TextField 2 : "
       + fld2.getText());
     return true;
   }
   else
     return false;
}
}
```

The salient feature of the applet above is the use of the **action()** event handler, which works in much the same way as **handleEvent()**, described earlier. However, because the value of **arg** is of type **Object** it must have its data type changed to **String** before it can be compared with other literal string values.

Note also the use of **getText()**, which allows the contents of a text field or text area to be accessed. Figure 8.10 illustrates our applet as seen through the Java AppletViewer utility. All **System.out.println()**s are directed to the standard

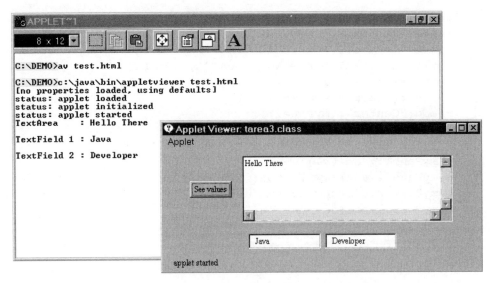

FIGURE **8.10** *The applet and DOS shell environment in our example.*

output, which in this case is the DOS shell. You can see the result of pressing the "*See values*" button in Figure 8.10.

TIP

The `setText()` method can also be used to place text within a text area. When using this method the complete text area field is replaced.

Consider the applet below, which uses `setText()` to manipulate a text area.

```
import java.lang.*;
import java.awt.*;
import java.applet.*;
public class TextFillApplet extends java.applet.Applet {
  public void init() {
    new MyFrame("");
  }
}
```

```
class MyFrame extends Frame {
  Panel  myPanel1 = new Panel();
  Panel  myPanel2 = new Panel();
  TextArea     ta1 = new TextArea("", 10, 60);
  MyFrame(String title) {
    super("Sample Applet");
    add("Center", myPanel1);
    add("South",  myPanel2);
    setLayout(new FlowLayout(FlowLayout.LEFT));
    myPanel1.add(ta1);
    myPanel2.add(new Button("Button 1"));
    myPanel2.add(new Button("Button 2"));
    myPanel2.add(new Button("Exit"));
    resize(500,250);
    show();
  }

  public boolean action(Event evt, Object obj) {
    String Ta_data1 = "This is some text for button 1";
    String Ta_data2 = "You pressed button 2";
    String label    = (String)obj;

    // See if any buttons were pressed:
    if (label.equals("Button 1")) {
      ta1.setText(Ta_data1);
      return true;
    } else
    if (label.equals("Button 2")) {
      ta1.setText(Ta_data2);
      return true;
    } else
    if (label.equals("Exit")) {
      // Bye bye...
      System.exit(0);
    }
    return true;
  }
}
```

In this applet we define a frame and create two panels. A series of buttons is placed in the lower panel which activates the **setText()** method using two different strings of text.

TIP

Here are some other useful methods for use with text fields and text areas that you can incorporate into your applets (see also the later section on colour-handling):

```
myObj.setForeground(Color.colorWord)
```

which sets the foreground (text) colour, where `colorWord` is a colour code word, as defined in `Color.class`, e.g. `Color.blue` for the colour blue. The value of `myObj` should be set to your text area or field name.

```
myObj.setBackground(Color.colorWord)
```

which sets the background colour (colour codes as described above). The value of `myObj` should be set to your text area or field name.

```
myObj.setEditable(true|false)
```

which toggles edit mode on or off (useful for stopping users from entering text into a field – perhaps the field is for displaying text only). Supply `true` to allow the current text field or area (`myObj`) to be edited, or `false` to disallow editing.

Creating checkboxes

A checkbox is an object that can hold either a `true` or a `false` value, i.e. selected or unselected. Checkboxes are used to obtain *mutually exclusive* options from the user, i.e. where a single response among many options is required. Consider the simple checkbox applet below, for example:

```
// A simple checkbox applet:
import java.applet.*;
import java.awt.*;

public class check extends java.applet.Applet {
  Panel myPanel;
  public void init() {
    myPanel = new Panel();
    CheckboxGroup MyChecks = new CheckboxGroup();
    myPanel.setLayout(new GridLayout(5, 1));
    myPanel.add(new Checkbox("Archie", MyChecks, false));
    myPanel.add(new Checkbox("Gopher", MyChecks, false));
    myPanel.add(new Checkbox("WWW",    MyChecks, false));
```

```
            myPanel.add(new Checkbox("Email",   MyChecks, false));
            myPanel.add(new Checkbox("WAIS",    MyChecks, false));
            add("Center", myPanel);
        }
    }
```

This applet starts by defining a panel area into which the checkboxes are to be drawn. There are five checkboxes in the example, each of which is added to the panel using the `Checkbox()` constructor. In order to create a new checkbox the `CheckboxGroup()` method must first be called. In the applet this is done with the statement:

```
    CheckboxGroup MyChecks = new CheckboxGroup();
```

which creates a checkbox called `MyChecks`. Individual checkbox options are added using statements of the form:

```
    myPanel.add(new Checkbox("Email", MyChecks, false));
```

where `myPanel` is a panel area which will hold the checkbox options. `Checkbox()` is called with three parameters, namely: (i) a label name; (ii) the name of the checkbox container created with `CheckboxGroup()`; and (iii) a `true` or `false` value indicating whether the current checkbox option is selected (by default). This latter option sounds slightly contradictory, since we already know that checkboxes only allow one option to be selected. If you did set every item to `true`, Java would ensure that only the last option is initially selected.

Processing checkbox selections

In order to ascertain which checkbox has been chosen by the user you will have to write an event handler to scan through each box and see which is set to `true`. The extended applet below does just this:

```
    // Checkbox applet with event handler:
    import java.applet.*;
    import java.awt.*;

    public class check extends java.applet.Applet {
        Panel myPanel;
        public void init() {
            myPanel = new Panel();
            CheckboxGroup MyChecks = new CheckboxGroup();
            myPanel.setLayout(new GridLayout(5, 1));
```

```
      myPanel.add(new Checkbox("Archie", MyChecks, false));
      myPanel.add(new Checkbox("Gopher", MyChecks, false));
      myPanel.add(new Checkbox("WWW",    MyChecks, false));
      myPanel.add(new Checkbox("Email",  MyChecks, false));
      myPanel.add(new Checkbox("WAIS",   MyChecks, false));
      add("Center", myPanel);
      // Add a button to see the selected checkbox:
      add("South", new Button("See Values"));
   }

   public boolean handleEvent(Event MyEvent) {
      if (MyEvent.id == Event.ACTION_EVENT) {
         if ("See Values".equals(MyEvent.arg)) {
            SeeValues();
            return true;
         }
      }
      return false;
   }

   public void SeeValues() {
      System.out.println("Checkbox status:\n\n");
      for (int n = 0 ; n < myPanel.countComponents() ; n++)
{
         Checkbox comp = (Checkbox)myPanel.getComponent(n);
         if (comp.getState()) {
            // It seems that this checkbox is selected:
            System.out.println(comp.getLabel());
         }
      }
   }
}
```

This applet now has two new methods, namely `handleEvent()` and
`SeeValues()`, the latter of which is responsible for printing the checkbox label that
has been selected by the user. This is done to the standard output, so AppletViewer
users should watch the DOS shell for output and Netscape 2.0 users should use the
Show Java Console feature located in the *Options* menu. Figure 8.11 illustrates the
extended applet in action.

In order to scan through a series of checkboxes the `countComponents()` method
has been used. We could have hard-coded the number of checkboxes of course (to 5 in
this case), although since the checkboxes exist by themselves within a panel we can scan

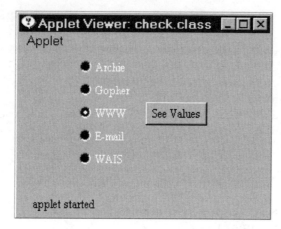

FIGURE 8.11 *The checkbox applet as seen through AppletViewer.*

the panel for components based on the value returned by the `countComponents()` method. A `for` loop scans through each component. In order to access each checkbox the `getComponent()` method is used. A variable, `comp`, is assigned the value of the current checkbox component, and an `if` statement then checks to see whether the checkbox is selected. This is done using `getState()`.

The `getLabel()` method simply returns the label of a checkbox option and is printed on the screen to the user for the purposes of this example, although any code-block can of course be executed. For example, a more extensive code-block would be needed to check to see which checkbox was selected. The extended `SeeValues()` method shown below does this:

```
// Extended SeeValues() method to handle individual
  checkboxes:
public void SeeValues() {
  System.out.println("Checkbox status:\n\n");
  for (int n = 0 ; n < myPanel.countComponents() ; n++) {
    Checkbox comp = (Checkbox)myPanel.getComponent(n);
    if (comp.getState()) {
      label = comp.getLabel();
        if (label == "Archie") {
          // etc ...
        } else
        if (label == "Gopher") {
          // etc ...
        } else
```

```
        if (label == "WWW") {
          // etc ...
        } else
        if (label == "Email") {
          // etc ...
        } else
        if (label == "WAIS") {
          // etc ...
      }
    }
  }
}
```

Creating checkboxes within a menu

Checkboxes can also be embedded within the options in a menu. Menu bars were discussed earlier in the chapter; they are created using the `MenuBar()` and `MenuItem()` constructs. Java provides the `CheckboxMenuItem()` construct for placing checkbox items within a menu. Rather than using round checkboxes, a tick is placed next to the item that is selected by the user. Since checkboxes are on/off values, the tick can be *toggled* on and off by subsequent clicks upon the same option. As before, only one option may be selected at any one time. Consider the small applet below, which creates a frame and then inserts a menu bar:

```
// Applet to create a frame, menu bar and checkbox list:
import java.awt.*;
import java.applet.Applet;

public class CheckMenu extends java.applet.Applet {
  Frame f;
  public void init() {
    // Create a frame with a single menu:
    f = new MyWindow("Sample Frame");
    f.resize(350,100);
    f.show();
  }

  // Event handler for menu events within the frame:
  public boolean handleEvent(Event evt) {
    switch(evt.id) {
      case Event.ACTION_EVENT: {
        System.out.println(evt.arg);
        return true;
```

```
          }
        }
        return false;
    }
  }

class MyWindow extends Frame {
  MyWindow(String title) {
    super("Sample Frame");
    // Create a menu-bar and options:
    MenuBar mybar = new MenuBar();
    Menu m = new Menu("Help");
    m.add(new CheckboxMenuItem("Checkbox item 1"));
    m.add(new CheckboxMenuItem("Checkbox item 2"));
    m.add(new MenuItem("-"));
    m.add(new CheckboxMenuItem("Checkbox item 3"));
    mybar.add(m);
    setMenuBar(mybar);
  }

  // Simple event handler for menu-options:
  public boolean handleEvent(Event evt) {
    switch(evt.id) {
      case Event.ACTION_EVENT : {
        System.out.println(evt.arg);
        return true;
      }
    }
    return false;
  }
}
```

A small event handler has also been included in the above applet. This prints the name of the checkbox that has been activated by the user. In order to actually process each event, simply adapt the event handler shown in the earlier example that scans through each checkbox. Figure 8.12 illustrates the previous applet as seen through the AppletViewer tool (with option two selected in this case – notice the tick).

Creating choice lists

A *choice list* is a series of options that pop up when clicked upon. Users can then scroll through a series of options in order to select the one they require. Once a

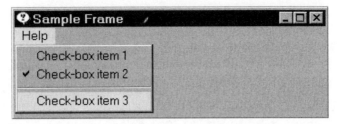

FIGURE 8.12 *The frame and checkbox menu list from the example.*

selection is made it is displayed as the currently selected item. Choice lists are created using `Choice()`, and items are added into the choice box using `addItem()`. The applet below implements a simple choice box scheme with five selectable options. In order to display the choice box a panel must first be created. This applet also includes a simple event handler to display the currently selected choice:

```
// Choice box and event handler applet
import java.awt.*;
import java.applet.Applet;
public class ChoiceTest extends java.applet.Applet {
  Choice ch;
    public void start() {
      // Create some panels:
      Panel Panel1 = new Panel();
      Panel Panel2 = new Panel();

      // Create a layout for the panels:
      setLayout(new BorderLayout());
      add("North", Panel1);
      add("South", Panel2);

      // Add some choice options:
      ch = new Choice();
      ch.addItem("Item 1");
      ch.addItem("Item 2");
      ch.addItem("Item 3");
      ch.addItem("Item 4");
      ch.addItem("Item 5");

      // Add the button to the 2nd panel:
      Panel2.add(new Button("See Values"));
```

```
        // Add the choices to the 1st panel:
         Panel1.add(ch);
    }

    public boolean action(Event evt, Object arg) {
       if ("See Values".equals(arg)) {
         System.out.println("Selected item is: " +
           ch.getSelectedItem());
         return true;
       }
       return false;
    }
}
```

In particular, notice how the choices are created and then added to our panel using the `add()` construct at the very end of the `start()` method. The event handler is implemented as an `action()` method and just checks to see if a button-press is made by the user. The button in the example applet is provided to allow the event handler to print the currently selected choice option. You would have to add some additional code to check which selection was currently active. Figure 8.13 illustrates the applet as seen through the AppletViewer utility.

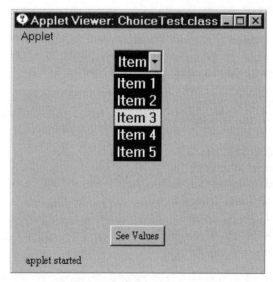

FIGURE 8.13 *The choice list in our example.*

Scroll bars

Scroll bars allow the user to move within an object that is itself larger than the area in which it appears. This can be the case for textual and for graphical objects. For example, a frame could have scroll bars to allow the user to move an image around in order to view it. The code to implement a scroll bar is fairly straightforward, although it can become confusing, because by itself the scroll bar controls are useless. It is when the scroll bar is combined with an event handler and a component to actually *scroll* around that their use becomes apparent.

In Java a scroll bar is created using the `Scrollbar()` constructor. Consider the more advanced applet below, `ScrollTest`, which allows the user to scroll around an image placed within a frame (i.e. window) structure:

```
import java.applet.*;
import java.awt.*;
public class ScrollTest extends java.applet.Applet {
   static Image img;
   public void init() {
      img = getImage(getCodeBase(), "images/myimage.gif");
      new MyFrame();
   }
}

class MyFrame extends Frame {
   DrawCanvas cv;
   Scrollbar horz;
   Scrollbar vert;
   public MyFrame() {
      super("MyFrame");
      add("Center",  cv = new DrawCanvas());
      add("East",  vert = new Scrollbar(Scrollbar.VERTICAL,
         cv.vert_axis, 0, 0, 30));
      add("South", horz = new
Scrollbar(Scrollbar.HORIZONTAL,
         cv.horz_axis, 0, 0, 100));
      resize(350,110);
      show();
   }

   public boolean handleEvent(Event evt) {
      if (evt.target == vert) {
         cv.vert_axis = ((Integer)evt.arg).intValue();
```

```
       cv.repaint();
       return true;
    }
    if (evt.target == horz) {
       cv.horz_axis = ((Integer)evt.arg).intValue();
       cv.repaint();
       return true;
    }
    return false;
  }
}

class DrawCanvas extends Canvas {
  int vert_axis = 0;
  int horz_axis = 0;
  public void paint(Graphics g) {
    g.translate(-vert_axis, -horz_axis);
    g.drawImage(ScrollTest.img, 0, 0, this);
  }
}
```

Our applet starts by defining an image object using the **Image** statement, where **img** is the variable that references the image. The **img** variable is defined as **static** because it will be referenced from a separate class that is defined later on in the program.

TIP

It is not possible to reference a variable defined within one class from another unless the variable being referenced is defined as **static**. A static variable can exist only once within a program, and is mainly used to create a unique instance of a variable. A compilation error will occur if you access a non-static variable that is defined outside the scope of the current class.

Next an image is loaded from disk using the **getImage()** method with the line:

```
img = getImage(getCodeBase(), "images/myimage.gif");
```

There are two ways of referring to the *location* of an image. The first uses the **getCodeBase()** method, which returns the name of the directory mentioned in the `<applet>` tag's `codebase` attribute. For example, the applet in our example could be loaded via the HTML applet tag shown below:

```
<applet code=ScrollTest.class
  codebase=classes
  width=100
  height=100>
```

So, in relation to our program `getCodeBase()` returns the string value `"classes"`. Java has another similar method called `getDocumentBase()`, which returns the name of the directory in which the HTML file referencing the current applet is located. The next argument to `getImage()` is the name of the actual image to load, and optionally the directory in which it is contained. In our context we are loading the image `MYIMAGE.GIF`, which exists in the directory `CLASSES/IMAGES.GIF` *relative* to the HTML file that is referencing the applet.

TIP

If we were using `getDocumentBase()` we would have to ensure that the directory `IMAGES` was located below the directory in which the HTML calling the applet was located. For example, if our HTML file was located in the directory `\DEMO`, `getCodeBase()` would assume that a directory named `\DEMO\CLASSES\IMAGES` exists, whereas `getDocumentBase()` would assume that the directory `\DEMO\IMAGES` exists instead. Confusing the location of a file is one of the easiest mistakes to make when referencing applets using relative directory names. The choice of using `getCodeBase()` instead of `getDocumentBase()` depends on whether or not you have a `codebase` attribute in your `<applet>` tag. Unfortunately you *cannot* specify a literal directory name (such as the string `"\CLASSES"`) as the first argument to `getImage()`.

Next in our example program we have the line:

```
new MyFrame();
```

This statement creates a new object called `MyFrame()`, where `MyFrame()` is the *constructor* of the class `MyFrame`. `MyFrame()` creates the frame in which our image will be displayed and is discussed in more detail later in this section. The `new` statement is used in this context since it allows us to invoke the class we require (it also allocates storage for the new object and calls the constructor for the class concerned – in this case the constructor is the public method `MyFrame()`). This completes the code for the `init()` method.

TIP

The `new` statement does two main things when invoking a class: (i) It allocates memory for the new object and (ii) it calls the appropriate *constructor* for that object – in the case of a class, the constructor is a method within the class that takes the same name.

Now come the main class definitions that make up the bulk of our program. The class `MyFrame` inherits its properties from the `Frame` class (or from `java.awt.Frame.class`, to be more precise). In other words, this entire class implements a frame – a separate window region that is detached from the main applet area, as defined by the statements:

```
class MyFrame extends Frame {
   DrawCanvas cv;
   Scrollbar horz;
   Scrollbar vert;
   ...
}
```

The two scroll bars can easily be identified – these are the objects `horz` and `vert` (horizontal and vertical scroll bars), both of which are defined as class type `Scrollbar` (from `java.awt.Scrollbar.class`). The object `cv` is of class type `DrawCanvas`. Since the class `DrawCanvas` is not part of Awt (i.e. there is no such file as `java.awt.DrawCanvas.class`), it must be *user-defined*. This is indeed the case, since the class `DrawCanvas` is defined later on in the program – it is a canvas region where we can draw objects in this instance. Within the class `MyFrame` is one constructor method, also called `MyFrame`, although you can see it is a method because it accepts arguments within the open and closed brackets (none in this case, however). Within the scope of `MyFrame()` are a number of Java statements that create a canvas region and two scroll bars. Here is the code again to remind you:

```
public MyFrame() {
   super("MyFrame");
   add("Center",  cv = new DrawCanvas());
   add("East",  vert = new Scrollbar(Scrollbar.VERTICAL,
     cv.vert_axis, 0, 0, 30));
```

```
add("South", horz = new Scrollbar(Scrollbar.HORIZONTAL,
   cv.horz_axis, 0, 0, 100));
resize(350,110);
show();
}
```

The **super()** statement calls the parent constructor, in this case **MyFrame()**, to create the frame region we require. Objects are then *added* to the frame in the normal way using the **add()** method. In this case three objects are added: a canvas region, a horizontal scroll bar and a vertical scroll bar. The canvas region is created by the class **DrawCanvas()**, which in this example simply places an image within the frame. The **Scrollbar()** constructor accepts a number of arguments; for example, the statement:

```
add("East",  vert = new Scrollbar(Scrollbar.VERTICAL,
   cv.vert_axis, 0, 0, 30));
```

creates an East-facing scroll bar, i.e. the bar will be vertical and placed on the right-hand side of the frame. The value of **VERTICAL** is taken from **java.awt.Scrollbar.class** and is a numeric value that specifies the *orientation* of the scroll bar. Literal values can be placed in here (0 for horizontal and 1 for vertical), but it is easier to use an exact identifier for readability. The next argument, **cv.vert_axis**, is a value representing the current position of the vertical scroll bar. Since **cv** references the **vert_axis** variable it must be defined within the **DrawCanvas** class. It is important to track the movement of the scroll bar so that the objects inside the frame can be moved accordingly (more on this later). The next two arguments represent the size of the visible scroll bar selector – the bar used to move within the scroll bar region. A value of zero (0) uses the default size. Finally, the last two arguments to **Scrollbar()** represent the minimum and maximum size of the scrollable region. In our example we are loading an image into a frame. It is therefore sensible to ensure that the user cannot move beyond the bounds of the image. You can adjust the maximum value until you are satisfied that the object scrolls properly within the frame.

Next we use the **resize()** method to specify the dimensions of the frame and the **show()** method to draw the frame on the screen.

TIP
Remember that a frame is *not* made visible until **show()** is specified.

Within the `MyFrame` class there is also an event handler, implemented using `handleEvent()`. Using a scroll bar without an event handler that tracks the position of each bar is a fruitless exercise. Here is the event handler in our example program:

```
public boolean handleEvent(Event evt) {
  if (evt.target == vert) {
    cv.vert_axis = ((Integer)evt.arg).intValue();
    cv.repaint();
    return true;
  }
  if (evt.target == horz) {
    cv.horz_axis = ((Integer)evt.arg).intValue();
    cv.repaint();
    return true;
  }
  return false;
}
```

This event handler uses the `target` variable defined in `java.awt.Event.class`. Whenever the user clicks on a scroll bar or drags it an event is generated. This event is stored in the `target` variable, which is itself of type `Object` (and hence why the direct '==' comparison is allowed, since the `new` statement creates a new object of type `Object` – in this case a scroll bar). When the vertical scroll bar is moved the value of `cv.vert_axis` is updated. The value of `arg` stores this pixel value. Vertical movement means that our image is being moved either up or down. The value of `arg` is coerced to an integer before it can be used, since it arrives as type `Object`. The method `intValue()` then extracts this integer (whole number) value and it is stored in `cv.vert_axis` accordingly. The `repaint()` method redraws the canvas, i.e. *refreshes* it, to reflect the new scroll bar position. The same is done for the horizonal scroll bar, except that `cv.horz_axis` is updated instead.

TIP
If you are unsure what *type* of value a method returns, simply look at the source code for the class concerned. For example, it is easy to see that the `target` variable in the `Event` class is of type `Object`, since you can edit `Event.java` and search for 'target' in order to see how it is defined (as `public Object target` in this instance). The JDK houses all of its class source code in the compressed archive named `SRC.ZIP`. You will have to decompress this archive to get at the source code file you need.

Finally, our program defines the class **DrawCanvas**, which inherits all of its properties from the **Canvas** class, and is used to draw an image into our frame region. As a reminder, here is **DrawCanvas** again in its entirety:

```
class DrawCanvas extends Canvas {
    int vert_axis = 0;
    int horz_axis = 0;
    public void paint(Graphics g) {
      g.translate(-vert_axis, -horz_axis);
      g.drawImage(ScrollTest.img, 0, 0, this);
    }
}
```

The **DrawCanvas** class also defines the variables **vert_axis** and **horz_axis**. Both are integers and are initially set to zero when the class is first invoked. The **paint()** method is called automatically by the Java run-time for the purposes of 'painting' graphical information into a region of the screen – the canvas area in this case. The **java.awt.Graphics** class is mentioned as an argument to **paint()** for this reason; the **Graphics** class has a number of methods designed solely for graphical operations, such as drawing shapes and loading images.

Probably the most important method in this class is **translate()**, which takes the **horz_axis** and **vert_axis** variables and translates these positions so that they are relative to the current component. The 'current component' in this case is the canvas region (identified by variable **cv**). The **translate()** method thus ensures that any movements made using the scroll bars update the canvas, i.e. move the image about. This works in conjunction with the event handler that repaints the screen after each movement. Without a **translate()** method our scroll bars would have no control over any objects that they were meant to control. Figure 8.14 illustrates our applet in action using the AppletViewer tool, and where the image being examined is a map.

TIP

In our example program the **translate()** method specifies that the **vert_axis** and **horz_axis** variables are negative, i.e. they are prefixed with a minus sign (–). Why is this? Well, when a vertical scroll bar moves downwards our (partially obscured) image should really move *upwards* so that we can see what exists below the current frame position. Likewise, moving a horizontal scroll bar to the right means that you really want the image to move to the left (relative to the current frame). This is achieved by making the values in the **translate()** method negative, so that, effectively, they perform the opposite action. If you leave out the minus

FIGURE 8.14 *The example applet with active scroll bars.*

signs the scroll bars will behave literally, i.e. moving a scroll bar upwards will make the image move upwards etc. Strange, but true!

The `drawImage()` method, as the name suggests, draws a bitmap image into a region of the screen at a specified `x`, `y` coordinate (0, 0 is the top left-hand corner of our canvas in this instance). The image in the example is named `ScrollTest.img`, which refers to the `img` variable in the `ScrollTest` class defined at the very top of the program (as the *root*, or top-level class definition). The variable `img` is defined as `static` so that it can be referenced outside the scope of its original definition. By looking at the applet you can see that it contains an image loaded from disk via the `getImage()` function.

TIP
`drawImage()` can handle both GIF and JPEG format images.

TIP
Any image that is loaded with `getImage()` will be transported to the user's machine automatically via the Internet if your applet is being

accessed from a Web server. The Java run-time system built into Netscape
2.0 will handle this for you. Be sure to place your applet, HTML file (and all
associated images etc.) on your Web server so that they can be accessed by
other Internet users.

Manipulating fonts

New font objects are created using the `Font()` constructor, and are set using
`setFont()`. Font alterations work with Awt functions that display text, including
`drawString()`, as well as other user interface components, such as text areas and
text fields. You can manipulate the font according to the user interface component
that you are creating for maximum flexibility. For example, consider the applet code
fragment shown below:

```
import java.awt.*;
import java.applet.*;
class FontTest extends Applet {
  public void init() {
    resize(300,200);
    ...
  }
  public void paint(Graphics g) {
    Font myFont;
    ...
    myFont = new Font("Courier", Font.PLAIN, 12);
    g.setFont(myFont);
    g.drawString("Hello World!", 10, 10);
    ...
  }
}
```

which uses `Font()` to create a new font that has the `Courier` typeface and is 12 points
in size. The `PLAIN` argument is defined in the `java.awt.Font` class and specifies that
the font will have no special attributes, such as **bold** or *italic* effects – the `Font` class also
has the variables `BOLD` and `ITALIC` for this purpose. The `drawString()` function
would therefore draw *'Hello World!'* using a plain 12 point Courier font.

TIP

Each font has a unique name, for example `Symbol`. In order to find a
particular font name you can run the Windows 95 Control Panel and select

Fonts. Font names in Java do not have spaces, so the Times Roman font is specified as `TimesRoman`. If a font cannot be located, no run-time error will occur; instead a default font will be used by Java.

Handling colour

The main class for handling colour is `java.awt.Color`. By examining the source code for this class you can see that a number of standard colours are supported by Java, as illustrated in Table 8.1.

There are no general-purpose colour manipulation methods, since colours are applied to components, of which there are many. The Awt `Component` class has the colour methods `setForeground()` and `setBackground()`, for example, which can be applied to a variety of graphical components, such as text areas. Objects such as text areas inherit from the `Component` class and thus have access to these methods. For graphical objects based upon *x*, *y* coordinates, such as shapes and lines, the `setColor()` method is provided as part of the `Graphics` class. For example, a solid blue rectangle could be drawn using the Java code:

```java
import java.awt.Graphics;
import java.awt.Color;
public Paint(Graphics g) {
  ...
  g.setColor(Color.blue);
  g.fillRect(0, 0, 200, 200);
  ...
}
```

TABLE 8.1 *Java's standard colours*

Colour	Java object reference
White	`Color.white`
Light Gray	`Color.lightGray`
Gray	`Color.gray`
Dark Gray	`Color.darkGray`
Black	`Color.black`
Red	`Color.red`
Green	`Color.green`
Magenta	`Color.magenta`
Cyan	`Color.cyan`
Blue	`Color.blue`

Drawing shapes

Awt has a number of shape-drawing methods. Appendix C lists these, along with their arguments. It is possible to draw both two- and three-dimensional objects in Java. Lines are drawn using `drawLine()`, ovals with `drawOval` and polygons with `drawPolygon()`. These methods draw outline objects, rather than filling the structure with any colour. Shapes can also be drawn with solid interiors, using methods such as: `fillOval()`, `fillPolygon()` and `fillRect()`. Three-dimensional drawing methods include: `draw3DRect()`, which draws a three-dimensional rectangle.

Handling mouse-based events

Java has a number of methods that allow mouse events to be captured and acted upon. The principal methods for detecting button clicks from a mouse are `mouseDown()` and `mouseUp()`, which detect button presses and button de-presses (a button release) respectively. In order to detect whether the mouse is within the applet's display area, Java provides the `mouseEnter()` and `mouseExit()` methods. Finally, there is `mouseDrag()`, which detects when the mouse is being *dragged* (that is the mouse is being moved while a button is being held down) and `mouseMove()`, which detects when the mouse is being moved. Being able to detect the actions of the mouse is as simple as defining a method such as:

```
// Detect when a mouse button is pressed:
public boolean mouseDown(Event event, int x, int y) {
   System.out.println("Mouse click.");
   return true;
}
```

TIP

The x and y integer variables passed to methods such as `mouseDown()` represent the x, y pixel coordinate of the mouse cursor (within the applet's display area) at the time the event was generated. See the later example for an applet that displays these x, y values.

First, consider the simple applet below, which uses all of the methods previously mentioned. Run this with the AppletViewer from within a DOS shell and watch the output that is generated while you move the mouse around in and out of the applet's display area.

```
// Applet to detect Mouse events:
```

```
import java.awt.*;
import java.applet.Applet;
public class MouseTest extends Applet {
  public void init() {
    System.out.println("Initializing applet...");
  }
  public boolean mouseDown(Event event, int x, int y) {
    System.out.println("Mouse button click.");
    return true;
  }
  public boolean mouseEnter(Event event, int x, int y) {
    System.out.println("Mouse entered applet area.");
    return true;
  }
  public boolean mouseExit(Event event, int x, int y) {
    System.out.println("Mouse exited applet area. ");
    return true;
  }
  public boolean mouseDrag(Event event, int x, int y) {
    System.out.println("Mouse being dragged. ");
    return true;
  }
  public boolean mouseMove(Event event, int x, int y) {
    System.out.println("Mouse moving.");
    return true;
  }
}
```

TIP
Each of the mouse events mentioned earlier only works when you are currently *within* the applet's display area. Be sure to place the appropriate method within the scope of the object in which you want to detect mouse events. For example, if you have an applet that creates a frame (i.e. a window), you will need mouse event methods within the scope of the applet and the frame in order to detect events in *both* areas.

The final applet example illustrates how the *x, y* coordinate of a mouse click can be detected. The applet simply waits for a mouse click using `mouseDown()`, and then uses `System.out.println()` to display the values of `x` and `y` that the method returns.

```
// Applet to detect Mouse click and return x,y coordinate:
import java.awt.*;
import java.applet.Applet;
public class MouseXY extends Applet {
  public boolean mouseDown(Event event, int x, int y) {
    System.out.println("Mouse click at coordinate: " +
      x + "," + y);
    return true;
  }
}
```

C H A P T E R

9

Threads

In this chapter you will learn:

- Why threads are beneficial to the Java programmer
- How to implement single and multiple threads in Java by extending the `Thread` class and by defining a `Runnable` interface
- How to program image animations and other real-time threaded programs
- How to allocate thread priorities

Introducing threads

Threads are Java's way of implementing *multitasking*, that is, multiple processes that execute simultaneously. In fact 'simultaneous' is a slightly inaccurate description; *concurrent* would be more accurate, because threading allocates a *slice* of time to each thread process, thus giving the impression that multiple processes are running simultaneously when in fact they are running very quickly one after the other. So why use threads? Tasks that can be performed in the *background*, such as downloading files, waiting for network messages or updating information are all prime candidates for a thread. Allocating time to each such process will allow other tasks to be undertaken by the user that require immediate attention. Many of the standard software packages use threads. For example, the Netscape Navigator Web browser allows you to browse a page and download an image via the use of threads.

> **TIP**
> A *thread* is defined as 'a single sequential flow of control within a Java program'.

Threads can be used for a variety of other tasks, including the following:

- Playing an image animation
- Playing and manipulating sounds
- Updating and retrieving data in the background
- Waiting for and processing data over a network connection

Once a thread is started it is allocated its own resources. In this way it can run by itself, allowing the user to engage in other tasks, such as scrolling within a hypertext document or interacting with another applet.

Threads are said to have a *body* in which the Java statements that make up that thread are located. In Java, the `run( )` method is used to house the body of a thread.

> **TIP**
> When should I use a thread? Threads are useful for activities that need to be updated on a continual basis. If such a task also needs to be paused and re-started, threads offer a convenient way of doing this (as will be demonstrated in later examples). It is possible to code many iterative tasks without a thread, such as the animation of an image, although this *hogs* the applet's resources in the process, and can lead to a degradation in system performance. Threads are designed to run *concurrently*, so that each task receives an equal share of processor time.

Implementing a thread in Java

Java provides the programmer with two ways of implementing the *body* of a thread:

- Defining a `Runnable` interface and using the `run()` method
- Extending your applet from the `java.lang.Thread` class.

Defining a `Runnable` interface

In the case of a *runnable* interface you define your applet in the normal way except that you use the `implements` keyword with the interface name `Runnable`. For example, we could have:

```
class MyApplet extends java.applet.Applet implements
Runnable {
  ...
  public void run() {
    // Body of the thread
  }
}
```

where `MyApplet` is the name of your applet. The statement `implements Runnable` dictates that the applet contains a thread, and that the body of the thread is located in the `run()` method. The `run()` method will be executed automatically by the Java run-time when it encounters a `Thread()` constructor.

TIP

As a rule of thumb, if your class is derived from some other class (most commonly this will be `java.applet.Applet`) you should use a `Runnable` interface, as described above.

Extending your applet from the `Thread` class

The second way of implementing a thread is by extending (or *subclassing*) your applet to inherit its behaviour from the `java.lang.Thread` class. In this way a `run()` method is still required, although it is *overridden* by the extended class definition. For example, we could have:

```
class MyThread extends java.lang.Thread {
  ...
```

```
public void run() {
   ...
  }
}
```

TIP
When should I use **Runnable** and when should I subclass? This is an interesting question, which arises out of one of Java's limitations. An applet that uses the **Runnable** interface makes use of the **run()** method to house the body of a thread. In order to run with a Web browser that is Java-compatible, such as Netscape 2.0 or Sun's HotJava browser, an applet must be derived from the **java.applet.Applet** class, that is to say that you use the **extends** keyword with the **Applet** class. Since a class may also need to use a thread, this class cannot inherit from both the **Applet** *and* **Thread** classes at the same time (in other words Java does not support *multiple inheritance*). Hence some classes use the **Runnable** interface to implement threads.

TIP
Another reason why many people choose to create a subclass of the **Thread** class, rather than using a **Runnable** interface, is that it is more straightforward to create multiple threads when subclassing. For a start, with only one **run()** method it is not immediately clear how more than one threaded task can be implemented. See the later section on implementing multiple threads for more information.

Creating a thread

Threads are created by first defining an object of type **Thread** and then using the **new** statement with the **Thread()** constructor. For example, we could have the following applet fragment, which uses a **Runnable** interface and creates its thread within the **start()** method:

```
Class MyApplet extends java.applet.Applet implements
   Runnable {
   Thread threadObj;
   ...
```

```
       public void start() {
         threadObj = new Thread(this, "MyThread");
         threadObj.start();
       }
       ...
     }
```

where `threadObj` is a reference to our newly created thread. This object allows us to control the thread, i.e. to stop, start or delay the thread. The `Thread()` constructor then creates the thread and is passed the name of the applet and a name for the thread as arguments. The `this` variable refers to the *current applet* (`MyApplet` in this case) and is passed in as the first argument to the `Thread()` constructor. This argument must implement the `Runnable` interface and by doing so becomes the thread's *target*. In this way our thread (`threadObj`) gets its `run()` method from its target `Runnable` object, in this case the `MyApplet` applet.

TIP

The `start()` constructor is used to start a thread object, i.e. to call the `run()` method in this case. There is also a `suspend()` routine that pauses a thread and a `stop()` routine that stops the thread.

You may also see a slight alteration in an applet that uses threads so that it that checks to see if a thread is running before it is started, for example:

```
     Class MyApplet extends java.applet.Applet implements
       Runnable {
       Thread threadObj;
       ...
       public void start() {
         if (threadObj == null) {
           threadObj = new Thread(this, "MyThread");
           threadObj.start();
         }
       }
       ...
       public void stop() {
         threadObj.stop();
         threadObj = null;
       }
     }
```

The null value is assigned to a variable that has not yet been initialized. In the second line of the applet above we have defined a thread, but we have not yet started it. This is known as a null thread. It could be the case that the thread is already running of course, in which case it is commonplace to find code that checks the thread before actually running it. It is possible to stop and start a thread while you are in the same applet, for example by moving the mouse cursor over an applet's display area (an application to be examined later on in the chapter).

TIP
Threads are started and stopped automatically by the Java run-time system. For example, when you *leave* a hypertext page containing a thread the stop() method is called automatically. Likewise, if you *return* to a page that has an applet that is using a thread, the start() method is invoked.

A real-time clock applet

Consider the applet below, which implements a real-time (24-hour) clock that can appear anywhere within a hypertext (HTML) page. This applet uses a thread to continuously fetch the current time from the computer (the time arriving courtesy of the *local* computer):

```
// Clock applet:
import java.awt.Graphics;
import java.util.Date;
public class Clock extends java.applet.Applet implements
Runnable {
  Thread clockThread;
  public void start() {
    // Check to see if thread is running:
    if (clockThread == null) {
      clockThread = new Thread(this, "Clock");
      clockThread.start();
    }
  }
  // Thread body:
  public void run() {
    while (clockThread != null) {
      repaint();
```

```
          try {
            clockThread.sleep(1000);
          } catch (InterruptedException e) {}
      }
  }
  public void paint(Graphics g) {
    Date now = new Date();
    g.drawString(now.getHours() + ":" + now.getMinutes() +
                              ":" + now.getSeconds(), 5, 10);
  }
  public void stop() {
    clockThread.stop();
    clockThread = null;
  }
}
```

TIP

The `java.util.Date` class contains the routines `getHours()`,
`getMinutes()` and `getSeconds()`, which are used in the clock applet.
`Date()` returns the current date, which includes both the time and date,
and should be used to access individual elements such as the current hour.

In this applet we start by defining a thread, `clockThread`:

```
Thread clockThread;
```

The `start()` method is then used to create a new thread and start it. The thread is
examined to see whether it is running already before being started, as shown below.
The thread will always be null the first time the `start()` method is executed, of
course, so the thread will always be started:

```
public void start() {
  // Check to see if thread is running:
  if (clockThread == null) {
    clockThread = new Thread(this, "Clock");
    clockThread.start();
  }
}
```

Next we have the *body* of the thread itself – the `run()` method. This has been set up as a loop that runs while the thread is not set to `null` (`clockThread != null`), i.e. while the `stop()` method is not invoked, such as when a new hypertext document is loaded. The `repaint()` method redraws the applet's display area, since this will be constantly changing as the clock updates. The `paint()` method houses the code that actually draws the current time. Without a `repaint()`, each number that makes up the string containing the current time would be continuously drawn over itself. Then we encounter a new statement called `try`, which is used to catch an *exception*.

TIP
An exception is essentially an event that is generated by the Java run-time when an error occurs within a program. Many of the standard Java methods, such as `sleep()`, which is defined within `java.lang.Thread.class`, 'throw' an exception which should ideally be 'caught' and then dealt with accordingly (e.g. by showing an error message and terminating the applet). You must process all such exceptions, otherwise a compiler error will be generated. By examining the `Thread` classes source code in `Thread.java` (contained in `SRC.ZIP`) you can see that `sleep()` throws an exception called `InterruptedException`, which is in fact the class of the same name called `InterruptedException.class`.

An exception is dealt with using an *exception handler*, which is implemented using the `try` and `catch` statements. The `try` statement specifies a code-block with the statement that generates, or *throws* the exception. The `try` and `catch` statements in our example program resemble:

```
try {
  clockThread.sleep(1000);
} catch (InterruptedException excpt) {}
```

where the variable `excpt` is an arbitrary exception identifier variable. The `{}` represents a code-block to deal with the exception that has been raised, and for the purposes of the example has simply been left empty.

The `sleep()` method is found in the `Thread` class. It allows a thread to be 'put to sleep', i.e. paused for a specified amount of time, measured in milliseconds (ms). Hence the statement:

```
clockThread.sleep(1000);
```

pauses the `clockThread` thread for 1 second (where 1000 ms = 1 second), effectively leading to a clock update time of one second (just like a normal clock).

We could have rewritten the `run()` method in a more simplified way, omitting the exception handler, although as mentioned this will cause a compiler warning:

```
public void run() {
  while (clockThread != null) {
    repaint();
    clockThread.sleep(1000);
  }
}
```

Figure 9.1 shows the clock in action, embedded within an HTML file, as seen through Netscape 2.0. The HTML file itself resembles the following. Be sure to make the applet's height small so that the time can be included within the rest of your HTML document.

```
<html>
<head>Clock Demonstration Applet</title>
<body>
Time: <applet code=Clock.class codebase=classes
  width=50 height=10>
<hr>Clock animation would normally appear here<hr>
</applet>
<hr>This hypertext document has a real-time clock in the
    top left-hand corner of the page.
```

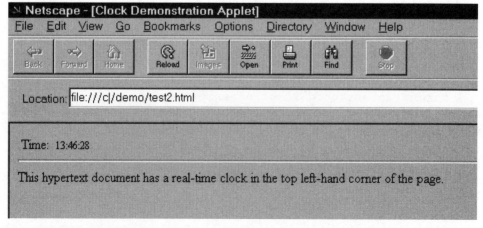

FIGURE 9.1 *The clock applet running within the Netscape 2.0 browser.*

```
</body>
</html>
```

From the HTML file we can see that the `Clock.class` file resides in the `CLASSES` directory, so place your HTML file (as above) in a directory above this. From the URL in Netscape's *Location:* field, shown in Figure 9.1, you can see that the HTML file that invokes the clock applet is called `test2.html` and that it resides in the `\DEMO` directory. Since the `codebase` attribute of the `<applet>` tag specifies the value `"CLASSES"`, the applet `Clock.class` must reside in the directory `\DEMO\ CLASSES` in this instance. Ensure that you have a similar directory structure so that you can see the results. If you want to upload this applet to a Web server, copy the same directory structure that you use locally.

Implementing an image animation using a thread

Here is another example, this time using a thread for an image animation. The animation in question contains two still picture GIF files which are drawn in succession to one another to give the impression of movement.

TIP
If you need the images for this animation applet you will find them at *Essential Internet Home Page* on the Web at the URL:

> `http://www.gold.net/users/ag17/index.htm`

When you arrive click on the *Java Book Support* option.

Our applet starts in the normal way. It imports all of the required classes, including Awt, so that we can draw the images. We will also use the `Math` class to use Java's `random()` routine to generate a random delay between the loading of each image to make the animation more realistic. The animation itself can be any two images you choose, although I am using two pictures of Arnold Schwarzenegger (of *Terminator* fame) to animate his eyes by flashing them on and off. What is different about this applet is that we are using the mouse event methods `mouseEnter()` and `mouseExit()` to control the thread: the thread in the applet is only activated when the mouse cursor is over the applet's display area. Here is the applet in its entirety:

```
import java.awt.Graphics;
import java.applet.Applet;
```

```
import java.awt.*;
import java.lang.Math;

public class arnieAnimation extends Applet implements
  Runnable {
  Image images[];
  int picNum = 0;
  Thread arnieThread;
  public void init() {
    resize(70,103);
  }
  public void Paint(Graphics g) {
    update(g);
  }
  public void update(Graphics g) {
    g.drawImage(images[picNum], 0, 0, this);
  }
  public boolean mouseEnter(Event e, int x, int y) {
    arnieThread = new Thread(this);
    arnieThread.start();
    return true;
  }
  public boolean mouseExit(Event e, int x, int y) {
    arnieThread.suspend();
  return true;
  }
  public void run() {
    images = new Image[2];
    images[0] = getImage(getCodeBase(),
      "images/arnie1.gif");
    images[1] = getImage(getCodeBase(),
      "images/arnie2.gif");

    for (;;) {
      repaint();
      picNum = (picNum == 0) ? 1 : 0;
      try {
        Thread.sleep( (int) (Math.random() * 500));
      } catch (InterruptedException e) {}
    }
  }
}
```

> **TIP**
> Threads can be suspended and resumed using `suspend()` and `resume()` respectively. To stop a thread use `stop()`; to destroy a thread, without *cleaning up*, use `destroy()`.

An array, `images[]`, is used to store both of the images that make up the animation (the images being `arnie1.gif` and `arnie2.gif` in this case). When the thread `arnieThread` is constructed in the `init()` method the `run()` method is automatically invoked. The `run()` method starts by loading the two images into the `images[]` array at position 0 and 1. The method then uses a `for(;;)` loop to iterate infinitely – hence the omission of any control arguments to the loop. Infinite loops are useful for tasks such as animation, and are frequently used with threads of this type. Within this loop the variable `picNum` determines which image will be shown. The applet knows which image will be displayed next using the statement:

```
picNum = (picNum == 0) ? 1 : 0;
```

which is a 'shorthand' version of the Java `if` statement. The statement is basically saying: 'Set the value of *PicNum* to 1 if PicNum is 0, else set *PicNum* to 0'. We could have replaced this with:

```
if (picNum == 0)
    picNum = 1;
else
    picNum = 0;
```

although the former method is much more compact, as you can see. The numbers 0 and 1 do of course refer to positions 0 and 1 in the array `images[]`. Notice how the value of `PicNum` is used as an array index to `images[]`, which is then passed to `drawImage()`. In order to place a delay between the loading of each image the `sleep()` routine is used again, as in the clock applet shown earlier, except that this time the argument to `sleep()` is not hard-coded. Instead, it is specified as a random value using the `random()` routine, which is part of Java's `Math` class. The value passed to `sleep()` is coerced to an integer so that the value is a whole number, which `sleep()` expects as an argument. This value cannot exceed 500, so we end up with delays that reach a maximum of 500 milliseconds (or half a second).

TIP
You could do away with the use of a random delay generator, and just hard-code a delay factor into the `sleep()` method, e.g. `sleep(500)` for a half-second (500 ms) pause.

All of the other methods in the applet are self-explanatory: `mouseEnter()` simply starts the thread, while `mouseExit()` stops it. The `repaint()` routine calls the `update()` method, which updates the applet's display area, and which is also used to draw the image into our applet. Remember that you will have to move the mouse over the picture in order for it to animate. So you see, pictures really do come to life with Java!

TIP
By using the `<param>` tag within the `<applet>..</applet>` container, you can pass different images to an application. This saves hard-coding the names of the images into the program, and provides maximum flexibility to quickly change the images you want to display. Use `getParameter()` to load the name of the image you require into `drawImage()`, for example:

```
<applet code=arnieAnimation.class codebase=classes
  height=100 width=75>
<param name="image1" value="images/pic1.gif">
<param name="image2" value="images/pic2.gif">
<img alt="Arnie Image" src="arnie.gif">
</applet>
```

Figure 9.2 illustrates the animation in our example applet, as seen through Netscape. Of course, you can't see the *actual* animation, although you can see how the applet can be laid out with some additional HTML. An HTML table structure has been used to place some text by the side of the applet. Notice also how non-Java-aware users can see just a static picture instead of the applet.

The HTML file to invoke the animation applet shown in Figure 9.2 is therefore as follows:

```
<!-- TEST.HTML: Invoke the Arnie applet -->
<html>
<head>
<title>Arnie Animation Applet</title>
```

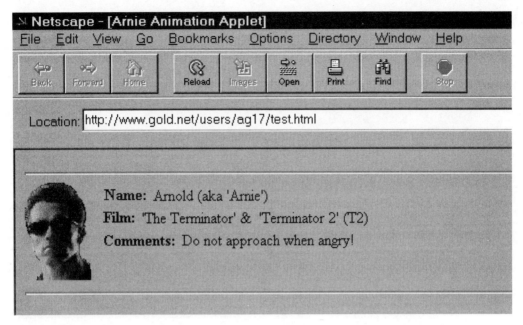

FIGURE 9.2 *The animation applet as seen through Netscape 2.0 (with added HTML).*

```
<body>
<hr>
<table border=0>
<!— Table row #1: vertically aligned to the top —>
<tr valign="top">
  <!— Table cell #1: The arnie applet / static image —>
  <td>
    <!— Reference the applet —>
    <applet code=arnieAnimation.class codebase=classes
      height=100 width=75>
    <!— Allow non-Java browsers to see Arnie! —>
    <img alt="Arnie Image" src="arnie.gif">
    </applet>
  </td>

  <!— Table cell #2: Some descriptive text —>
  <td>
    <b>Name:</b> Arnold (aka 'Arnie')<br>
```

```
    <b>Film:</b> 'The Terminator' & 'Terminator 2'
(T2)<br>
    <b>Comments:</b> Do not approach when angry!<br>
  </td>
</tr>
</table>
<hr>
</body>
</html>
```

TIP

Build your applets into the HTML page so they blend in as much as possible. You can place applets on the page using a number of HTML tags such as `<table>..</table>` (table structure container); `<center>..</center>` (centre object container); `<div align="left | center | right">..</div>` (HTML 3 align paragraph tag).

TIP

If you need to animate more than two images simply alter your `run()` method accordingly, for example as shown below, which animates six images (with a tenth of a second delay):

```
public void run() {
  images = new Image[6];
  images[0] = getImage(getCodeBase(),
   "images/img1.gif");
  images[1] = getImage(getCodeBase(),
   "images/img2.gif");
  images[2] = getImage(getCodeBase(),
   "images/img3.gif");
  images[3] = getImage(getCodeBase(),
   "images/img4.gif");
  images[4] = getImage(getCodeBase(),
   "images/img5.gif");
  images[5] = getImage(getCodeBase(),
   "images/img6.gif");

  for (;;) {
```

```
      repaint();
      imageThread.sleep(100); /* 10th sec delay */
      imgIndex ++;
      if (imgIndex >= 5) {
        // Reached the last array elementm so
        // reset and continue looping:
        imgIndex = 0;
        continue;
      }
    }
  }
```

TIP

Be patient with Netscape when viewing animations loaded over the Net.
They can take a while to load and then start up. They will appear,
eventually. Try to keep your images small. Animations tend to run more
smoothly with smaller image files.

Allocating thread priorities

Threads can be allocated priorities using the `setPriority()` routine. The priorities
themselves fall into three types, each of which has its own identifier: `MIN_PRIORITY`
for *minimal* priority tasks, `NORM_PRIORITY` for *normal* priority tasks and
`MAX_PRIORITY` for *maximum* priority tasks. Altering the priority of a thread alters the
amount of time awarded to the thread. Priorities can be changed at any time during
the lifetime of an executing thread. The default priority for all newly created threads is
`NORM_PRIORITY`. For example, we could have:

```
...
Thread myThread;
public void init() {
  myThread = new Thread(this);
  myThread.setPriority(Thread.MAX_PRIORITY);
  ...
}
```

which allocates maximum priority to the thread named `myThread`. The use of thread priorities becomes more apparent when using multiple threads.

Implementing multiple threads

Up until now, all of the applet examples in this chapter have used single threads. This has mainly been as a consequence of using a `Runnable` interface via the `run()` method. However, if you allow a class to inherit its characteristics from the `Thread` class you can implement multiple threads. Consider the fragment of Java code below for example:

```
import java.applet.Applet;
class CreateTwoThreads extends Applet {
  public void CreateTwoThreads() {
    new CreateThread1().start();
    new CreateThread2().start();
  }
}

class CreateThread1 extends Thread {
  ...
  public void run() {
    ...
  }
}
class CreateThread2 extends Thread {
  ...
  public void run() {
    ...
  }
}
```

In this skeletal applet, the class `CreateTwoThreads` creates two new threaded objects and starts them immediately. `CreateThread1` and `CreateThread2` are separate classes that inherit their behaviour from the `Thread` class. Effectively, both of these classes are now separate threads in their own right, and thus anything declared with their `run()` methods will be executed as a threaded process. In fact, we could even take the two applets shown earlier and place their code in `CreateThread1` and `CreateThread2`, the result being two threaded applications that are allocated equal priority (although you can of course allocate higher priorities by using the `setPriority()` method, as was illustrated earlier).

CHAPTER

10

Streams

In this chapter you will learn:

- How to use streams to process local files: `InputStream`s and `OutputStream`s
- How to pull textual and graphical information from remote Internet servers
- How to load URLs directly into Netscape

Introduction

Up until now all of the applets that have been demonstrated are designed to run locally. What about actually linking up to other Internet resources from within an applet? To understand this you first have to consider how the Internet works, and which standards are already in place. The Internet is based around a framework known as the *client–server* model. The *client* and *server* are similar in that they are both computers that are connected to the Internet (indeed both are frequently implemented on a single computer). The main difference between client and server lies in the *location* of information. After all, information is what every *client* is after. All those who use Web browsers, such as Netscape, are clients because they are accessing Web servers for information – hypertext documents in this case. Servers are the entities that offer information to clients. All Web servers serve information to you in the HTML format primarily, although they do of course serve other formats, such as still images and audio/video content.

TIP

Clients are computers *requesting* information from a server machine. Web servers handle client requests by sending them the information they request, such as a hypertext page or an image. Web servers are machines running special software that allow clients to request hypertext documents from them. The NCSA HTTPD server, CERN Server and EMWAC (Microsoft) are popular Web server software systems in common use (the first two also being *freeware*).

Java doesn't do away with the need for a server entity, although it does shake the client–server model up a bit. The server element in the model will always exist, since the information a client requires will most probably be located elsewhere on the Internet. However, Java doesn't need a 'Web server' specifically; applets could quite easily be transported to a host using another Internet protocol, such as FTP (file transfer protocol).

TIP

Many of the applets and applications in this chapter require an Internet connection, e.g. a TCP/IP SLIP/PPP connection via an Internet provider. Windows 95 users have an in-built 32-bit TCP/IP stack which arrives as part of the Dial-up Networking Module. You will have to install this software first in order to gain Internet access to work with Java.

Java allows the developer to get information back from a server in one of two ways:

- By using a *stream* to read data from a URL, file or CGI-script
- By using a *socket* connection

Streams are an important concept, since they are also used to manipulate files locally, i.e. to read and write data to and from disk.

TIP
In order to read and write data to disk you will have to use a *stream* (see the later section on manipulating files using streams).

Battle of the interactive standards: CGI vs. Java

A number of standards currently address the task of implementing *interactive content* on the Internet. CGI, or the Common Gateway Interface, is the system upon which the vast majority of 'interactive' systems on the Internet are presently built. CGI is a very successful standard that allows the client and server to exchange information using conventional programming language features, such as *environment variables* and *data streams*. CGI works very well when the 'interaction' required is typically straightforward, i.e. the user sends some information to a Web server and a CGI compliant *script* (a program or other script parser) receives the information, decodes it and then (optionally) sends back some further information, e.g. the results of a database search. CGI development is somewhat limited in that the developer must author both sides of the equation. The vast majority of CGI-driven applications are built around HTML forms, since these offer the only facilities for user input.

In the main, CGI solutions are useful where simple send-and-receive (essentially *half-duplex*) responses are required, for example: *I'll send you my name and email address; you receive the information, store it and send me back a confirmation*. Anything beyond this level of interaction requires a system with Java's capabilities. Take the game of chess for example, which has already been successfully implemented using a CGI-based solution whereby the user can play against the computer via the Internet. Every time a new move by either player is made a response must be sent across the network in order to update the chessboard and then inform both players. In contrast, Java could implement the entire game as a single applet and transport this directly to the client. This in turn would eliminate the need to send data across the Internet, thus eliminating problems such as the dreaded *'waiting for a new page to load'* syndrome. All of the drawing functions could also be handled locally, since Java has a dedicated graphics library. In essence the Java applet merely houses the rules of the game and the graphical functionality that allows both players to compete.

Another significant limitation of CGI is that the Web server must be running a script that is itself *platform-dependent*, that is to say that the script requires a specific operating system (such as DOS or UNIX) in order to function. A CGI developer's nightmare has frequently been to have developed a script under one operating system (such as MS-DOS) that does everything the developer wants, flawlessly, and yet it can't be 'ported' to a UNIX-based Web server simply because the script doesn't operate in that particular environment. Java applets are platform-independent, so after you have written an applet and then compiled it into a neutral format it can be uploaded to a Web server *anywhere* on the Internet and then accessed by *anyone* who is running a 'Java-aware' browser.

In comes as a surprise to many that Java does not even need HTTP (HyperText Transfer Protocol) in order to function; Java applets can *piggyback* on just about any Internet protocol. Nevertheless, HTTP is still the chosen transport mechanism, since it is a *low-overhead* protocol. It also forms the foundation of the World-Wide Web itself, of course, and in any event the introduction of yet another new protocol might only confuse matters further.

The popularity of CGI cannot be overlooked, however. While CGI is an established *de facto* standard, its features pale in comparison with Java's. Java's superior code portability and programming facilities speak for themselves. Java programs can be embedded within Web pages and through a library of dedicated windowing functions can provide real-time graphical user interfaces, animation and audio. There are even dedicated libraries for interfacing with existing Internet entities (e.g. USENET News and FTP servers).

The only other standard for interactive content at the time of writing is VRML (Virtual Reality Modelling Language). VRML has a tendency to detach the user from the hypertext document. Java *is* content, since applets run embedded within a hypertext page. Another tool to view the applet is therefore not required.

TIP

Java and CGI are currently the only methods used for implementing 'interactive content' on the World-Wide Web. CGI is dominant, although Java is predicted to reach and surpass CGI as the main way of achieving *executable content*. CGI requires the author to develop server applications within a particular environment; Java is 100 per cent portable. Ironically, some Java applets actually link into CGI scripts on other servers to exchange information, so don't rule out CGI (just) yet.

CGI-based systems use a `<form>` tag within an HTML document to facilitate the entry of some information (e.g. for a database search). HTML allows the fields within a form to be assigned unique names and for that form to be assigned a server script that will process the information in the form. CGI scripts are implemented in a wide range of computer languages, such as C, Icon, BASIC and Perl, as well as 'real' scripting languages, such as the UNIX shell scripts `csh` and `sh`.

The socket solution

Sockets are the building blocks of the Internet. Every TCP/IP-based application uses sockets in order to communicate with other computers on the Internet. The *WinSock* (Windows Sockets) standard is based upon the use of sockets as a communications mechanism. Sockets are themselves described as an IPC (interprocess communications) mechanism, since they allow processes (programs in this case) to communicate with each other over the Internet. Programming languages such as C have dedicated socket libraries that allow 'Internet-aware' applications to be built from scratch.

TIP

Whether or not CGI is killed off by Java remains to be seen. Netscape was reported to have said that CGI will be 'replaced' using technologies such as JavaScript and Java. Nevertheless, CGI is a dominant force, a *de facto* standard which is popular because of the ability to create solutions using a variety of programming and *scripting* languages. Java can quite easily read the data generated by a CGI-script using a data-transport mechanism known as a *stream* (to be discussed below).

Sockets are not considered in this chapter since work is still under way within Netscape 2.0 to allow them to function properly and securely. Streams form the basis of this chapter.

Manipulating files using streams

One of the commonest questions that arises is how to manipulate files in Java. It turns out that streams have an important part to play in such matters, since Java does not have any methods that specifically open and close *files*. The concept of reading and writing data to a file in Java is slightly different: you have to envisage *pushing* and *pulling* data from a 'stream' connected to that file. Java provides a number of stream mechanisms for handling most data types; for example, a `FileInputStream` is required to read and write data to and from a file on disk.

TIP

The source code for Java's stream classes is to be found in the `\JAVA\IO` subdirectory (the *input/output* class directory) after decompressing the

SRC.ZIP file that arrives with the JDK. Use the FileInputStream and FileOutputStream classes to handle direct file manipulation.

Consider the simple Java application below, for example, which reads a single character from a file passed to the program through the command line using the value of args[0]:

TIP

Quick recap: Applications are passed command line parameters using the string array args[ ]. The value of args[0] is the first argument, in this case a filename that we want to establish a stream to in order to read data from.

```
import java.io.*;
class ReadFileChar {
  public static void main(String args[]) {
    try {
      FileInputStream f = new FileInputStream(args[0]);
    } catch (FileNotFoundException e) {
      System.println("File not found.");
      System.exit(0);
    }
    int c;
    try {
      c = f.read();
    } catch (Exception e) {}
    System.out.println( (char) c);
    try {
      f.close();
    } catch (Exception e) {}
  }
}
```

In order to run this program, create an ASCII file which can be passed as an argument and then run the application using the Java interpreter JAVA.EXE. Alternatively, pass the name of any existing ASCII file to the program. For example:

```
java ReadFileChar c:\autoexec.bat
```

would read the first character from the file `autoexec.bat`, which resides in the root directory of drive C.

TIP
Once you have initiated a stream, the `read()` method can be used to *pull* data from the stream. To close the stream use `close()`. Streams, like file connections, should be closed when you are finished with them in order to avoid possible file corruption.

The `try` and `catch` statements have been mentioned already. Be aware that many *input/output* (I/O) activities (such as initiating, opening and closing streams) all raise exceptions. For example, the creation of a new `FileInputStream` causes a `FileNotFoundException` to be generated in the case that the file mentioned was not found. Catching and dealing with these exceptions does prove to be a bit tiresome, although a necessity if you wish to build robust Java programs. The generic exception-class `Exception` can also be used if you are not too fussy about dealing with specific program exceptions. Remember to process all exceptions, otherwise Java will produce a fatal compile-time error (this is new in JDK 1.0 beta 2; warnings used to be issued).

TIP
The `FileInputStream`'s `read()` method throws an `IOException` error when an error retrieving data over the stream is encountered.

Admittedly, reading a single character from a file is a pretty worthless exercise, although it demonstrates the point that `read()` only retrieves *single* characters from a stream. Note also that the `read()` method requires an integer argument, that is to say that it treats characters as integer values based on their unique ASCII code (A being **65** and X being **88** etc.). In order to actually see the character retrieved, rather than its ASCII value, we must coerce the output to a character – which is what the `println()` method does in the example. Try out the program, and feed it some non-existent filenames to see the exception handler jump into action.

The next application reads the contents of a complete file from disk. The program is similar to the previous one in that it uses `args[0]` as a filename. All that is different here is the method used to read data from the input stream:

```
import java.io.*;
class ReadAFile {
  public static void main(String args[]) {
    InputStream myStream = null;
    int aChar;
    try {
      myStream = new FileInputStream(args[0]);
    } catch (FileNotFoundException e) {
      System.out.println(args[0]+": file not found.");
      System.exit(0);
    }
    try {
      while ((aChar = myStream.read()) != -1) {
        System.out.print( (char) aChar);
      }
    } catch (IOException e) {
      System.out.println("I/O Read Error!");
      System.exit(0);
    }
    try {
      myStream.close();
    } catch (Exception e) {}
  }
}
```

Again, to run this application, use a command line of the form:

```
java ReadAFile filename
```

where `filename` is the file to display in this case, and `ReadAFile` is the name of the Java application (taken from our example). The salient part of this application is the `while()` loop:

```
while ((aChar = myStream.read()) != -1) {
  System.out.print( (char) aChar);
}
```

which continuously reads characters from the stream. When no more data can arrive from the stream, i.e. we have reached the 'end-of-file' (to use that now *antiquated* phrase) the value of −1 is returned by `read()` and can be used in the `while()` loop's main looping condition accordingly.

TIP

Be sure to watch your bracketing within the `while()` statement. Remember that the condition within `while()` must evaluate to `true` in order to keep running. If you were to use the unbracketed expression:

```
(aChar = myStream.read() != -1)
```

an *error* would be returned by the compiler, since it is not apparent what we are checking the value of −1 against: is it `aChar` or the `read()` statement itself? In the above expression, Java would assume that you were trying to keep the loop running using a condition that uses an integer expression, when what is required is an expression that evaluates to `true` or `false`, i.e. a *boolean* expression. By bracketing off the expression as:

```
((aChar = myStream.read()) != -1)
```

we can see that we are testing −1 against the single value returned by `read()` itself, which in this case is an integer. So if the character currently being read was the letter 'A', the value of `aChar` would be 65. The expression `65 != -1` evaluates to `false`, and is therefore valid. The bracketing really serves two purposes, since we also assign the value read by `read()` into the variable `aChar`, which is used later within the loop to print the actual character read into the stream.

TIP

Another method called `readLine()` also exists, and is used to return a complete line of text from a file. In order to use this method you must define a `DataInputStream`, as described below.

Finally on the topic of reading data from files, consider the `showfile` application shown below. This program uses a `DataInputStream` to read and display the contents of a file. Data input streams are used to read *primitive* data types, such as characters and integers. When you use a `DataInputStream` you also get access to the `readLine()` method, which can be used to retrieve a complete line of text from a file:

```
import java.io.*;
class showfile {
  public static void main (String args[]) {
    String thisLine;
```

```
       if (args.length > 0) {
         FileInputStream fis = new FileInputStream(args[0]);
         DataInputStream fileInput = new
           DataInputStream(fis);
         while ((thisLine = fileInput.readLine()) != null) {
           System.out.println(thisLine);
         }
       }
       else {
         System.out.println("Syntax: showfile <filename>");
         System.exit(0);
       }
     }
   }
```

As with previous programs, this application processes the first command line argument passed to it (`args[0]`). It is necessary to create a `FileInputStream` first when reading data from disk, so this is done with the statement:

```
FileInputStream fis = new FileInputStream(args[0]);
```

which opens an input stream called `fis` to the file we specified on the command line. Next we create a `DataInputStream` and pass the `fis` variable as an argument in order to change the stream type.

TIP
Modifying the stream type may seem slightly clumsy, but it is necessary since there is no `DataInputStream()` constructor that accepts a filename argument. `DataInputStream()` only accepts a *stream* (of type `InputStream`) as an argument, hence the need to pass it the name of a existing `FileInputStream` that points to the file that we want to read from disk.

We can then read data from the file, using the loop statement:

```
while ((thisLine = fileInput.readLine()) != null) {
  System.out.println(thisLine)
}
```

The `readLine()` method reads a line of text from an input stream until there is no data left to read, in which case a `null` value is returned – which is why the `while` loop in the example only executes while the value of the `thisLine` variable is not null.

TIP

Why are there so many stream-types in Java? If you look in the `\JAVA\IO` subdirectory after decompressing the `SRC.ZIP` file you will see that there are a myriad of different input and output streams, each of which serves a specific purpose. Some streams track line numbers; some work with files; others may even work with different stream types altogether. The type of stream that you use will ultimately depend on the program you are developing. Take a few moments to examine each stream class to see its exact behaviour (a description can be found near the top of each such file). Unfortunately, a complete examination of every stream mechanism in Java is beyond the scope of this chapter.

Writing data to a file using a stream

So far we have examined applets that read data from a stream. What about writing data to a stream? Well, for this Java provides the stream facility called `FileOutputStream`, and this works in exactly the opposite way to `FileInputStream`. As you would expect, a method is also provided to allow data to be written to the stream. That method is `write()`. Consider the Java application below, which is a modified version of our previous example. Our application, `ReadAndWrite`, reads one file from disk and then writes it to another file. Effectively, this application is analogous to the DOS `COPY` command:

```java
import java.io.*;
class ReadAndWrite {
  public static void main(String args[]) {
    InputStream  inStream = null;
    OutputStream outStream = null;
    int aChar;
    try {
      inStream = new FileInputStream(args[0]);
      outStream = new FileOutputStream("results.txt");
    } catch (FileNotFoundException e) {
      System.out.println(args[0]+": file not found.");
```

```
      System.exit(0);
    }
    try {
      while ((aChar = inStream.read()) != -1) {
        outStream.write(aChar);
      }
    } catch (Exception e) {
      System.out.println("Read Error.");
      System.exit(0);
    }
    try {
      inStream.close();
      outStream.close();
    } catch (Exception e) {}
  }
}
```

The two streams in this example are called `inStream` and `outStream`, the first a `FileInputStream` and the second a `FileOutputStream` respectively. The output file is hard-coded in this case, and has been named `results.txt`, although this can be changed to an alternative name (or even integrated into a command line parameter such as `args[1]`). The looping structure in this application now uses the `write()` method, effectively writing out every character as soon as it has been read in, for example:

```
while ((aChar = inStream.read()) != -1) {
  outStream.write(aChar);
}
```

After compiling the application with `JAVAC.EXE` and running it with the hypothetical command line:

```
javac ReadAndWrite myfile.txt
```

we would end up with a new file, `results.txt`, which is an exact copy of `myfile.txt`.

TIP
Be aware that in our example the data written to the output stream will overwrite any existing data that is held within the file being referenced.

Viewing a URL using an input stream

There are a number of ways to receive information from a Web server using Java. In our solution we are going to use a number of Java packages that implement a communication mechanism known as a *stream*. A stream is essentially a flow of information back and forth between two processes – in our case the applet (the *client* process), and a Web server (the *server* process). Our applet can be used to view hypertext files, or to see the results returned from a CGI-based program running on a Web server.

TIP

As well as capturing the output of a CGI program, the example program can in fact be used to capture *any* hypertext page from the Internet – since we are capturing the *stream* of data returned from the URL that we specify. It doesn't really matter if the data originates from a CGI script, or is a verbatim copy of a file on that Web server – the results will still look the same. This type of program is known as a *content handler*.

Consider the Java application below, `PageGrabber`, which will show the text contents of any Web-based resource on the Internet, such as a hypertext page, and store this in a text area field for the user to view conveniently on the screen:

```
import java.applet.*;
import java.awt.*;
import java.io.*;
import java.net.*;
import java.lang.*;

class PageGrabber {
  static StringBuffer MyBuf;
  static URLConnection urlConn;
  static String UrlData;
  static URL myData = null;

  public static void main(String args[]) {
    String MyUrl = "";
    if (args.length > 0)
      MyUrl = args[0];
    else {
      System.out.println("Please supply a URL to see.");
```

```
      System.exit(0);
    }

    MyBuf = new StringBuffer(MyUrl);

    try {
      myData = new URL(MyBuf.toString());
    } catch (MalformedURLException ml) {
      System.out.println("Error: URL " +
        "syntax incorrect.");
      System.exit(0);
    }

    try {
      urlConn = myData.openConnection();
    } catch (IOException e) {
      System.out.println("Error opening a " +
        " URL connection.");
      System.exit(0);
    }

    int c = 0;
    InputStream is1 = null;
    StringBuffer sBuf = new StringBuffer();

    try {
      is1 = myData.openStream();
      while ((c = is1.read()) != -1) {
        sBuf.append((char)c);
      }
      is1.close();
    } catch(IOException e) {
      System.out.println("Error reading URL data.");
    }

    UrlData = sBuf.toString();
    new MyFrame("");
  }
}

class MyFrame extends Frame {
  Panel myPanel = new Panel();
```

```
TextArea  ta1 = new TextArea("", 15, 85);
MyFrame(String title) {
  super("URL Results");
  add("Center", myPanel);
  myPanel.add(ta1);
  ta1.setText(PageGrabber.UrlData);
  resize(500,300);
  show();
}
}
```

The program starts by defining a class, **PageGrabber**, to hold the body of our application. A number of variables are then defined:

```
class PageGrabber {
  static StringBuffer MyBuf;
  static URLConnection urlConn;
  static String myData;
  static URL myData = null;
  ...
}
```

including **myData**, a text string to hold the data returned by the Web Server, and **MyBuf** which is a string buffer of the **StringBuffer** type. String buffers are similar to text strings except that they can grow in size. We can append each character we receive from the server into this variable using a **StringBuffer** method called **append()**. The other variables defined at this point in the program are **urlConn** and **myData**, the former being derived from the **java.net.URLConnection** class, which allows an object to represent an active connection to a given URL, such as the URL for a hypertext page or CGI script. We can monitor the status of the connection to the URL using this variable. Then we have the **myData** variable, which is derived from the Java class **java.net.URL**. This will be used to open and maintain a data stream to the URL that specifies the location of the file that we wish to retrieve from the remote Web server.

Next we have the first method declaration. This program is implemented as an application, since we have defined a **main()** function. The other tell-tale sign is that we have not **extended** this applet from the **Applet** class.

TIP
You can make this application into an applet simply by changing the **main()** method to a method such as **init()** or **start()**, and then extending the applet accordingly (using the **extends** statement). You can

then create an HTML file with an `<applet>` tag in order to invoke the program.

Since our program is invoked from the command line (and not via the AppletViewer and an HTML file) we can allow command line arguments to be passed directly to it. This is done by mentioning them on the command line. Applets are run by loading them via an HTML file; applications are run from a DOS shell or by using the *Run* option after pressing the Windows 95 *Start* button, with the `JAVA.EXE` interpreter; for example, the command:

```
JAVA PageGrabber http://www.gold.net/users/ag17/index.htm
```

invokes `PageGrabber` with the URL `http://www.gold.net/users/ag17/index.htm`, placing the text of the file `index.htm` on the screen. Similarly, you could capture the output of a CGI script using the program. Try specifying the URL:

```
http://www2.infoseek.com:8001/IS/Titles?qt=%5Bessential+
    internet%5D
```

which uses the popular *Infoseek* search engine to conduct a search for the words `essential` and `internet` (the `%5B` and `%5D` are hexadecimal codes that represent the `[` and `]` brackets, which are used in Infoseek to search for keywords within the *same section* of text). Infoseek has a CGI script which handles search requests using the host `www2.infoseek.com`, which answers on port `8001`. You will not be able to ascertain the exact format of the search-phrase URL, so it is best to conduct a query and then note the *Location:* field in Netscape to see the exact URL returned. You can then use this for future searches – without having to use the normal form-driven interface, of course.

TIP
All non-alphabetic characters are specified using their hexadecimal representation within a given URL (for example a space has the ASCII value of `32`, which is `%20` in hexadecimal). The per cent sign (`%`) specifies that the following number is coded in the hexadecimal system.

TIP
When an application is defined using the `main()` method, the argument `args[]` represents an array of command line arguments (text strings) that are passed to the program (from a DOS shell prompt). The variable

length can be used with the array **args** to see how many arguments
have been entered on the command line (see below).

For example, in the program we have:

```
public static void main(String args[]) {
  if (args.length > 0)
    MyUrl = args[0];
  else {
    System.out.println("Please supply a URL to see.");
    System.exit(0);
  }
  ...
```

which defines the **main( )** method as accepting a string of arrays as arguments. The
variable **MyUrl** stores the URL of the CGI script that we going to invoke, and is
altered according to the first argument that is passed to the program. We shall only
deal with the first argument in this case, so the value of **MyUrl** is set to **args[0]** –
the first argument. If an argument is not supplied an error message is shown and the
program terminates at this point.

Next we create a string buffer variable to hold the data captured from the stream
we are about to create. This is done with the statement:

```
MyBuf = new StringBuffer(MyUrl);
```

Now we arrive at a series of **try** statements that perform all of the network
functionality in the program. It is important to remember that some Java methods
throw *exceptions*, which are basically errors that can occur during the execution of a
task. For example, the **URL( )** method is used to specify the URL of a resource
located on the Internet. If you look at the source code for **URL( )** in
java.net.URL.java (in the **\JAVA\NET** subdirectory after decompressing the
SRC.ZIP file) you will see that there is a syntax for the **URL( )** method defined as:

```
public URL(String spec) throws MalformedURLException {
  this(null, spec);
}
```

and that it takes a string representing a URL and may throw a
MalformedURLException. This exception is thrown when the URL is itself
malformed, i.e. when its syntax is incorrect. For example you might mistype
http:// as **htto://**. In such a case, the **catch** statement specifies the code-block

that will be executed when the exception occurs. In the program we simply output an error message and terminate the application at that point:

```
try {
    myData = new URL(MyBuf.toString());
} catch (MalformedURLException ml) {
    System.out.println("Error: URL syntax incorrect.");
    System.exit(0);
}
```

A connection to the URL is opened with the `openConnection()` method, which is appended to the `myData` object that was created previously with `URL()` in order to open and reference the URL we want to connect to. In the program we have the following:

```
try {
    urlConn = myData.openConnection();
} catch (IOException e) {
    System.out.println("Error opening a URL connection.");
    System.exit(0);
}
```

which is another exception handler, this time for the `openConnection()` statement to establish a stream to the URL previously opened. The `openConnection()` method will throw an `IOException` (input/output exception) when a stream cannot be established. Nothing is guaranteed on the Internet; servers go off-line and break down without prior warning, so catching this exception is a definite requirement (it is also needed because exceptions that are not caught will generate a compile-time error from `JAVAC.EXE`).

In order to read data from the stream that we have established we have to create a variable in which to store the incoming data. This is done using a string buffer variable (`sBuf`). The stream on which data arrives is termed the *input stream*, and a variable is declared of this type (`is1`) and set to null, i.e. empty to begin with. Data is read from the stream a character at a time using the `read()` method. When the stream is read, data arrives in numeric format as a series of integers that represent each ASCII letter or symbol. In order to write out the character representation (rather than the numeric representation) we use `(char)` to ensure that all of the data written into the string buffer are characters. `append()` is a `StringBuffer` method that expands the string buffer by one character. We read characters using a `while` loop. The value of −1 is returned when the stream is finished, and this is used to terminate the loop (you can also use the condition '> 0', rather than '!= −1', which detects whether data is *still* being returned). The code from the program that does this is:

```
int c = 0;
InputStream is1 = null;
StringBuffer sBuf = new StringBuffer();
try {
  is1 = myData.openStream();
  while ((c = is1.read()) != -1) {
    sBuf.append((char)c);
  }
  is1.close();
} catch(IOException e) {
  System.out.println("Error reading URL data.");
}
```

Notice how `openStream()` opens the input stream prior to reading from it. After the stream has been read, `close()` is used to close it (streams, and indeed *sockets,* are rather like *files* in that they are opened for reading and are closed when no longer required). We encapsulate the stream functions in an exception handler and use the generic class `Exception` to trap any errors at this stage. This saves declaring exception handlers for both `openStream()` and `read()`. The program then converts the input buffer into a string and calls the class `cgiFrame`. We convert the data to a string so that it can be read into a text area (explained below). The class `cgiFrame` inherits its behaviour from the `Frame` class, i.e. it appears as a separate window. Finally, we have a class that creates a window and draws the results received into a text area. The text area is drawn within a centred panel within the frame, and the `setText()` method places the text retrieved from the server we have contacted into the text area, where it can be conveniently viewed:

```
class MyFrame extends Frame {
  Panel myPanel = new Panel();
  TextArea  ta1 = new TextArea("", 15, 85);
  MyFrame(String title) {
    super("URL Results");
    add("Center", myPanel);
    myPanel.add(ta1);
    ta1.setText(PageGrabber.UrlData);
    resize(500,300);
    show();
  }
}
```

Figure 10.1 illustrates the `PageGrabber` program used with the URL `http://www2.infoseek.com:8001/IS/Titles?qt=%5Bjason+manger%5D`. Try some other URLs to see what you can retrieve.

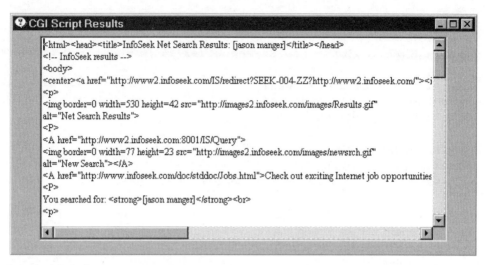

FIGURE 10.1 *The* `PageGrabber` *program in action with a CGI script.*

TIP
Remember that the text retrieved by the `PageGrabber` program will
probably be HTML-formatted (i.e. full of HTML tags) unless the server
returns an unformatted 'plain text' file. Experiment with the program to see
which files you can receive. Any valid URL that retrieves a text file can be
used. Try entering some *malformed* (i.e. invalid URLs) also, in order to see
the results.

Viewing an image using an input stream

By modifying the previous applet, we could also view images. Consider the applet
below, which works pretty much the same as the other examples, except that it uses a
`FileOutputStream` to write the data collected via the input stream to a file. This
file is then opened using `GetImage()` and is then drawn into a frame using Awt's
`drawImage()` method. The image that is viewed can be stored in the JPEG or GIF
formats. The name of the image has been hard-coded into the applet, although it
could arrive from another source (such as via a `<param>` tag using
`getParameter()`). Remember that this program is an applet, and can be viewed

either through the AppletViewer or via Netscape 2.0. The image URL shown can be used if you need to test the applet, although any valid URL can be used:

```java
import java.applet.*;
import java.awt.*;
import java.io.*;
import java.net.*;
import java.lang.*;

public class ShowAnImage extends java.applet.Applet {
  static StringBuffer MyBuf;
  static URLConnection urlConn;
  static URL myData = null;
  static Image img;

  public void start() {
    //
    // This is the URL of the image we want to load:
    //
    String MyUrl="http://www.gold.net/users/ag17/" +
                    "netnav2.gif";
    MyBuf = new StringBuffer(MyUrl);

    showStatus("Checking URL...");
    try {
      myData = new URL(MyBuf.toString());
    } catch (MalformedURLException m1) {
      showStatus("Error: URL syntax incorrect.");
      System.exit(0);
    }

    showStatus("URL OK. Opening URL Connection...");
    try {
      urlConn = myData.openConnection();
    } catch (IOException e) {
      showStatus("Error opening a URL connection.");
      System.exit(0);
    }

    int bytesRec = 0;
    int c = 0;
    InputStream  is1 = null;
```

```java
    OutputStream is2 = null;

    showStatus("Establishing Stream to URL...");
    try {
      is2 = new FileOutputStream("_tmp.gif");
    } catch (IOException e) {
      showStatus("Error opening stream. Exiting...");
      System.exit(0);
    }

    showStatus("Stream to URL opened OK.");
    try {
      is1 = myData.openStream();
        while ((c = is1.read()) != -1) {
          is2.write( (char) c);
          bytesRec++;
          showStatus("Bytes received: "+bytesRec);
        }
      is1.close();
      is2.close();
    } catch(IOException e) {
      showStatus("Error reading URL data.");
      System.exit(0);
    }

    showStatus("File received. Loading image...");
    img = getImage(getDocumentBase(), "_tmp.gif");
    new ImageFrame("");
  }
}

class ImageFrame extends Frame {
  ImageFrame(String title) {
    super("Viewing image");
    resize(500,300);
    show();
  }

  public void paint(Graphics g) {
    g.drawImage(ShowAnImage.img, 0, 0, this);
  }
}
```

TIP
This applet views an image, not a plain text file (such as an HTML file). If you give the name of a file other than an image, the program will try to load it as an image, causing an exception (i.e. a run-time error) to occur – mainly because `getImage()` and `drawImage()` only work with image file formats. To overcome this problem you could check the *type* of the file retrieved and then view each file accordingly.

In fact, the `ShowAnImage` applet is extremely long-winded, and could have been implemented in about a third of the code. This is because the `getImage()` method also accepts a URL argument. Rather than opening streams to URLs and then capturing the output of a stream, we can specify the location of the image URL within `getImage()` and then load this without writing any data to disk. Consider the `ShowImageURL` applet below, for example:

```
import java.applet.*;
import java.awt.*;
import java.io.*;
import java.net.*;
import java.lang.*;

public class ShowImageURL extends java.applet.Applet {
  static Image img;
  public void start() {
    try {
      img = getImage(new URL(getParameter("RESOURCE")));
    } catch (MalformedURLException e) {
      System.print.out("There is a URL Syntax error.");
      System.exit(0);
    }
    new ImageFrame("Image");
  }
}

class ImageFrame extends Frame {
  ImageFrame(String title) {
    super(title);
    resize(500,300);
    show();
  }
```

```
public void paint(Graphics g) {
  g.drawImage(ShowImageURL.img, 0, 0, this);
}
}
```

As you can see, this code is vastly simplified, although it has probably been beneficial to show how both methods function. In the `ShowImageURL` applet the `getImage()` function resembles:

```
img = getImage(new URL(getParameter("RESOURCE")));
```

where `img` is the name of our image. The `URL()` method actually handles all of the stream mechanisms for us in this instance. The name of the URL that we wish to view is stored in a `<param>` tag within the HTML file that calls this applet, and could be structured as:

```
<applet code=ShowImageURL.class codebase=classes
  width=300 height=100>
<param name=RESOURCE
  value=http://www.gold.net/users/ag17/netnav.gif>
</applet>
```

Of course, this new applet does not store the file on disk. Instead it uses the `URL()` method to open the file (using an `InputStream`) and then reads the data into the `img` variable, whereupon it is viewed on screen immediately using `showImage()`.

TIP

The `URL()` method opens a connection to a resource using an `InputStream` stream. The stream is opened automatically by the `URL()` method. Passing `URL()` to `getImage()` saves you from coding what has already been done for you in the `URL` class.

Viewing multiple formats

The `PageGrabber` and `ShowAnImage` programs are designed to view a certain *type*, i.e. format, of file: ASCII files in the former case and image files in the latter. To allow our programs to deal with a variety of formats we could implement a simple checking scheme whereby we examine the file to see what format it is stored in. This is possible because most image files are allocated a header which has a keyword describing their contents. For example, GIF images have the string GIF87 or GIF89 as the first five characters. Consider the Java application below, which determines the internal format of a GIF image:

```java
import java.io.*;
class FileTest {
  public static void main(String args[]) {
    char hdr[] = new char[5];
    try {
      InputStream f = new FileInputStream(args[0]);
    } catch (Exception e) {
      System.out.println("Stream error.");
      System.exit(0);
    }
    int c;
    int b = 0;
    try {
      while ((b < 5) && (c = f.read()) != -1) {
        hdr[b] = (char)c;
        b++;
      }
    } catch (IOException e) {
      System.out.println("I/O error.");
      System.exit(0);
    }
    f.close();
    String theHeader = new String(hdr);
    if (theHeader.equals("GIF87"))
      System.out.println(args[0]+": GIF 87 format.");
    else
    if (theHeader.equals("GIF89"))
      System.out.println(args[0]+": GIF 89 format.");
    else
      System.out.println(args[0]+": Not a GIF file.");
  }
}
```

In order to run this program we pass the name of a file to it as the first argument. Here is a typical command line and program output for a GIF87-formatted file:

```
java FileTest myfile.gif
myfile.gif: GIF 87 format.
```

If we pass the application a file it doesn't recognize, such as a `.class` file, we see the default output:

```
java FileTest FileTest.class
FileTest.class: Not a GIF file.
```

Notice how the input stream is set up and how the first five bytes are read into a character array (called `hdr[ ]`). After five characters are read in the `while` loop terminates and the input stream is closed. A series of `if..else` statements then check to see whether the codes `GIF87` or `GIF89` have been found, and the result is shown to the user on the standard output using a suitable message with `System.out.println()`.

TIP
In order to convert a character array into a string simply use the `String()` constructor with the name of the character array as an argument, for example:

```
char hdr[] = new char[5];
...
String theHeader = new String(hdr);
```

A much easier way of ascertaining the *type* of file is to examine the filename extension. For example, if you load the URL `http://www.gold.net/users/ag17/index.htm` it is immediately apparent that you are requesting an HTML file (from the `.htm` extension). The Java application below, `CheckFile`, uses the `subString()` method to extract the last four characters of a URL to see what file type is being referenced (`subString()` is one of Java's string-handling functions):

```
class CheckFile {
  public static void main(String args[]) {
    try {
      ImageOrText(args[0]);
    } catch (FileNotFoundException e {
      System.out.println("File not found:"+args[0]);
      System.exit(0);
    }
```

```
    }

    // Get the last four characters:
    static public void ImageOrText(String aUrl) {
      String Ext = aUrl.substring((aUrl.length())-4,
        aUrl.length()).toLowerCase();
      if (Ext.equals("html"))
        System.out.println("HTML file.");
      else
      if (Ext.equals(".gif"))
        System.out.println("GIF file.");
      else
        System.out.println("File type not known.");
    }
  }
```

CheckFile is passed the name of a URL in args[0], the first command line argument. It then invokes the ImageOrText() method with this URL (which is stored as a string) which stores the last four characters of the URL into the string variable Ext. This is subsequently checked and a message is output according to the type of file that has been found – based on the filename extension. This approach has the drawback that a file could be renamed as something else (although this is very unlikely of course) – a problem the previous applet did not suffer from since it examined data actually stored *inside* the file.

This code could be integrated into our earlier ShowAnImage applet in order that we could view both images and text from within a single applet. Consider the applet below, TextImgView, which does just this. This applet examines the URL passed to it via a <param> tag and, depending on the extension, loads an image or a text file. In the case of an image the getImage() and loadImage() methods are used, and the image is displayed within a frame for the user to see. If a text file is loaded (we assume it has an .html extension) the file is read into a string buffer and then placed into a text area field for the user to read instead. This code implementation could be reduced by passing a URL() directly to getImage(), rather than opening all of the necessary streams, as illustrated earlier in the ShowImageURL applet:

```
import java.applet.*;
import java.awt.*;
import java.io.*;
import java.net.*;
import java.lang.*;

final public class TextImgView extends java.applet.Applet
```

```
{
static StringBuffer MyBuf;
static URLConnection urlConn;
static URL myData = null;
static String TextData;
static Image img;

public void start() {
  String MyUrl = getParameter("RESOURCE");
  String Ext   = MyUrl.substring((MyUrl.length())-4,
    MyUrl.length()).toLowerCase();
  System.out.println("Extension of URL " + MyUrl +
    " was ["+Ext+"]");
  MyBuf = new StringBuffer(MyUrl);
  showStatus("Checking URL...");
  try {
    myData = new URL(MyBuf.toString());
  } catch (MalformedURLException ml) {
    showStatus("Error: URL syntax incorrect.");
    System.exit(0);
  }

  showStatus("URL OK. Opening URL Connection...");
  try {
    urlConn = myData.openConnection();
  } catch (IOException e) {
    showStatus("Error opening a URL connection.");
    System.exit(0);
  }
  int c          = 0;
  InputStream  is1 = null;
  OutputStream is2 = null;
  StringBuffer sBuf = new StringBuffer();

  showStatus("Establishing Stream to URL...");
  try {
    is2 = new FileOutputStream("_tmp.gif");
  } catch (IOException e) {
    showStatus("Error opening stream. Exiting...");
    System.exit(0);
  }
```

```java
      showStatus("Stream to URL opened OK.");
      try {
        is1 = myData.openStream();
          if (Ext.equals(".gif")) {
            while ((c = is1.read()) != -1) {
              is2.write( (char) c);
            }
          }
          else
          if (Ext.equals("html")) {
            while ((c = is1.read()) != -1) {
              sBuf.append((char)c);
            }
          }
          is1.close();
          is2.close();
      } catch(IOException e) {
          showStatus("Error reading URL data.");
          System.exit(0);
      }

      showStatus("File received. Loading...");
      if (Ext.equals(".gif")) {
        img = getImage(getDocumentBase(), "_tmp.gif");
        new ImageFrame("Image");
      }
      else
      if (Ext.equals("html")) {
        TextData = sBuf.toString();
        new TextFrame("Text");
      }
      else {
        System.out.println("File format not recognized.");
        System.exit(0);
      }
    }
}

class ImageFrame extends Frame {
  ImageFrame(String title) {
    super(title);
    resize(500,300);
```

```
      show();
    }
    public void paint(Graphics g) {
      g.drawImage(TextImgView.img, 0, 0, this);
    }
  }

class TextFrame extends Frame {
  Panel aPanel = new Panel();
  TextArea ta1 = new TextArea("", 15, 85);
  TextFrame(String title) {
    super(title);
    add("Center", aPanel);
    aPanel.add(ta1);
    ta1.setText(TextImgView.TextData);
    resize(500,300);
    show();
  }
}
```

TIP

The **TextImgView** applet uses the last four characters of a URL to ascertain the *type* of file being accessed. Since extensions can run to four characters on UNIX-based computers the extension **html** has been used for HTML-formatted files, whereas **.gif** has been used for GIF image files (these are still given a three-letter extension simply because GIF is the full acronym in this case). You can alter the program to detect other file type extensions. The applet will also show JPEG-formatted images (Java can now handle these in the JDK pre-beta 1 version), as well as ASCII files with extensions other than **.html**, e.g. **.txt** or **.asc**.

The salient points of this program are the *two* **while** loops, each of which handles a different file format. Text files are loaded into a string buffer, while image files are written to a temporary file (**_tmp.gif** in this case). In the case of the latter it is easier to write the file to disk since **loadImage()** can then be used with a local filename. The two classes **ImageFrame** and **TextFrame** simply create a window and display the files accordingly. Liberal use of the **showStatus()** method has been made to illustrate how system messages can be sent to the applet's environment, i.e. to the AppletViewer.

TIP

If you need to change the URL loaded, modify the `<param>` tag that launches the applet. Here is a simple HTML file that could be used to run the `TextImgView` applet:

```
<html>
<body>
<applet code=TextImgView.class codebase=classes>
<param name=RESOURCE
  value=http://www.gold.net/users/ag17/side2.gif>
</body>
</html>
```

Loading URLs using `showDocument()`

You can make Java automatically load a URL of your choice into the Netscape browser. This is done using the `URL()` and `showDocument()` methods. Allowing the current URL to be changed is useful since it can be controlled independently by the applet, rather than by the user. For example, an applet could load random URLs, or it could call URLs in a pre-specified order.

TIP

The *applet context* is an interface that corresponds to the applet's display environment. The display environment in this context is either the AppletViewer tool or the Netscape browser. In order to gain access to the Netscape browser, the `getAppletContext()` method must be used.

Consider the `UrlLoader` applet, shown below. This Java program loads a URL into the Netscape browser (or alternatively the AppletViewer) using the `showDocument()` method. In order to connect to a given URL the `URL()` method must first be called along with a string that represents the URL you want to contact – in this case my own home page, although any valid URL can of course be used:

```
import java.applet.*;
```

```
import java.net.URL;
public class UrlLoader extends java.applet.Applet {
  public void init() {
     // This is the URL to be loaded:

LoadThisUrl("http://www.gold.net/users/ag17/index.htm");
     }
     public void LoadThisUrl(String aUrl) {
       URL loadedUrl;
       try {
         // Open a URL & stream connection...
         loadedUrl = new URL(getDocumentBase(), aUrl);
       } catch (MalformedURLException e) {
         System.out.println("Malformed URL detected.");
         System.exit(0);
       }
       // Ok, fetch the URL...
       getAppletContext().showDocument(loadedUrl);
     }
  }
```

`URL()` throws the exception `MalformedURLException` if the URL's syntax is invalid, hence the provision of the `try` and `catch` statements in the program, which simply print an error message and terminate the applet in such cases. The method that does all of the work in this applet is `LoadThisUrl()`, which accepts a single string representing the URL to be loaded and then fetches this accordingly. When the applet is loaded into Netscape it causes the browser to perform a DNS lookup on the host `www.gold.net`, after which it retrieves the file specified (`index.htm` in this case). The file is then loaded into Netscape just as if you had directly typed in the URL yourself.

TIP
Note that only the URL service type `http://` can be loaded with `showDocument()`. Local files loaded using the `file://` URL will not work. You will therefore have to be on-line in order to test your program. Remember that you should use a 32-bit Winsock with the 32-bit version of Netscape and/or AppletViewer; Windows 95 has this built into it as standard, although you must install it first as part of the Dial-Up Networking module (see `http://www.windows95.com` for more details on installing TCP/IP connections under Windows 95). The `http://` protocol can load much more than HTML files; it can also load images such as GIFs

and JPEGs, as well as any other type of binary file. Netscape will launch an appropriate *helper application* if a particular file format cannot be viewed within the browser (e.g. a `.PCX` formatted image file, which Netscape cannot handle internally in this instance).

APPENDIX

A

Questions and answers

This appendix presents a series of questions and answers on all aspects of Java, including the programming language, Java Developer's Kit, the World-Wide Web and the Netscape 2.0 Web browser.

'Where is?' questions

Q: Where can I obtain a copy of Java?
A: The Java Developer's Kit (versions 1.0b2 and 1.0) can be found on the CD-ROM that accompanies this book.

For further updates from the Internet: The Java Developer's Kit (JDK) comprises the tools for preparing applets to run as standalone applications and within the Netscape 2.0 browser. You will need the JDK in order to convert your applets into a format recognizable by the Java run-time module that is built into Netscape Navigator 2.0

Web browser. The JDK is available from the Internet at Sun's FTP site, located at `ftp.javasoft.com` in the `/pub` directory. Windows 95 users require the file named `JDK-1_0-win32-x86.exe`, which is a self-extracting archive for a 32-bit environment, including Windows NT and Windows 95. Run it from your hard disk's root directory (e.g. `C:\`), and then back up and/or delete the original `.exe` archive. There are mirror sites for the JDK, which may be faster to use if they are located geographically nearer to your computer. Remember that if you want to see applets running within a Web browser environment you will also need a copy of Netscape 2.0 (or any other 'Java-aware' Web browser that supports the beta-API).

Q: Where can I obtain the Netscape Navigator Web browser?

A: Netscape's FTP server (and mirror sites) are the main sources. Netscape's FTP server is located at the URL `ftp://ftp.netscape.com` (see the `/2.0` directory). It goes without saying that this site can get *very* busy, so you are advised to try a Netscape *mirror site* instead, such as those documented in the appendices.

Q: Where is the Java documentation to be found?

A: Good question – it doesn't arrive in the JDK archive (as mentioned above). Instead it is available from Sun's Internet FTP site located at `http://java.sun.com` in the `/pub` directory as the file named as `progGuide.html.zip`. The file is compressed with PKZIP. All documentation arrives in the HTML format. You will need to have a 32-bit version of Netscape in order to read the documentation, since all of the files have long filenames (a feature new to Windows 95) – see below also.

TIP
See Appendix B for details of other Java documentation resources.

Q: My current version of PKUNZIP will only unzip files in a 16-bit environment. All of the filenames are truncated. Where can I get some software to unzip my files properly?

A: Get hold of a 32-bit unzip utility, such as the shareware Windows 95 program *WinZip* – available from `http://www.winzip.com` (there is a link to the FTP site for the Windows 95 version of this popular software). You do not have to unzip the Java classes in the beta-API since they can be left compressed – the Java compiler can now handle compressed files (this has been done to save disk space).

Q: Where is the best source of information for Java developers?
A: There are now dozens of Java-related Web sites on the Internet, although USENET is the best place for person-to-person chats. The group `comp.lang.java` is the best Java-related group, and receives many thousands of postings. Get chatting! As for Web sites, `http://java.sun.com` has pointers to all the best sites. See the appendices for the definitive list of Java-related Web sites and other resources.

Netscape-related questions

Q: What is special about Netscape 2.0 in the context of Java?
A: Netscape Navigator 2.0 is the second Java-aware Web browser, which means that Java applets can run within the browser environment. HotJava (from Sun Microsystems) was the first 'Java-aware' Web browser to arrive on the Internet, although Netscape Navigator remains the *de facto* Web browser.

Q: How can I see what is happening as I run an applet inside of Netscape?
A: Click on *Options* and enable the *Java Console Window* option. You can then see what the applet is up to as it is loaded into Netscape. The Java Console is also the only method of obtaining output using methods such as `System.out.println()` – which is useful for debugging purposes during development (e.g. for printing values during the lifetime of a program).

Q: Do applets blend in with `<body background...>` images in Netscape?
A: Not in the beta 6 version that I have been using, unfortunately. This problem will doubtless be fixed at a later release.

Q: Images don't seem to appear in Netscape 'locally' using Java's `getImage()` and `drawImage()` methods. Why is this?
A: Try loading your applet via the Internet and it will work (assuming all of the `code` and `codebase` attributes are correctly set up). Image loading seems to require a network connection, although AppletViewer will function correctly.

Q: When I load an applet into Netscape how do I stop it?
A: In a nutshell, there is no option that stops an applet that is currently running. An applet's `stop()` method is normally called when you visit a new URL or if you load another document from disk etc. If you load a new document with an applet in it the current applet will be stopped, although Netscape 2.0 is very reluctant to interrupt an applet that is running when you use the ESC key or *Stop* button. Netscape provides messages to tell you of the current applet's status (Netscape 2.0N is much more verbose in this respect).

Q: If I want to run an applet locally in Netscape what should I do?
A: For a start, ensure that a `CLASSPATH` directory is defined in the `AUTOEXEC.BAT`
file, and that it includes the '`.`' (current directory) entry. Using `file://` URLs works
for some applets but not for others. Try using the *File/Open* command instead from
within Netscape (to open an HTML file that invokes an applet). Viewing images
locally has been a problem for many, although this works fine over the Internet, i.e.
when the applet is referenced from a Web server using an `http://` URL. See the
introduction for more details on installing Netscape and the Java Development Kit
(JDK).

JDK-related questions

Q: What actually is the JDK?
A: The Java Developer's Kit, or JDK, is a collection of tools that allows you to develop
programs written in the Java language. It comprises, essentially, a program compiler
(`JAVAC.EXE`), an interpreter (`JAVA.EXE`) and an AppletViewer utility
(`APPLETVIEWER.EXE`). A disassembler (`JAVAP.EXE`) is also provided with the JDK,
so that you can even convert compiled classes back into Java source code.

Q: How do I use the applet compiler, `JAVAC.EXE`?
A: Simply run it with the name of the applet or application that you want to compile.
`JAVAC.EXE` creates a `.class` file from your applet (upon successful compilation),
which you can then run either though the AppletViewer or Netscape 2.0. Be sure to
give the full name of the applet you want to compile, for example:

```
javac TicTacToe.java
```

`JAVAC.EXE` can be run from the Windows 95 DOS prompt or from the *Run*
option after pressing the *Start* button in Windows 95.

Q: How do I use the applet interpreter, `JAVA.EXE`?
A: This utility is used to run Java applications (not applets). Run it with the name of
the application's class (without quoting the `.class` extension). For example, to run
`MyApplet.class` (the compiled version of `MyApplet.java` – see above) you
would enter the following from the command line:

```
java MyApplet
```

`JAVA.EXE` can be run from the Windows 95 DOS prompt or from the *Run* option
after pressing the *Start* button in Windows 95.

Q: Can I view Java *applications* through the AppletViewer?
A: No, because a Java application has a `static void main(args[0])` method which is the 'entry point' for that program. An applet does start its life with the `main()` method, so AppletViewer will reject the file, saying that it does not have a `main()` method. You can use the method name `main()` in an applet, although it will not replace `init()` as the entry point for the applet.

Q: Are Sun releasing a non-byte-code (i.e. 'executable') applet compiler?
A: There have been a few references to this on the Net recently, so it could become a reality. Platform-specific compilers tend to make Java lose its 'architecture-neutral' capability, although many would argue that the JDK is not itself architecture-neutral, and many people would favour the performance benefit that such a compiler would bring. Directly executable applications (and applets) would run faster than their byte-code counterparts – even though they may be much larger – and Java programs could be used as direct CGI script replacements and truly standalone programs (at present Java applications require the `JAVA.EXE` interpreter and applets require a class library, such as the `MOZ2_0.ZIP` file in Netscape Navigator).

Q: What are the differences between the alpha JDK, JDK beta-1 and JDK beta-2, and what are future versions expected to bring?
A: JDK beta-1 and beta-2 differ in that beta-2 added more to the Java API. Some minor alterations to existing methods have also been implemented, and bug-fixes to existing classes have also been made. Beta-2 also uses a compressed archive of classes (called `CLASSES.ZIP`) for compilation purposes, which saves disk space. Another notable change is that all compiler warnings in beta-1 now generate fatal errors in beta-2, so for example you must catch and process all methods that throw exceptions (these generated warnings in beta-1). The alpha-API was used with the HotJava browser and is now outdated.

Q: What is the `CLASSES.ZIP` file?
A: This is where all of Java's classes are kept, in compressed form, in order to save space. This feature is new to JDK beta-2. Read the introduction on how to process this file. You can either leave it compressed (the `JAVAC.EXE` compiler can handle zipped class files), or you can uncompress it into a directory such as `\JAVA\SRC` if you need to see the source code. The ability to see the Java source code is useful if you want an insight into how the language is structured, and to see the various methods held in various classes.

Java terminology questions

Q: Why the name 'Java'?

A: Why not? Anyway, here is one answer that I was recently given, courtesy of one Sun Microsystems employee working on the Java project – anonymity preserved of course :-):

> *Hmmm, you want the real story? The name Java came from a bunch of people sitting in a meeting brainstorming a bunch of names and sending them off to a lawyer to see which ones weren't already obviously taken (trademarked), and picking from the ones that cleared. There was a little bit of effort to avoid certain over-used terms (like web-anything) and to avoid obviously bad connotations, but basically we needed a sequence of letters that was easy to pronounce and that we could trademark. First came Java and later came HotJava. They used to be called OAK (which stood for nothing in particular) and Webrunner, respectively, both of which are trademarked by other computer firms.*

So there you have it, straight from the horse's mouth. Not surprisingly, the name *Java* has spawned a whole series of other tools with coffee-related names. For example, *Mocha* is another name for Netscape's JavaScript language (and there is even a `mocha:` URL in Netscape 2.0), while *EspressoGrinder* is the name of a new public domain Java compiler. For more details on the *EspressoGrinder* compiler see the Web site at the URL `http://wwwipd.ira.uka.de/~espresso`.

Q: What is the difference between a Java *applet* and a Java *application*?

A: An *applet* is a Java program that runs within the Netscape 2.0 browser – effectively *executable content*. A Java *application* is similar, although it runs outside the browser environment, i.e. it is a 'standalone' program that is called from a DOS shell, and is run through the Java interpreter. Applets require a browser to run, such as Netscape 2.0, while applications can be run via the Java interpreter `JAVA.EXE`. Applets can also make use of the AppletViewer tool (see above). Applets have *milestones* that start with the `init()` method; applications have a `main(String args[])` method which is their main entry point in the program.

Q: What is 'Awt'?

A: Awt is the *Abstract Window Toolkit*, a package that allows graphical facilities to be incorporated into Java applets and applications. You can build a complete user interface using Awt 'components' such as buttons, windows (known as *frames* in Java), checkboxes and pull-down menus. Awt provides all of the methods to implement just about any graphical function. You can learn all about Awt in Chapter 8.

Q: What is an event handler?
A: An *event handler* is a section of a Java program that handles events that are generated during the lifetime of your Java program. Events include button-presses and all kinds of user-instigated actions (e.g. the shutting down of the current applet). The `action()` and `handleEvent()` methods are used to implement event handlers in Java.

Java programming questions

Q: How can I get input from the user into my Java program?
A: In order to do this within an applet, use an Awt facility such as a text area (multiple line input) or text field (single line input). This will allow the user to input data which can then be stored into a variable and processed accordingly. Without Awt (i.e. outside an applet) the only way to get input is via the `read()` method, which reads characters from the keyboard (from the standard input, that is). Another way would be to pass command line arguments to the application and use these for input. Awt's functions are by far the best, since they are graphical.

Q: How do I read and write data to and from a file?
A: You need to use a mechanism known as a *stream*. Streams are data paths to both remote files (via a URL) and local files. Using a stream you can read and write data to and from a file held on disk. See Chapter 10 for more information and source code examples.

Q: How do user-defined parameters get passed to *applets* and *applications*?
A: *Applets* use the `<param>` tag to pass values to an applet. The applet must use `getParameter("name")` to obtain the parameter value, where `name` is the name of the parameter in this instance. `<param>` tags must occur within the `<applet>..</applet>` container that references your applet from within an HTML file. *Applications* use a different method to obtain user parameters. When an application is invoked it is done so via the `JAVA.EXE` interpreter, for example:

```
java MyApplication
```

Arguments placed immediately after the name of your application are automatically stored in the array `args[]`, which the `main(String args[])` method uses. Hence the first argument is `args[0]`, the second `args[1]` and so forth. All such parameters are `String` values, so for example:

```
java MyApplication hello there
```

would store "hello" in args[0] and "there" in args[1].

Q: My image animations seem to *flicker* when they run. Is there a cure?
A: You could use smaller image files. Smaller images get loaded and updated more quickly than larger images. Animations also tend to flicker at the start, since they are not yet *cached* into memory (or on disk). Try the sample applet named *'Tumbling Duke'* (stored in \JAVA\DEMO\TumblingDuke by default) and see how the flicker disappears after all of the images have been loaded. Another way around this problem is not to use multiple image files, but to use one image file with multiple 'frames' (i.e. pictures) inside of it. By slicing up the image you can then animate accordingly. See the \JAVA\DEMO\UnderConstruction applet for an example of this faster, albeit more complex, solution.

Q: I want to use mouse events in my Java applet. How do I do this?
A: Use the standard methods such as mouseUp() and mouseExit(), which catch mouse events such as movement, button clicks, and x, y coordinates. See Chapter 8 for more information.

Q: How can I send status bar messages to the user from within a Java program?
A: Use the setStatus() method, for example:

```
setStatus("Hello Maria ;-)");
```

Q: How can I set the title of a window (*frame*) in Java?
A: Use the setTitle() method that is defined in the Frame class. For example:

```
myFrame.setTitle("This is a title");
```

Q: How can I load a new HTML file into the Netscape browser using Java?
A: Use the showDocument() method with a valid URL.

Q: How can I draw an image into an applet?
A: Use the getImage() and drawImage() methods. If you need to get an image from a particular URL use the call getImage(new URL(myUrl)), where myUrl is the URL of the image (using http:// etc.). If you want to load an image from disk use: getImage(getDocumentBase(), "filename.gif") instead, where getDocumentBase() returns the directory location where the HTML file that called your applet resides (use getCodeBase() if you need to refer to the directory in which the applet's class is stored instead).

Q: How do I arrange my user interface components within an applet?
A: This facility is expected to be improved, although with the JDK 1.0b2 you must use a series of *panels* that are arranged using compass-like coordinates, e.g. `North`, `South`, `Center`. The `Panel()` constructor creates a new panel. See Chapter 8 on the Awt package for more information on panels and UI components.

Q: Can I attach a menu bar to anything else but a frame?
A: No. Only *frames* can have menu bars attached to them. A panel cannot have a menu bar attached to it, for example (so you can't add new menus to the Netscape browser itself – nice idea though).

Q: How are the `<applet>` tags `WIDTH` and `HEIGHT` attributes related to Java's `resize()` method?
A: The `resize(rows,cols)` method is used to change the dimensions of the applet's *display area*. When you use AppletViewer the `WIDTH` and `HEIGHT` attributes control the initial size of the applet on the screen, i.e. the size of the AppletViewer window. However, as soon as `resize()` is called this will override the `WIDTH` and `HEIGHT` settings (at which point you see the AppletViewer's window change size). A frame can also be resized with the `resize()` method, although since the frame is not shown until the `show()` method is called the frame appears with its correct dimensions from the outset. Viewing an applet within Netscape is another matter, since the `WIDTH` and `HEIGHT` attributes take precedence over `resize()`. It is therefore important to allocate enough space to the applet so that the components within it are visible.

Q: What is the current state of play regarding the use of *sockets* in Netscape and the AppletViewer?
A: There has been a large debate on the use of sockets within Netscape 2.0 using the `net.*` classes. It seems that it is possible to open sockets *ad hoc* to just about any site when using AppletViewer, but when using Netscape 2.0 an *exception* is thrown that denies access to create an external socket. It seems that Netscape (and Sun) are worried about possible security problems, and have thus not allowed external socket calls to a Web server. It is possible to read and write data via a CGI script, however, using a Java stream mechanism to read the data and an HTML form to write the data by submitting it to the CGI script directly (see below). You may also want to check out USENET's `comp.lang.java` newsgroup for more information on the Java/CGI connection. Many companies are now starting to offer Java/CGI integration tools (check out `http://weblogic.com` for instance). Netscape announced (December 1995) in USENET that Netscape v2.0b4 and above will solve the 'socket problem', thus allowing applets within Netscape to make external socket calls.

Q: Can I implement a clickable imagemap (clickable image regions) within my applet?

A: Yes, but it is no easy task. See the sample imagemap program in `\JAVA\DEMO\ImageMap`. This sample applet catches a mouse event within an image (to get the x, y coordinate) and then maps this into a series of regions that activate different URLs. The `showDocument()` method is used to launch a new URL after clicking on a specific 'hot-spot' region. If you are using Netscape 2.0 you can of course use client-side imagemaps. See my home page on the Web for details of this.

Q: What is the difference between `getCodeBase()` and `getDocumentBase()`?

A: `getDocumentBase()` and `getCodeBase()` return pathname information based upon the location of an applet or the HTML file that references the applet. `getCodeBase()` returns a pathname according to the `CLASSES` attribute that is used in the `<applet>` tag (this attribute specifies the location of an applet's `.class` file). The `getDocumentBase()` method returns the name of the HTML file that invoked the current applet, and is not a *pathname* in the true sense of the word (it is an *absolute* pathname to a file). Both methods are defined in `Applet.class` and are used in functions that retrieve information from disk, e.g. `getImage()`.

Q: How can I link my Java program to a CGI script?

A: Open a stream to the URL that calls the CGI script, remembering to include any arguments that the script requires, e.g. `http://www.mysite.com/cgi-bin/myscript?name=wombat`, where `wombat` is the argument and `name` is the form field variable, both of which are passed to the CGI script `myscript`. The question-mark (`?`) is used to separate the data you are sending from the actual script name. The stream will then return the data from the CGI script, whereupon you can store it in a variable or output it into a text area field. If your CGI script wrote the results to another file on the Web server (perhaps HTML-formatted) you could even load that file into Netscape using Java's `showDocument()` method in order to view it properly. See Chapter 10 for more on Java's stream facilities. Java applications can read from the standard input, effectively allowing them to be CGI scripts. However, since there is not (yet) a Java compiler that will create platform-dependent executable files, a Java application cannot be called via a hyperlink in a `<form>`'s `action=` attribute. Remember that 'platform-dependent' tools are really what Java is rigorously trying to avoid. A whole new approach to CGI and Java must therefore be adopted. Perhaps we shouldn't really be using CGI at all, but rather opening a direct server connection in order to get to the data needed. CGI is platform-specific; applets are not, since they are stored in an architecture-neutral byte-code format. Java programs can send data to a CGI script by opening a `FileInputStream` to the exact URL where the script resides. The CGI script can then read the standard input stream to gather the data.

Q: How can I optimize my Java applets and applications?
A: Use the **-O** (optimize code) argument to **JAVAC.EXE** when compiling your Java programs. For example, use the command-line:

```
javac -O MyApplet.java
```

You can also declare your classes as being **final**, for example:

```
final public class MyApplet extends ... {
  ...
}
```

which will speed up program execution. The compilation process will be longer, however.

Q: What is an *exception*?
A: An exception is an event that is generated at run-time (when an applet or application is running), specifically notifying that an error has occurred. Many different types of exception are supported by Java. For example, if you directly referred to a file that did not exist, Java would raise (or *throw*) a **FileNotFoundException** exception. In order to process an exception Java provides the **try {...}** and **catch** statements. The **try {...}** statement specifies a code-block that may contain statements that throw a particular exception, while **catch** deals with the exception. Exceptions may cause fatal errors that stop program execution. By trapping such exceptions you can build safety mechanisms into your programs. When you come to compile a Java program the compiler (**JAVAC.EXE**) will generate an error for each exception that you have not caught (this is new to the beta-2 Java API).

Q: How can I play an audio file in Java?
A: By using the **play(filename)** method. If you need to load an audio file from a given URL, use the **getAudioClip(URL)** method, as is also defined in **\JAVA\SRC\JAVA\APPLET\Applet.class** (assuming you have unzipped the **CLASSES.ZIP** file into a directory called **\JAVA\SRC**).

Javascript-related questions

Q: What is JavaScript?
A: JavaScript (previously known as *LiveScript*) is a Java-like programming language that allows Netscape events such as page updates and mouse events to be caught and

acted upon. It also integrates with Java, allowing applets to be called and for data to be exchanged. JavaScript can also invoke Netscape plug-ins (such as Macromedia media files, Adobe PDF files, and QuickTime video), and can interface with fill-out-forms created in HTML for field-validation activities etc. JavaScript *scripts* can be embedded within an HTML document, unlike a Java applet whose code is stored separately. You can write complete JavaScript applications, although it is mainly the 'glue' that bonds applets, scripts and plug-ins together. JavaScript is also great at dynamically creating HTML documents, based upon external events and values, e.g. dates and times. It can also be used to automate many repetitive tasks. The JavaScript language is covered in detail in Chapters 1–6.

Q: How do HTML and JavaScript integrate together?
A: Netscape-enhanced HTML has been altered significantly to include new attributes for integration with JavaScript. Most tags are now treated as *objects* within Netscape, so for example an anchor created using `<a name>...</a>` is now called an *anchor object*. Such tags have also been given a `name` attribute so that they can be named as JavaScript objects by the author. HTML forms are now JavaScript-aware in that objects such as text fields, text areas, checkboxes, radio buttons and selection lists all *trigger* JavaScript events. For example, the `onChange` attribute can specify some JavaScript code to invoke when a field value is changed (see Chapter 6 for more details on JavaScript event-handling attributes).

Q: What is a JavaScript alert box?
A: This appears when an error in the current JavaScript program has been detected. Press OK to continue, and make a note of the line number of the error so that it can be corrected. See Chapter 5 for more details.

Q: How do I go about writing and viewing a JavaScript program?
A: Read Chapters 1–6 and then create an HTML file with the `<script>..</script>` container that stores the body of your JavaScript program. You can then load your HTML file into Netscape 2.0 to see the results.

Q: Why does the `<script>..</script>` container need to be enclosed inside `<!—` and `—>` HTML comment tags?
A: In a sentence: for *backwards compatibility* with other Web browsers. Non-Netscape 2.0 browsers cannot handle JavaScript programs (not yet anyway), so the body of the JavaScript program must be commented in order that its contents are not seen literally within the HTML document. Netscape 2.0 understands the `<script>` tag and thus looks into the comment in order to access the JavaScript program that resides there. Other browsers will ignore the program completely because of the comments. Because you cannot guarantee which browser a person

will be using when viewing your pages, it makes sense to make all of your pages backwards compatible. Leave the comments out at your peril. Flames may ensue!

Q: Are semicolons (;) required at the end of JavaScript statements?
A: Yes and no. Semicolons are optional in JavaScript statements that exist on separate lines. However, if you use statements within event-handling attributes (as part of a string) you will need to terminate each statement with a semicolon (excluding the final statement). I would recommend that you use semicolons as a general rule, even after normal statements. For example:

```
<a href="http://www.host.com/dir/page1.html"
   onClick="window.status='Click here for page 1' ;
   return true;">
```

requires a semicolon to separate the two JavaScript statements in an `onClick` event attribute (note the use of different quotes as well), although:

```
function myFunc() {
   HoursinYear = 8760
   PetName = "Tortoise"
}
```

does not require semicolons – they are optional in this case. See Chapters 1–6 for more examples of the use of semicolons. The `window.status` property allows the Netscape status bar message to be changed – see Chapter 4.

Q: How can I get input from the user into my JavaScript application?
A: By using the `prompt()` method, for example:

```
var num = prompt("Enter a number", 12);
```

where `12` is the default value in this case. Strings can also be entered using the `prompt()` method. Another method is to use an HTML form and then define fields for input. JavaScript can access and even modify form fields dynamically by direct assignment to the field in question (see Chapter 5).

Q: Can I invoke a JavaScript function *after* a page is loaded ?
A: Yes, by using the new `onLoad` attribute within an HTML <body> tag. For example:

```
<html>
<body onLoad="ShowLogo();">
...
```

```
</body>
</html>
```

The meaning of `onLoad` can be confusing, since the event is not triggered when the document is *initially* loaded, but rather when the document has finished loading (see the next question).

Q: The `onLoad` event-handling attribute doesn't do what I want. I want to create HTML documents *dynamically* when a document is loaded. How do I do this in JavaScript?
A: If you need to write a function that writes data into an HTML document when it is first loaded, create a simple function that writes out a `<body>` tag (and whatever other HTML-formatted text and HTML attributes that you need) and then call the function immediately after you have defined it (i.e. it is a compulsory call). Then you can put a literal `</body>` tag into your text at the end of your document and you are done, for example:

```
<html>
<head>
<script language="JavaScript">
<!— start of script
function StartBody() {
  document.writeln("<html><body " +
                   "background=back.gif text=#FFFF00>");
}
// Call the function to start the body:
StartBody();
<!— end of script —>
</script>
</head>
This is where your actual HTML body text goes...
</body>
</html>
```

See Chapter 5 for details of how JavaScript can be used to alter background patterns and colours according to the value of a `Date` object. See the section on the `onUnLoad` event also.

Q: How can I invoke a JavaScript function?
A: Defining a button within an HTML form is one solution, whereby you use the event handler attribute `onClick` to reference the JavaScript function that you want to call, for example:

```
<form name="myForm">
<input type="button" value="Click me" onClick="myFunc()">
</form>
```

would create a button on the page, which when clicked activates the JavaScript function named `myFunc()`. You can also invoke a JavaScript function automatically, without user involvement. This is done by defining a function and then calling it immediately, for example:

```
<script language="JavaScript">
function myFunc() {
  ...
}
myFunc();
</script>
```

which calls the user-defined function called `myFunc()`.

Q: How can I send HTML-formatted text from JavaScript into the Netscape browser?
A: By using the `document.write()` and `document.writeln()` functions (the latter sends a carriage return code at the end of the string that is written). For example:

```
document.writeln("<table><tr><td>This is some " +
   "HTML-formatted text within a table</td></tr></table>");
```

sends an HTML-formatted string – which creates a simple table structure – into the Netscape browser. Since you can control the exact HTML that is sent to the browser it is possible to alter the appearance of documents according to pre-specified rules (e.g. you could return differently formatted HTML-documents depending on the output of a JavaScript function). Remember that string codes such as `"\n"` (line break) do not work in HTML – use `<br>` and `<p>` to break lines instead.

Q: How can I change document-based properties within JavaScript, rather than using HTML?
A: Some properties allow direct modification. For example, if you placed the JavaScript statement:

```
document.bgColor="#0000FF";
```

in your application, the background colour would be set to blue. This saves having to use the `<body background="#rrggbb">` tag. See Chapter 4 for more details on such JavaScript properties.

Q: How can you access files locally from within JavaScript?

A: This is a feature not yet in Netscape 2.0, although future versions are likely to have simple and secure file-opening and manipulation routines similar to those found in Java, such as `read()`.

Q: How do I invoke a Java applet from within JavaScript?

A: If you dynamically create an HTML document (using the `document.writeln()` method) that includes an `<applet>` tag this may provide a solution. Some problems have been encountered with this approach, however. It is best to create a JavaScript function that creates a complete HTML document from scratch, rather than using the HTML `<body>` container for such text, since Netscape has been known to crash when a `write()` method attempts to update the current document. Try to use frameset documents where possible, rather than writing data into an existing window. Remember that a JavaScript function is only invoked after an HTML document is loaded, and not before.

Q: How can I find out which browser the user is accessing my page with?

A: The `userAgent` property can be used for this, which is part of the new `navigator` object. Using this property it would be possible to dynamically alter your HTML document accordingly; for example, a Netscape 1.2 user could be served non-JavaScript documents, whereas Netscape 2.0 users could be served embedded applets and JavaScript programs. Non-Netscape users could be served documents without any of Netscape's HTML enhancements, or you could add new tags depending on the browser's capability, e.g. a `<marquee>` container for scrolling text for people accessing your page with the Microsoft *Internet Explorer* browser.

Q: I'm confused about how to refer to a text field within an HTML form. Please clarify.

A: Well, suppose you have a form defined in the following way:

```
<html>
<body>
<form>
<input name="field1" type="text" size=30>
</form>
</body>
</html>
```

You could then refer to the field named `field1` within a JavaScript program as:

```
document.forms[0].field1.value
```

since `forms[0]` is the JavaScript property that refers to the first form within the current document. The `value` property extracts the *literal* value from the field. You must use this property when assigning values to the field or when trying to retrieve a value from the field. Alternatively, you could define a form in the following way:

```
<html>
<body>
<form name="myForm">
<input name="field1" type="text" size=30>
</form>
</body>
</html>
```

which uses the `name` attribute of the `<form>` tag to create a form object. You can now access the field named `field1` within this form using the JavaScript expression:

```
document.myForm.field1.value
```

since `myForm` is the name of the form in which this field exists. This method of referring to a form also has the added benefit that you do not have to worry about the number of the form, which, to say the least, can become very confusing to remember, especially when you may have more than one form within a document. Remember that non-text fields, such as checkboxes, radio buttons and selection lists are still accessed in a similar way, in that the `document.formname.field` prefix remains the same; all that changes is the *access method*. Text fields are simple repositories for text since they are one-dimensional entities. Items such as selection lists require more effort to process since they are multi-dimensional. Refer to the chapter on using JavaScript's event attributes for more examples.

Q: How do I access fields located in forms within different frames?
A: In this instance use the `frames` property (also an array, just like `forms`) to access the frame in which a form exists. For example:

```
document.frames[0].forms[0].field1.value
```

refers to the text field named `field1` that exists in the first form of the first frame in the parent `<frameset>` container, e.g. the `<frame src>` tag. Frameset documents are separate documents loaded into different regions (*frames*) of a screen. You must therefore specify the frame *and* the form to access a given field.

Q: What is a *recursive* JavaScript function?
A: Essentially, a recursive function is one that calls *itself*. Read Chapter 5, where there is an example of a recursive timeout routine that invokes itself in order to provide a real-time clock. JavaScript functions are permitted to invoke themselves in this manner.

Q: How can I carry out base conversions, e.g. hexadecimal to decimal?
A: Use the `parseInt()` method. See Chapter 5 for more details.

Q: What is a 'timeout function' in JavaScript?
A: Timeouts are handled using the `setTimeout()` and `clearTimeout()` methods. The first method allows an event to be executed after a pre-specified number of milliseconds, where 1000 milliseconds is equal to 1 second, whereas the latter method cancels such an event. `setTimeout()` returns a timeout ID that can be used for such cancellations. See Chapter 5 for more details and examples of these timeout methods in general use.

Q: How can I obtain random numbers using JavaScript?
A: The `random()` function could be used, although this only works in an *X-Window* environment (a UNIX platform GUI implementation). You could use a `Date` object and then extract the seconds using `getSeconds()`. You could also use one of the `Math` functions to alter this value further, of course.

Q: How can I obtain the numeric ASCII code of a character?
A: Use the JavaScript `escape()` and `unEscape()` functions. See Chapter 5 for more details on this.

Q: Is it always necessary to use a `<script>..</script>` container?
A: No, you can embed JavaScript statements directly in event attributes such as `onClick`. For example:

```
...
<input type="button"
  value="Press Me!"
  name="button1"
  onClick="alert('This is a JavaScript alert box!')">
```

Q: Is it possible to use the same quotes inside event-handling attributes, rather than using a combination of single (') and double (") quotes?
A: Yes, by *escaping* the quote required with a \ character, for example:

```
...
<input type="button"
```

```
      value="Press Me!"
      name="button1"
      onClick="alert(\"This is a JavaScript alert box!\")">
```

Q: When I use the `onLoad` event handler within a <body> tag to call a JavaScript function and I load a completely new document, Netscape still associates the new document with the previous function. How can I stop this?
A: This seems to be a bug (in 2.0 beta 6 anyway). Use `onLoad=" "` in the <body> tag within any subsequently loaded documents and the problem will go away.

APPENDIX

B

A–Z of Java and JavaScript resources

This appendix details a variety of Java and JavaScript resources that can be found on the Internet. Entries are organized into two sections, namely **Java resources** and **JavaScript resources**.

Entries have been rated out of a total of 5 stars for general content and usefulness. Java resources are now appearing in their hundreds, and more appear each day. Any search engine of your choice will yield such resources; this appendix represents a cross-sample of the better resources that I would recommend visiting on your travels through the Web.

A–Z of Java resources

Web sites

Awt tutorial ★★★

```
http://ugweb.cs.ualberta.ca/~nelson/java/JavaTutorial.html
```

Nelson Yu's Awt tutorial contains many useful examples for building applets with graphical user interfaces.

Besiex software – Java resources ★★★

- ```
  http://amber.wpi.edu/~thethe/Documents/Besiex/Java/
     index.html
  ```
- ```
  http://amber.wpi.edu/~FEMur/Java/
  ```

A collection of classes and other useful Java-related information from Java guru Benjamin Cabell. Some of the applets here are engineering-related.

Calender applet ★★

```
http://www.oclc.org:5046/~tkac/classes/Wiz.java
```

A useful applet for implementing a calender system.

Digital Espresso ★★★★

```
http://www.io.org/~mentor/J___Notes.html
```

Digital Espresso (formerly J*** News) is a repository for USENET postings, all of which have been organized into various categories, for example *Help Wanted* and *Questions & Answers* etc. Clearly, not every USENET article is stored, only the most useful and important postings. Digital Espresso is expected to go commercial because of its popularity. The site includes a section on Java classes that people kindly want to share. The site is updated regularly and is a definite bookmark candidate (NB: there are three underscores in the URL).

Ed Snible's guide to the JDK beta release of Java ★★

```
http://www.goodnet.com/~esnible/
```

A good Web page containing miscellaneous notes on the JDK.

From Hello World to Ticker Tape in Seven Steps ★★

```
http://www.well.com/user/yimmit
```

One of the better applet-tutorials on the Web, including details on Awt (a mix of alpha and beta API the last time I had a look).

GameLan ★★★

```
http://www.gamelan.com
```

GameLan is a Web site that deals mainly in Java source code and Java resources. Here you will find a wealth of hyperlinked Java-based resources.

HotJava resources at NASA ★★

```
http://vision.gsfc.nasa.gov:2000/GUI.html
```

HotJavan HTML form-filling applet ★★

```
http://www.micrognosis.com/~ajack/inForm/index.html
```

HotJavan HTML DTD document ★★

```
http://www.halsoft.com/html/hotjava.html
```

Java Applet Library ★★★

```
http://www.applets.com
```

With a name like that, it must be good.

The Java Developer ★★★★

```
http://www.idsonline.com/digitalfocus/faq
```

An excellent resource including Java resources and Java Q&As. This resource collects material from a number of Java developers and places the results in a Frequently Asked Questions (FAQ) list for easy viewing.

Java Developer's Kit (JDK) FAQ (beta API) ★★★

```
http://java.sun.com/JDK-prebeta1/faq.html
```

A useful FAQ-style guide to the pre-beta 1 JDK from Sun.

Java FAQ ★★★★

```
news://comp.lang.java  (posted weekly)
http://java.sun.com/faq2.html
```

The main Java FAQ (Frequently Asked Questions) document is posted to `comp.lang.java` on a weekly basis. It contains a wealth of information on all aspects of Java, including resources, programming and contact information. The USENET Java FAQ is currently maintained by Elliote Harold (email: `elharo@inch.com`).

Java Message-Exchange Board ★★★

```
http://porthos.phoenixat.com/~warreng/WWWBoard/
    wwwboard.html
```

This is a new service offering Java and JavaScript developers the chance to meet up and exchange messages and ideas via the Net.

Multi-user game server in Java ★★★

```
http://www.vpro.nl/www/interaktief/java/gameserver.html
```

Netscape's Java applets page ★★

```
http://home.netscape.com/comprod/products/navigator/
    version_2.0/java_applets/
```

Information on Netscape's Java support. Not much in the way of resources, although useful to keep up-to-date with to see what has been changed.

PC Week's review of Java ★★

```
http://www.ziff.com:8002/~pcweek/reviews/june_1995/
    java.html
```

PC Week's article on the implications of Java. Reference material.

Perl and Java-related topics ★★★

```
http://www.perl.com/perl/versus/java.html
```

Notes and discussion on the differences (and benefits) of using Java and Perl (Practical Extraction and Report Language) from Perl expert Tom Christiansen.

Rapid Systems Solutions' Java Resources ★★

```
http://www.rssi.com/info/java-info.html
```

An updated guide to various Java resources on the Net.

Sun's Java Web sites ★★★★★

- ```http://java.sun.com```
- ```http://www.javasoft.com```

Sun Microsystems' Web site is the main repository of archive material for Java information (Sun having originally developed Java and HotJava). This site has been revamped recently, and contains a wealth of information on Java, including documentation, API guide and links to other Java resources (including sites using Java applets). If you want applets for the beta-API look under the following URL:

- ```http://java.sun.com/applets/applets```

Mirror sites for ```http://www.javasoft.com``` are available at:

- ```http://www.dnx.com/Java/```
- ```http://sunsite.informatik.rwth-aachen.de/Mirror/Java/```
- ```http://www.cdt.luth.se/Java/```

The main *documentation* page for Java itself is located at:

- ```http://www.javasoft.com/documentation.html```

The Wild, Wild World of HotJava ★★

```
http://www.science.wayne.edu/~joey/java.html
```

A variety of 'non-technical' articles on the Java and HotJava technologies can be found here.

Unicorn's Java Pages ★★

```
http://www.cdt.luth.se/~unicorn/Java
```

Virtual Rendezvous Java Page ★★

```
http://rendezvous.com/java
```

Yahoo's Java resources ★★★

The Yahoo! search-engine has a number of Java/HotJava-related resources, including the following:

- ```
  http://www.yahoo.com/Computers/Languages/Java/
  ```
- ```
  http://www.yahoo.com/Computers_and_Internet/Internet/
  World_Wide_Web/Browsers/HotJava
  ```

Mailing lists (LISTSERVs)

Sun's Java mailing-lists ★★★

- ```
  http://www.javasoft.com/mail.html
  ```
- ```
  http://java.sun.com/mail.html
  ```

A number of mailing lists are maintained by Sun. These are useful to receive up-to-date information on Java and the Java Developer's Kit (JDK) as changes are introduced. By subscribing to a mailing list you can receive information conveniently via email. A number of lists are maintained, including `java-announce` (latest announcements from Sun, e.g. software releases); `hotjava-interest` (a low-volume list that deals with the HotJava browser); `java-interest` (a high-volume list which discusses the Java language); and `java-porting` which discusses the porting (moving) of Java to other computer platforms. In order to subscribe to any of these lists send the word `subscribe` in the *body* of an email message to **listname**-request@www.javasoft.com, where **listname** is the name of the mailing list that you wish to subscribe to. For example, sending the message:

```
subscribe
```

to the email address

java-interest-request@www.javasoft.com

would register you with the `java-interest` mailing list. Details of cancelling your list subscription will arrive with the first acknowledgement message from Sun.

USENET newsgroups

comp.lang.java ★★★★

The USENET group `comp.lang.java` is an excellent place to pick up tips, bug information and general gossip on Java. Posting a Java question here will generate many replies; this is a *high-posting* newsgroup that attracts many thousands of articles on all aspects of Java, including platform installations and problems, programming questions and the future of Java. Make sure that you use a *threaded* newsreader (such as *WinVn*) so that you can retrieve separate discussion-paths.

alt.www.hotjava ★★

This is not a spill-over group from `comp.lang.java`; indeed it generates nowhere near as many posts. Still, it may be useful to subscribe in order to pick up snippets of information that you may have missed in `comp.lang.java`, although most of the articles are cross-posted from here in any event. This group was originally started for the discussion of Sun's *HotJava* browser.

A–Z of JavaScript resources

Web sites

GameLan ★★★

```
http://www.gamelan.com/Gamelan.javascript.html
```

This site is mainly concerned with Java, although A new JavaScript section has appeared.

JavaScript Resources Page ★★★★

```
http://www.c2.org/~andreww/javascript
```

In my opinion, one of the best JavaScript Web resources. Contains hundreds of links for new scripts, books, resources and general *Mocha gossip*.

Java documentation via Windows ★★★

```
http://www.jchelp.com/javahelp/javahelp.htm
```

A series of Windows-based help files with JavaScript documentation (downloadable files are available).

K2 Monico's JavaScript HomePage ★★

```
http://www.flinet.com/~k2/jsindex.html
```

JavaScript demo programs, and a voting form for the `comp.lang.javascript` resource (if not already available).

Morphic Molecules ★★★

```
http://www.txdirect.net/users/everett
```

This site has a series of tutorials for advanced JavaScript topics such as array-handling etc.

Netscape's JavaScript pages ★★★★

- ```
  http://home.netscape.com/comprod/products/navigator/
      version_2.0/script/index.html
  ```
- ```
  http://home.netscape.com/comprod/products/navigator/
      version_2.0/script/script_info/index.html
  ```

These pages contain all of the JavaScript documentation, as well as examples of JavaScript running under Netscape 2.0.

Verifying Input with JavaScript (white paper) ★★

```
http://ourworld.compuserve.com/homepages/gmccomb/valid.htm
```

A white paper from Gordon McComb, with numerous examples for validation routines written in JavaScript.

Miscellaneous Web resources

A variety of sites now contain JavaScript-related information, including sample programs and information. These sites are best viewed using Netscape 2.0, since many use frames and JavaScript-embedded commands. If you just want to '*view source*' at these sites to pick up tips, use Netscape 1.2 instead (it will be quicker).

- `http://flamenco.icl.dk:8000/~sjm/java/index.en.html`
- `http://www.cs.rit.edu/~atk/JavaScript/`
  `javascriptinfo.html`
- `http://www.cris.com/~raydaly/javatell.html`
- `http://ws2.scripting.com/playingwithjavascript.html`
- `http://www.hotwired.com/davenet/95/47/index3a.html`
- `http://www.wineasy.se/robban/jsindex.htm`
- `http://www.gatech.edu/amnesty/writingtest.html`
- `http://porthos.phoenixat.com/~warreng/WWWBoard/`
  `wwwboard.html`
- `http://www.zeta.org.au/~rodos/JavaScript.html`
- `http://www.dannyg.com`
- `http://www.metrowerks.com/products/announce/java.html`
- `http://www.webacademy.com/jscourse`
- `http://www.zdnet.com/~pcmag/dvorak/jd1211.htm`
- `http://www.center.nitech.ac.jp/ml/java-house/hypermail/`
  `0000`

Mailing list

http://www.obscure.org

Mail to: `majordomo@obscure.org`
Message body: `subscribe javascript`

USENET newsgroups

The main USENET groups at the time of writing are as follows:

- `comp.lang.java`
- `comp.lang.javascript`

Netscape news

Netscape's *secure news* service can be accessed by anybody using the Netscape browser.

- `snews://secnews.netscape.com/netscape.devs-javascript`

APPENDIX
C

Awt methods

This appendix documents Java's Awt package and catalogues the methods that comprise it. Awt, Java's Abstract Window Toolkit, is a collection of methods that are used to create graphical objects, such as user interface components. Awt is a large package; this appendix will help you to quickly locate the methods you need for your application (but note that this is not a complete contents list of Awt). If you need to examine Awt in detail, unzip the `SRC.ZIP` file that arrives with the JDK into a directory such as `\JAVA\SRC` and then examine the files with an ASCII editor, e.g. the Windows 95 Notepad.

AWTError.class

`AWTError.class` is used to catch errors from the Awt package. It is extended from the `java.lang.Error` class. The `msg` variable stores the error message.

```
public AWTError(String msg)
```

AWTException.class

AWTException is used to signal that an Awt *exception* has occurred. This class is an extension of java.lang.Exception and can be used in try statements. The msg variable stores the exception message.

```
public AWTException(String msg)
```

Button.class

The Button class produces a labelled button component that the user can click on in order to generate events. Button() creates the button; getLabel() returns the button's label and setLabel() sets a button label.

```
public Button(String label)
public String getLabel()
public void setLabel(String label)
```

Canvas.class

The Canvas class is used to create a canvas component. The canvas is an area that can be drawn within in an *ad hoc* manner. This is a generic class that must be subclassed in order to provide the functionality you require. The paint() method that Canvas defines is used to paint graphical objects into the canvas (see Graphics.class).

```
public void paint(Graphics g)
```

Checkbox.class

Implements a checkbox component that returns a boolean state. Checkbox() creates the checkbox, getLabel() returns the checkbox label, setLabel() sets a checkbox label, getState() returns a true or false value based on whether or not the checkbox is set, and setState() sets a checkbox state to true or false, i.e. on or off.

```
public Checkbox(String label)
public Checkbox(String label, CheckboxGroup group,
  boolean state)
public String getLabel()
public void setLabel(String label)
public boolean getState()
public void setState(boolean state)
```

CheckboxMenuItem.class

CheckboxMenuItem is used to place a visible on/off tick next to a pull-down menu option. CheckboxMenuItem() creates the item, getState() returns a boolean value representing whether or not the checkbox is active and `setState()` sets a checkbox state on or off.

```
public CheckboxMenuItem(String label)
public boolean getState()
public void setState(boolean t)
```

Choice.class

The `Choice` class implements a *pop-up* menu of items, where the current selection is displayed as the title of the menu. `Choice()` creates the menu, `countItems()` returns the number of items in the menu, `addItem()` adds a new menu item, `getSelectedItem()` returns the selected item's label, `getSelectedIndex()` returns the item based on an index number, `select()` selects the item with the index number passed to it, and `select` selects the item with the label specified.

```
public Choice()
public int countItems()
public synchronized void addItem(String item)
public String getSelectedItem()
public int getSelectedIndex()
public synchronized void select(int pos)
public void select(String str)
```

Color.class

The `Color` class stores the methods for colour manipulation, as well as defining a number of identifiers that can be used to specify particular colours. `Color()` creates a colour with the specified red, blue and green (RGB) values (three methods are supplied for this which take different arguments). The `getRed()`, `getGreen()` and `getBlue()` methods return the amount of each respective colour. The `getRGB()` method returns a red, green and blue tuplet value. Finally, the `brighter()` and `darker()` functions alter a colour so that it either becomes brighter or darker.

```
public Color(int r, int g, int b)
public Color(int rgb)
public Color(float r, float g, float b)
public int getRed()
public int getGreen()
public int getBlue()
public int getRGB()
public Color brighter()
```

```
public Color darker()
```

Component.class

The `Component` class defines an Awt component. It is a large class that houses many of the methods that have been explained earlier in the book. Here are some of the principal methods in this class:

Miscellaneous
```
public Color getForeground()
public synchronized void setForeground(Color c)
public Color getBackground()
public synchronized void setBackground(Color c)
public Font getFont()
public synchronized void setFont(Font f)
public void move(int x, int y)
public void resize(int width, int height)
public boolean handleEvent(Event evt)
```

`getForeground()` returns the foreground colour of the component, whereas `setForeground()` sets the colour of the component. `getBackground()` and `setBackground()` get and set the background colour. `getFont()` returns the currently selected font, whereas `setFont()` uses the font specified. The `move()` method is used to move a component to a new location based upon an x, y coordinate. `resize()` is used to resize the component in terms of its width and height and is normally used to size the applet's display area (although it can be used to resize frames etc. as well). The `handleEvent()` method is the main event-handling routine in the Java language.

Mouse events
```
public boolean mouseDown(Event evt, int x, int y)
public boolean mouseDrag(Event evt, int x, int y)
public boolean mouseUp(Event evt, int x, int y)
public boolean mouseMove(Event evt, int x, int y)
public boolean mouseEnter(Event evt, int x, int y)
public boolean mouseExit(Event evt, int x, int y)
```

`mouseDown()` is activated when the user presses a mouse button, whereas `mouseUp()` detects when the key has been let go. `mouseDrag()` detects when the mouse is being moved and one of its buttons is being held down. `mouseMove()`, as the name suggests, is activated when the mouse is moving. Finally, we have `mouseEnter()` and `mouseExit()`, which are used to detect when the user moves in and out of the applet's display area respectively.

Key events
```
public boolean keyDown(Event evt, int key)
public boolean keyUp(Event evt, int key)
public boolean action(Event evt, Object what)
```

Key events in Java include `keyDown()` which detects the pressing of a specific key (using its ASCII value). `keyUp()` detects when a specific key is let go. The `action()` event is another event handler used by Java and can be used to trap user events such as key and button presses.

Event.class

The `Event` class defines a number of events that can be caught by the user. It is mainly used as an argument to event-handling routines, such as `handleEvent()` and `action()`.

```
public boolean shiftDown()
public boolean controlDown()
public String toString()
```

The `shiftDown()` and `controlDown()` methods detect when the SHIFT and CTRL (control) keys are held down, respectively. The `toString()` method converts a given object event into a string so that it can be used as a label (perhaps for testing purposes when catching events etc.).

Font.class

The `Font` class is responsible for providing font manipulation tasks in Java.

```
public Font(String name, int style, int size)
public String getFamily()
public String getName()
public int getStyle()
public int getSize()
public boolean isPlain()
public boolean isBold()
public boolean isItalic()
```

`Font()` implements the font specified based upon a name, style and size. The family from which a font is derived is returned by `getFamily()`. The name, style and size of a font can be examined using `getName()`, `getStyle()` and `getSize()` respectively. Boolean functions include `isPlain()`, which returns a true or false value depending on whether or not a font is 'plain', i.e. has no effects such as *italicizing* or **emboldening**; `isBold()`, which returns whether or not a font is emboldened; and `isItalic()`, which tests to see whether a given font has the italic style enabled.

Frame.class
The `Frame` class provides the user with the facility to create a window area that is physically separate from the applet area (or browser area). Frames can have other user interface objects placed within them, such as pop-up menus and buttons.

```
public Frame(String title)
public String getTitle()
public void setTitle(String title)
public Image getIconImage()
public void setIconImage(Image image)
public synchronized void setMenuBar(MenuBar mb)
public synchronized void remove(MenuComponent m)
public synchronized void dispose()
public void setCursor(Image img)
```

`Frame()` creates a new frame with a title; `getTitle()` returns the current frame's title. A frame's title can be set using `setTitle()` – the title appears at the top of the window in the left-hand corner. Minimized frames are normally *iconized*, i.e. they are represented by an icon. The `getIconImage()` returns the image used for the icon. You can choose a new icon using `setIconImage()`. Menu bars are groups of pull-down menus that are placed under the frame's upper title bar. The `setMenuBar()` method places a new bar within the frame (as explained in detail in Chapter 8). Menu bars and other components within a frame can be removed with the `remove()` method. The `dispose()` method should be used to destroy the current frame. Finally, the `setCursor()` method can be used to change the cursor that is seen within the frame (this takes an image as an argument).

Graphics.class
The `Graphics` class is widely used in Awt, especially within methods such as `paint()`, which allow the user to draw objects into their applet. Among the methods in the `Graphics` class are:

```
public abstract boolean drawImage(Image img, int x,
  int y, ImageObserver observer);
public abstract void clearRect(int x, int y, int width,
  int height);
public abstract void copyArea(int x, int y, int width,
  int height, int dx, int dy);
```

```
public abstract void drawLine(int x1, int y1, int x2,
    int y2);
public abstract void drawOval(int x, int y, int width,
    int height);
public abstract void drawPolygon(int xPoints[],
    int yPoints[], int nPoints);
public abstract void drawString(String str, int x, int y);
public abstract void fillOval(int x, int y, int width,
    int height);
public abstract void fillPolygon(int xPoints[],
    int yPoints[], int nPoints);
public abstract void fillRect(int x, int y, int width,
    int height);
public void draw3DRect(int x, int y, int width,
    int height, boolean raised)
public void drawPolygon(Polygon p)
public void drawRect(int x, int y, int width, int height)
public void fill3DRect(int x, int y, int width,
    int height, boolean raised)
public void fillPolygon(Polygon p)
public abstract void setFont(Font font);
```

The shape-drawing and filling functions are all self-explanatory. These simply draw and fill a variety of different-shaped objects into the applet's display area (normally a canvas area).

Applet example: A sample drawing applet

```
import java.awt.*;
import java.applet.Applet;
public class SampleDraw extends Applet {
  public void init() {
    resize(150,150);
  }
  public void paint(Graphics g) {
    g.draw3DRect(5, 5, 25, 100);
    g.drawString("Hello!", 15, 10);
  }
}
```

Image.class
The Image class contains a small number of methods for dealing with bitmapped images.

```
public abstract int getWidth(ImageObserver observer);
public abstract int getHeight(ImageObserver observer);
```

The getWidth() and getheight() methods are used to return the width and height of a given image.

Menu.class

A menu is a component of a pull-down menu bar. The Menu class provides the programmer with a number of methods for manipulating menus.

```
public Menu(String label)
public int countItems()
public MenuItem getItem(int index)
public void add(String label)
public void addSeparator()
public synchronized void remove(int index)
public synchronized void remove(MenuComponent item)
```

Menu() is used to create a new menu and add() is used to add new menu items to it. The countItems() method returns the number of such items. addSeparator() adds an item to the menu, which consists of a single horizontal line known as a *separator*, and is used to group different menu items together (see Chapter 8). getItem() returns an item in a menu bar, given its index position. The remove() methods allow menu items to be removed on the basis of a index position or its actual name.

MenuBar.class

This class is used to allow menu bars to be bound to a frame, and is used in conjunction with the Menu class. Refer to Chapter 8 for more details on menus and menu bars.

```
public MenuBar()
public synchronized Menu add(Menu m)
public synchronized void remove(int index)
public synchronized void remove(MenuComponent m)
public int countMenus()
public Menu getMenu(int i)
```

MenuBar() creates the menu bar and add() is used to add new menus (notice that the Menu class has been mentioned as an argument to the add() method). The remove() methods allow menu bars to be removed on the basis of an index number or actual component name. countMenus(), as the name suggests, returns the number of menus within a menu bar, and `getMenu()` returns the menu with a given index number.

Panel.class

A *panel* is an area that groups together components. The `Panel` class provides a generic class for the creation of a panel area.

```
public Panel()
```

The `Panel()` method creates a new panel and invokes `setLayout()` to arrange the objects that are later placed in that panel.

Scrollbar.class

This class implements a scroll bar component.

```
public Scrollbar(int orientation)
public Scrollbar(int orientation, int value, int visible,
   int minimum, int maximum)
public int getOrientation()
public int getValue()
public void setValue(int value)
public int getMinimum()
public int getMaximum()
```

Scroll bars are created with the `Scrollbar()` method. This can be done in a number of ways, depending on which arguments you pass to `Scrollbar()`. Use `getOrientation()` to return the orientation of a scroll bar (vertical or horizontal) and `getValue()` to return the value of the current scroll bar setting (measured in pixels). The `getMinimum()` and `getMaximum()` methods return the minimum and maximum values associated with the scroll bar (as set with the `Scrollbar()` method).

TextArea.class

Text areas allows text spanning more than one line to be input by the user. They are essentially fields that can be filled with text.

```
public TextArea(int rows, int cols)
public TextArea(String text)
public TextArea(String text, int rows, int cols)
public void replaceText(String str, int start, int end)
public void insertText(String str, int pos)
public int getRows()
public int getColumns()
```

A text area can be created using one of the three different `TextArea()` methods – each of which accepts slightly different arguments. The `replaceText()` and `insertText()` methods are useful for modifying the text within a field. `getRows()` and `getColumns()` simply return the dimensions of the text area, based upon the `rows` and `cols` variables supplied to `TextArea()`.

Applet example: A sample text area applet

```
import java.awt.*;
import java.applet.Applet;
public class aTextArea extends Applet {
  public void init() {
    Panel mainPanel = new Panel();
    setLayout(new BorderLayout());
    add("Center", mainPanel);
    mainPanel.add(new TextArea("Hi!", 10, 30));
  }
}
```

TextField.class

Text fields are similar to text areas, detailed above, except that they occupy only a single line.

```
public TextField(int cols)
public TextField(String text)
public TextField(String text, int cols)
public int getColumns()
```

The `TextField()` method is used to create the text field object, and can be of a specified size by using the `cols` (columns) variable – measured in characters.

Applet example: A sample text field applet

```
import java.awt.*;
import java.applet.Applet;
public class aTextField extends Applet {
  public void init() {
    Panel aPanel = new Panel();
    add("Center", aPanel);
    aPanel.add(new TextField("A text field!", 20));
  }
}
```

APPENDIX

D

FTP sites for the Java Developer's Kit

Notes

■ This appendix documents each of the main Internet FTP sites where the Java Developer's Kit (JDK) is stored. At the time of writing the main archive name for the Windows 95 JDK (Release 1.0) is called `JDK-1_0-win32-x86.exe`. As new releases of the JDK are made available you can visit these sites to download the latest version. Be sure to visit the nearest server in order to speed up file downloads. Sun's main server can become very busy. A ✓ indicates a mirror server, i.e. a duplicate of Sun's main FTP server `java.sun.com`.

- You can use any FTP client program to access the JDK archive, including Netscape via the `ftp://` URL; for example, `ftp://ftp.javasoft.com/pub` would place you in the **pub** directory, whereupon you can click on the file you want to download. Ensure that you enable `binary` mode if you are using a command-driven FTP client.
- In order to process the JDK archive use a 32-bit UNZIP utility such as WinZip. Also ensure that the archive is extracted in the root (top-level) directory of your hard disk, e.g `C:\`.
- The JDK documentation is normally held in a **pub** subdirectory, and is compressed into a `.ZIP` file. The relevant archives are named `progGuide.html.zip` and `JDK-beta2-htmldocs.zip`, all of which are formatted in HTML. You must view the resulting files with a 32-bit version of Netscape because the directory structures use long filenames.
- JDK version 1.0 is now available from `ftp://ftp.javasoft.com/pub/JDK-1_0-win32-x86.exe`.

JDK FTP sites

China

- `math01.math.ac.cn/pub/sunsite` ✓

Germany

- `sunsite.informatik.rwth-aachen.de/pub/mirror/java.sun.com/JDK-1_0-win32-x86.exe` ✓

Korea

- `ftp.kaist.ac.kr/pub/java/JDK-1_0-win32-x86.exe` ✓

Japan

- `ftp.glocom.ac.jp/mirror/java.sun.com/JDK-1_0-win32-x86.exe` ✓

Singapore

- `ftp.iss.nus.sg/pub/java/JDK-1_0-win32-x86.exe` ✓

Sweden

■ ftp.luth.se/pub/infosystems/www/hotjava/pub/
   JDK-1_0-win32-x86.exe ✓

UK

■ sunsite.doc.ic.ac.uk/packages/java/
   JDK-1_0-win32-x86.exe ✓

USA

■ ftp.javasoft.com/pub/JDK-1_0-win32-x86.exe
■ www.blackdown.org/pub/Java/pub/JDK-1_0-win32-x86.exe ✓
■ ftp.science.wayne.edu/pub/java/JDK-1_0-win32-x86.exe ✓
■ sunsite.unc.edu/pub/languages/java/
   JDK-1_0-win32-x86.exe ✓
■ java.dnx.com/pub/JDK-1_0-win32-x86.exe ✓

APPENDIX

E

FTP Sites for Netscape Navigator 2.0

Notes

■ This appendix documents each of the main Internet FTP sites where Netscape Navigator 2.0 is stored. Netscape's main FTP server can become very busy. A ✓ indicates a mirror site, i.e. a duplicate of Netscape's main FTP server. Netscape 2.0 occupies just under 3 Mbyte of disk space when compressed, and 'expands' to around the same size when decompressed (this is because the archive contains further compressed files). After a full installation you can expect around 5 Mbyte of files to be installed. Be sure to download the 32-bit version of Netscape (this has the N32 prefix).

■ Netscape 2.0 is stored in a subdirectory commonly called `2.0` (e.g. on Netscape's FTP server the file is stored as the URL `ftp://ftp.netscape.com/2.0`). Look for a `2.0` directory when you are trying to locate the Netscape 2.0 software from an FTP server.

■ You can use any FTP client program to access the Netscape archive, including Netscape itself via the `ftp://` URL. For example, `ftp://ftp8.netscape.com/2.0` would place you in the `2.0` directory, whereupon you can click on the file you want to download. Ensure that you enable `binary` mode if you are using a command-driven FTP client (Netscape does this automatically). Note also that you may have to find the relevant directory when browsing a given FTP site.

■ When you have downloaded the Netscape archive, run it in a *temporary* directory (e.g. `C:\TEMP`) and the program will install itself. Just follow the screens to choose a directory location in which to install the Netscape software. You can delete the contents of the temporary directory after this. Ensure that you shut down all other programs before installing Netscape. It is also advisable to make backups of `netscape.ini` (Netscape's initialization file) and `bookmark.htm` (personal bookmarks file) *before* installing.

■ The URL `http://home.netscape.com/comprod/mirror/index.html` has an interactive system for finding the nearest mirror site and most up-to-date version of Netscape.

Netscape 2.0 FTP sites

Africa
■ `ftp://ftp.sun.ac.za/pub/archiving/www/mcom/netscape` ✓

Australia
■ `ftp://ftp.adelaide.edu.au/pub/WWW/Netscape` ✓
■ `ftp://ecto.curtin.edu.au/pub/internet/clients/netscape` ✓

Hong Kong
■ `ftp://sunsite.ust.hk/pub/WWW/netscape` ✓

Japan
■ `ftp://SunSITE.sut.ac.jp/pub/archives/WWW/netscape` ✓
■ `ftp://bash.cc.keio.ac.jp/pub/inet/netscape` ✓
■ `ftp://ftp.glocom.ac.jp/pub/net/netscape` ✓

- `ftp://ftp.pu-toyama.ac.jp/pub/net/WWW/netscape` ✓
- `ftp://ftp.elcom.nitech.ac.jp/pub/netscape` ✓
- `ftp://ftp.cs.titech.ac.jp/pub/net/WWW/netscape` ✓
- `gopher://SunSITE.sut.ac.jp:70/11/archives/WWW/netscape` ✓
- `http://SunSITE.sut.ac.jp/arch/archives/WWW/netscape` ✓

Sweden

- `ftp://ftp.sunet.se/pub/www/Netscape` ✓
- `ftp://ftp.luth.se/pub/infosystems/www/netscape/netscape` ✓

UK

- `ftp://sunsite.doc.ic.ac.uk/computing/`
  `information-systems/www/Netscapes` ✓

USA

- `ftp://ftp.netscape.com/2.0`
- `ftp://ftp2.netscape.com/2.0`
- `ftp://ftp3.netscape.com/2.0`
- `ftp://ftp4.netscape.com/2.0`
- `ftp://ftp5.netscape.com/2.0`
- `ftp://ftp6.netscape.com/2.0`
- `ftp://ftp7.netscape.com/2.0`
- `ftp://ftp8.netscape.com/2.0`
- `ftp://wuarchive.wustl.edu/packages/www/Netscape` ✓
- `ftp://ftp.cps.cmich.edu/pub/netscape` ✓
- `ftp://ftp.utdallas.edu/pub/netscape` ✓
- `ftp://ftp.micro.caltech.edu/pub/netscap` ✓
- `ftp://server.berkeley.edu/pub/netscape` ✓

APPENDIX

F

Netscape HTML/ JavaScript colour codes

Notes

- This appendix documents Netscape 2.0's colour codes. These codes can be used in a variety of HTML tags and with JavaScript's colour properties. Colour codes are represented by a red–green–blue (RGB) triplet that is encoded in the hexadecimal numbering system, ranging from `00` to `FF` (0–255) – `00` being the minimum colour intensity and `FF` being the maximum intensity. The colour blue is thus the code `0000FF`, i.e. no red, no green and the maximum blue intensity.
- A variety of standard HTML and JavaScript-enhanced tags in Netscape 2.0 can specify colour codes. The font container `<font`

`color="#rrggbb">..</font>` is one such example, where `rrggbb` specifies the colour-code (use the table below to identify each RGB value). The HTML `<body>..</body>` container also uses a number of colour-related attributes, including `bgcolor` (background colour), `fgcolor` (foreground colour), `link` (hyperlink colour), `alink` (active hyperlink colour), `vlink` (visited hyperlink colour) and `text` (text colour).

■ JavaScript colour properties, such as `document.alinkColor`, `document.bgColor` , `document.fgColor`, `document.linkColor` and `document.vlinkColor`, can also make use of the RGB colour codes documented in the table below.

■ As well as RGB codes, specific colour *names* can also be used within tags. For example, rather than specifying `<font color="#008000">..</font>` for the colour green, you could use `<font color="green">..</font>` instead. Colour names are shown in the first column of the table.

■ The table has four columns. The first column shows the textual colour name. Columns 2–4 show the decimal and hexadecimal representation of that colour (in the format `dec/hex`). The decimal values are useful to know since they can be used with JavaScript functions such as `parseInt()` to convert between decimal (base 10) and hexadecimal (base 16). If you are using colour codes of the form `#rrggbb`, be sure to use the right-hand (hexadecimal) entry. So, for example, if you wanted to use the colour 'aquamarine' you could use the RGB code `#7FFFD4`, noting that a hash (#) must prefix all RGB codes within HTML tags, such as `<font>` and `<body>`, and in JavaScript properties, such as `document.fgColor`.

Colour name	Red (dec/hex)	Green (dec/hex)	Blue (dec/hex)
aliceblue	240/F0	248/F8	255/FF
antiquewhite	250/FA	235/EB	215/D7
aqua	0/00	255/FF	255/FF
aquamarine	127/7F	255/FF	212/D4
azure	240/F0	255/FF	255/FF
beige	245/F5	245/F5	220/DC
bisque	255/FF	228/E4	196/C4
black	0/00	0/00	0/00
blanchedalmond	255/FF	235/EB	205/CD
blue	0/00	0/00	255/FF
blueviolet	138/8A	43/2B	226/E2
brown	165/A5	42/2A	42/2A
burlywood	222/DE	184/B8	135/87
cadetblue	95/5F	158/9E	160/A0

Colour name	Red (dec/hex)	Green (dec/hex)	Blue (dec/hex)
chartreuse	127/7F	255/FF	0/00
chocolate	210/D2	105/69	30/1E
coral	255/FF	127/7F	80/50
cornflowerblue	100/64	149/95	237/ED
cornsilk	255/FF	248/F8	220/DC
crimson	220/DC	20/14	60/3C
cyan	0/00	255/FF	255/FF
darkblue	0/00	0/00	139/8B
darkcyan	0/00	139/8B	139/8B
darkgoldenrod	184/B8	134/86	11/B
darkgray	169/A9	169/A9	169/A9
darkgreen	0/00	100/64	0/00
darkkhaki	189/BD	183/B7	107/6B
darkmagenta	139/8B	0/00	139/8B
darkolivegreen	85/55	107/6B	47/2F
darkorange	255/FF	140/8C	0/00
darkorchid	153/99	50/32	20/144
darkred	139/8B	0/00	0/00
darksalmon	233/E9	150/96	122/7A
darkseagreen	143/2B	188/BC	143/2B
darkslateblue	72/48	61/3D	139/8B
darkslategray	47/2F	79/4F	79/4F
darkturquoise	0/00	20/14	20/149
darkviolet	148/94	0/00	211/D3
deeppink	255/FF	20/14	147/93
deepskyblue	0/00	191/BF	255/FF
dimgray	105/69	105/69	105/69
dodgerblue	30/1E	144/90	255/FF
firebrick	178 B2	34/22	34/22
floralwhite	255/FF	250/FA	240/F0
forestgreen	34/22	139/8B	34/22
fuchsia	255/FF	0/00	255/FF
gainsboro	220/DC	220/DC	220/DC
ghostwhite	248/F8	248/F8	255/FF
gold	255/FF	215/D7	0/00
goldenrod	218/DA	165/A5	32/20
gray	128/80	128/80	128/80
green	0/00	128/80	0/00
greenyellow	173/AD	255/FF	47/00
honeydew	240/F0	255/FF	240/F0

Colour name	Red (dec/hex)	Green (dec/hex)	Blue (dec/hex)
hotpink	255/FF	105/69	180/50
indianred	20/14	92/5C	92/5C
indigo	75/4B	0/00	130/1E
ivory	255/FF	255/FF	240/F0
khaki	240/F0	230/1E	140/8C
lavender	230/1E	230/1E	250/FA
lavenderblush	255/FF	240/F0	245/F5
lawngreen	124/7C	252/FC	0/00
lemonchiffon	255/FF	250/FA	20/14
lightblue	173/AD	216/D8	230/1E
lightcoral	240/F0	128/80	128/80
lightcyan	224/E0	255/FF	255/FF
lightgoldenrodyellow	250/FA	250/FA	210/D2
lightgreen	144/90	238/EE	144/90
lightgrey	211/D3	211/D3	211/D3
lightpink	255/FF	182/B6	193/C1
lightsalmon	255/FF	160/A0	122/7A
lightseagreen	32/20	178/B2	170/AA
lightskyblue	135/87	20/146	250/FA
lightslategray	119/77	136/88	153/99
lightsteelblue	176/B0	196/C4	222/DE
lightyellow	255/FF	255/FF	224/E0
lime	0/00	255/FF	0/00
limegreen	50/32	20/14	50/32
linen	250/FA	240/F0	230/1E
magenta	255/FF	0/00	255/FF
maroon	128/80	0/00	0/00
mediumaquamarine	102/66	20/14	170/AA
mediumblue	0/00	0/00	20/14
mediumorchid	186/BA	85/55	211/D3
mediumpurple	147/93	112/70	219/DB
mediumseagreen	60/3C	179/B3	113/71
mediumslateblue	123/7B	104/68	238/EE
mediumspringgreen	0/00	250/FA	154/9A
mediumturquoise	72/48	20/149	20/144
mediumvioletred	199/C7	21/15	133/85
midnightblue	25/19	25/19	112/70
mintcream	245/F5	255/FF	250/FA
mistyrose	255/FF	228/E4	225/E1
moccasin	255/FF	228/E4	181/B5

Colour name	Red (dec/hex)	Green (dec/hex)	Blue (dec/hex)
navajowhite	255/FF	222/DE	173/AD
navy	0/00	0/00	128/80
oldlace	253/FD	245/F5	230/1E
olive	128/80	128/80	0/00
olivedrab	107/6B	142/2A	35/23
orange	255/FF	165/A5	0/00
orangered	255/FF	69/45	0/00
orchid	218/DA	112/70	214/D6
palegoldenrod	238/EE	232/E8	170/AA
palegreen	152/98	251/FB	152/98
paleturquoise	175/AF	238/EE	238/EE
palevioletred	219/DB	112/70	147/93
papayawhip	255/FF	239/EF	213/D5
peachpuff	255/FF	218/DA	185/B9
peru	20/14	133/85	63/3F
pink	255/FF	192/C0	20/143
plum	221/DD	160/A0	221/DD
powderblue	176/B0	224/E0	230/1E
purple	128/80	0/00	128/80
red	255/FF	0/00	0/00
rosybrown	188/BC	143/2B	143/2B
royalblue	65/41	105/69	225/E1
saddlebrown	139/8B	69/45	19/13
salmon	250/FA	128/80	114/72
sandybrown	244/F4	164/A4	96/60
seagreen	46/2E	139/8B	87/57
seashell	255/FF	245/F5	238/EE
sienna	160/A0	82/52	45/2D
silver[a]	192/C0	192/C0	192/C0
skyblue	135/87	20/146	235/EB
slateblue	106/6A	90/5A	20/14
slategray	112/70	128/80	144/90
snow	255/FF	250/FA	250/FA
springgreen	0/00	255/FF	127/7F
steelblue	70/46	130/1E	180/50
tan	210/D2	180/50	140/8C
teal	0/00	128/80	128/80
thistle	216/D8	191/BF	216/D8
tomato	255/FF	99/63	71/47
turquoise	64/40	224/E0	20/148

Colour name	Red (dec/hex)	Green (dec/hex)	Blue (dec/hex)
violet	238/EE	130/1E	238/EE
wheat	245/F5	222/DE	179/B3
white	255/FF	255/FF	255/FF
whitesmoke	245/F5	245/F5	245/F5
yellow	255/FF	255/FF	0/00
yellowgreen	154/9A	20/14	50/32

[a]Netscape default background page colour.

APPENDIX

G

JavaScript addendum

While this book was being finalized, a number of small additions were made to the JavaScript language for the full Netscape 2.0N release. The most important additions are documented in this appendix.

The new `navigator` object

A new JavaScript object, `navigator`, contains information about the version of Netscape Navigator that is being used to access the current hypertext document. It is a valuable object since it can allow dynamic HTML to be created according to the particular version of the Netscape browser being used.

The `navigator` object has four main properties, namely:

- ■ `appCodeName`   specifies the code name of the browser being used
- ■ `appName`   specifies the name of the browser being used
- ■ `appVersion`   specifies version information for the Netscape browser being used
- ■ `userAgent`   specifies the user-agent header of the current browser

No methods or event-handlers accompany the `navigator` object. As more browsers adopt JavaScript (which is likely in the future, bearing in mind that the likes of IBM and Microsoft have already licensed Java), these new properties will become more useful. Since non-JavaScript aware browsers will not be able to use these properties, or any of the JavaScript language for that matter, the `navigator` object is currently only of use to Netscape 2.0 and Netscape 2.0 Gold clients. Remember that these properties are set by the *client*, not the server, so only the browser can use them. You can write a CGI script to access such values as well, however, which can then be changed to values that are set by the Web server (and which will thus work irrespective of the client browser).

Examples

This example outputs each property value so that you can see the values returned by JavaScript:

```
<!—Output the navigator.* properties—>
<script language="JavaScript">
<!—:
document.write("<tt>appCodeName: " +
navigator.appCodeName + "<br>");
document.write("appName: " + navigator.appName + "<br>");
document.write("appVersion: " + navigator.appVersion +
   "<br>");
document.write("userAgent: " + navigator.userAgent +
"<br></tt>");
<!—>
</script>
```

The output from this example (assuming we are using Netscape 2.0N in a Windows 95 environment) is as follows:

```
appCodeName: Mozilla
appName: Netscape
appVersion: 2.0 (Win95; I)
userAgent: Mozilla/2.0 (Win95; I)
```

where `Mozilla` is the codename for Netscape Navigator (this codename is browser-specific), `Netscape` is the application name, `2.0 (Win95; I)` is the version of Netscape being used and the operating system that it is being used under and `Mozilla/2.0 (Win95; I)` is a combination of `appCodename` and `userAgent`.

Using `appVersion` it would be possible to alter the contents of your HTML documents dynamically, for example using the following skeletal example:

```
<script language="JavaScript">
<!— start:
browserVers = navigator.appVersion;
// Are we using Netscape?
if (appName == "Netscape") {
  // But is it Netscape version 2.0?
  if browserVers.substring(0,3) == "2.0" {
    // Yes, it is Netscape version 2.0, so we can
    // include JavaScript / Java and any of the
    // Netscape 'enhanced' tags.
    // ...
  }
  else {
    // No, it is not version 2.0, so we can't
    // include any JavaScript or Java programs etc:
    // ...
  }
}
else {
  // We're not using Netscape, so leave out all
  // Netscape additions and use 'vanilla-HTML':
  // ...
}
<!— end —>
</script>
```

Glossary

If you are stuck with a particular definition use the on-line technical glossary at Imperial College, London. This contains definitions for thousands of Internet-related terms and acronyms. The address is `http://wombat.doc.ic.ac.uk`.

Anchor
An anchor is an HTML object that is the target for an HTML `<a href>` hyperlink. Anchors allow sections of a hypertext document to be marked, thus allowing quick movement to that region of the document. They are used to allow quick navigation through a document (e.g. for indexes). *See also* Hyperlink.

Applet
A Java program that runs within the Web browser, effectively providing *executable content*. Applets can be embedded within existing HTML documents allowing the user to interact with them. *See also* Application.

Application
A Java program that runs outside the Web browser environment. Applets are most commonly run from within a DOS shell environment, i.e. from the command line. *See also* Applet.

ASCII
An acronym for American Standard Code for Information Interchange. A *plain text* file, such as an HTML file. *See also* Binary file.

Awt
Acronym for Abstract Window Toolkit. Essentially a collection of classes, known as a *package*, that allow the user to access graphical functions. Awt allows user interface components such as buttons, menus and windows to be created, as well as providing functions to draw and fill shapes etc.

Binary file
A non-text file, e.g. an executable program or an image, as opposed to an ASCII file (e.g. an HTML file). *See also* ASCII.

Browser
Synonymous with Web browser, Client or Client browser, which all refer to graphical programs such as Netscape Navigator. *See also* Netscape.

CGI
Abbreviation for Common Gateway Interface. CGI is currently the dominant standard that allows clients to interface with back-end programs running on a Web server. CGI essentially allows a degree of interactivity to be built into a hypertext document, although it always requires a server connection. Java applets can connect to servers and can run interactive programs autonomously. *See also* HTTP.

Client
Another name for a Web browser such as Netscape 2.0. The term is coined from the *client–server* model, which the Internet is based upon. The term 'client' can also refer, more loosely, to a process that is requesting information from a server, where the *process* is a program – perhaps a Java applet. *See also* Applet, Client–server model, Netscape.

Client pull
A *dynamic document* technique used by Netscape that makes use of the HTML `<META>` tag in order to update the request for a document within a specified time period. *See also* Netscape, Server push.

Client–server model

The Internet is based upon this model, where computers are either *servers* or *clients* (or both). Clients are hosts requesting information, whereas servers are hosts serving, or providing, information. *See also* Host, Internet.

DOS

An acronym for Disk Operating System. The operating system found on all IBM-compatible personal computers. A 32-bit version of MS-DOS has been integrated into the Windows 95 operating system. *See also* DOS shell.

DOS shell

A DOS shell is a separate window running the DOS pre-processor `COMMAND.COM`. It is necessary to run Java *applications* from a DOS shell, since they do not run with the assistance of a Web browser. Applets do not need a DOS shell.

DNS

An abbreviation for Domain Name Server. A DNS is a an Internet host that converts textual addresses, e.g. `www.wombat.com`, into numeric IP addresses, e.g. `164.8.8.68`. Once an address has been *resolved* and the numeric IP address found, a route to the host can then be set up across the Internet. You will be allocated your own DNS server by your IAP, although just about any DNS server can be used as long as you know the numeric IP address allocated to it. *See also* IAP.

DTD

An abbreviation for Document Type Definition, a specific implementation of document description using SGML, and which is contained within a file. HTML is referred to as an SGML DTD. *See also* HTML, SGML.

Email

Electronic mail (or just *email*) is a method of delivering text messages across the Internet (and indeed other computer networks). Messages are sent as plain text, although binary files can be sent using a suitable encoding scheme, such as MIME. *See also* ASCII, Binary file, MIME.

Expression

In programming, an expression is any valid set of variables, identifiers, operators and indeed other items (which may include other expressions) that evaluate to a *single value*.

FAQ

An acronym for Frequently Asked Questions. FAQs are documents that explain Internet fundamentals for new users (although many FAQs are very advanced as well). Many FAQs are distributed via USENET. *See also* Internet, USENET.

Flame war

A *flame* is a message posted to a USENET group or directly to an individual (via email) that criticizes the person regarding an article that person previously posted. A flame war is a whole series of *flames* originating from different people. *See also* Email, USENET.

Firewall

A firewall is a security scheme that protects one or more computers with Internet connections from intrusion by external computers which also have Internet connections. A firewall is essentially an *invisible boundary* created through software that distinguishes networked computers within the firewall from those outside the firewall. Those computers within the firewall possess internal access capabilities and shared resources that are not granted to those on the outside. External requests are therefore filtered and examined before they are allowed through the firewall, if at all. *See also* Proxy, Internet.

FOF

An acronym for Fill-Out-Form. FOFs are areas within an HTML document that allow user input to be passed from a client application such as Netscape to a server entity on another Internet host. HTML forms are created using the `<form>` container. *See also* Container, HTML.

FTP

An abbreviation for File Transfer Protocol (or File Transfer Program, if referring to the *application program*). FTP is a tool and protocol that defines how files of information are transferred over the Internet. FTP is the principal tool used for moving files between different Internet hosts, and is supported in Netscape via the `ftp://` URL. *See also* Host, Internet, Netscape.

GIF

An acronym for Graphics Interchange Format, a ubiquitous image format for still images used on the Internet. Web browsers such as Netscape use the GIF format for in-line images that appear within HTML documents. The GIF format was originally developed by CompuServe for use over its network. *See also* HTML, JPEG.

Helper application

A third-party program that can be used with the Netscape browser to view proprietary file formats, such as images, audio files and animations. Examples are *WinGif* and *Lview* for GIF/JPEG images and *Naplayer* for audio files.

Host

A term referring to a computer that is connected (or can be connected) to the Internet.

HotJava

A Web browser developed by Sun Microsystems that allows Java applets to be embedded within HTML documents. HotJava was the first 'Java-aware' Web browser. *See also* Applet, Browser, HTML, Java.

HTML

An abbreviation for HyperText Mark-up Language. HTML is a mark-up language for documents and is the *lingua franca* of the World-Wide Web. HTML was born out of the larger ISO SGML standard, but is a *looser*, less strict implementation. The HTML language itself is made up of a series of *tags* that encapsulate parts of the text within a document and provide document mark-up features, such as paragraphs, bold/italic/pre-formatted text, headers, in-line images and so forth. *See also* SGML, In-line images, ISO, Tags.

HTTP

An abbreviation for HyperText Transfer Protocol, the principal protocol used by the World-Wide Web. HTTP is encapsulated within TCP/IP packets for transmission over the Internet. *See also* FTP, TCP/IP, URL.

Hyperlink

Hypertext link. Synonymous with hyper-reference. A hyperlink is an item of text (or an image) that the user can click on in order to be led to another item, or source of information. Hyperlinks give the Web its hypertext and hypermedia functionality. Hyperlinks are created using the HTML container `<a href>` *See also* Container, HTML, Hypermedia, Hypertext.

Hypermedia

Hypermedia is similar to hypertext, although bringing together many more other media, typically of an audio and visual nature. Hypermedia has been made possible through tools such as Netscape and the World-Wide-Web. *See also* Hypertext.

Hypertext

Hypertext is a way of cross-referencing textual information. A hypertext document is made up of many cross-references (hyperlinks) to other, related items of information, perhaps in the same document or located in other external documents. *See also* Hyperlink, Hypermedia.

IAP

An abbreviation for Internet Access Provider – the organization that provides your access to the Internet, e.g. *dial-up* access via a modem.

Identifier

In programming, the name of a variable. *See also* Variable.

Imagemap

An imagemap is an image that has one or more hot-spot regions within it. Each region can be clicked on by the user (using the mouse) in order to activate a particular URL that is associated with that hot-region. Netscape supports HTML *client-side* imagemaps which do away with the need for a server entity. *See also* GIF, HTML, Netscape, URL.

In-line image

An in-line image is a graphic file placed within an HTML document. Netscape, for example, can handle GIF and JPEG formatted images within documents (as well as any external image format using an appropriate helper application). The HTML `<img src>` tag is used to place an image within a hypertext document. *See also* GIF, Helper application, HTML, JPEG, Netscape.

Internet

The world's largest computer network: a network of networks all interlinked to form one collective entity, and all of which run the TCP/IP protocol to communicate. The Internet is known by many names, including *The Net*, *The Information Superhighway* and *CyberSpace*. The World-Wide Web now makes up a large proportion of the Internet, although it is not the Internet *per se*. *See also* TCP/IP, World-Wide Web.

ISO

An abbreviation for International Organization for Standardization, a major standard-setting body in the computing world.

Java

A secure, object-orientated and highly portable programming language. A Java *engine* is built into Netscape Navigator 2.0 to provide executable content. *See also* JavaScript, Netscape.

JavaScript

Loosely based on the Java language, JavaScript is a scripting language that is closely linked to the Netscape program interface – allowing browser events such as page navigation to be detected within an HTML document and acted upon. JavaScript also brings *executable content* to the Web; it is primarily of use to HTML authors who do not wish to delve to deeply into Java. JavaScript was announced to the world in late 1995. JavaScript was previously known as 'LiveScript' (which formed part of Netscape's LiveWire project). *See also* Java, Mocha, Netscape.

MIME

An acronym for Multipurpose Internet Mail Extensions. MIME defines a number of different internal file formats whose names take the form *file-type/sub-type*. For example HTML text is specified as `text/html`, whereas plain (or ASCII) text is specified as `text/plain`. MIME allows standard email (which is entirely text-based, and 7-bit only) to carry other file formats (typically binary formats that have 8 bits in each byte). All results passed via the HTTP protocol over the Internet are done via MIME-formatted messages. *See also* HTTP, Internet.

Mocha

The name of Netscape's scripting language, named after Java because of its 'coffee connections' (*mocha* being a type of coffee). Netscape 2.0 has a `mocha:` URL for testing JavaScript expressions. *See also* Expression, JavaScript, Netscape.

Mozilla

Another name for the popular Netscape Navigator browser. *Mozilla* is a dinosaur mascot. *See also* Netscape.

Netscape

1. The company that built the immensely popular Web browser, located on the World-Wide Web at `http://home.netscape.com`.

2. The shortened name of the graphical Web browser Netscape Navigator, a tool that facilitates access to an area of the Internet known as the World-Wide Web. Netscape is an HTML version 1.0, 2.0 and 3.0 browser with enhanced features such as secure network support, dynamic documents, and Java/JavaScript programming. *See also* HTML, World-Wide Web.

Netsite

> *Netsite* is a term coined by Netscape, developers of the Netscape Navigator browser, to refer to a Web server that is running their own server software with secure HTTP enabled, i.e. data encryption is enabled for all client–server activity, allowing sensitive information to be transmitted without fear of interception. *See also* HTTP, Netscape, SSL.

NNTP

> An abbreviation for Network News Transfer Protocol. A ubiquitous protocol used to distribute USENET news over the Internet. Netscape can interface to an NNTP server to gain access to USENET. *See also* Netscape, URL.

PC

> An abbreviation for Personal Computer.

POP

> An acronym for Post Office Protocol. An email protocol used to collect messages from a mail server. Netscape supports POP3 (the third and most recent protocol version). SMTP is used to relay mail across the Internet between different hosts. *See also* Email, SMTP.

PPP

> An abbreviation for Point-to-Point Protocol, the more advanced predecessor to the SLIP protocol, which allows TCP/IP to run over serial line connections. SLIP and PPP are the two most common protocols supported for *dial-up* Internet connections. PPP enhancements include an error-correction capability. *See also* Internet, SLIP.

Proxy

> A proxy is an entity, i.e. a server (hardware and software) that allows access to the Internet from within a *firewall*. A proxy server runs in conjunction with some suitable firewall software. The proxy server waits for a client request from inside the firewall, forwards the request to the remote server located outside the firewall, and then reads the response and sends it back to the client. *See also* Firewall.

Push–pull

> A term that refers to Netscape 1.1's *dynamic document* capability, whereby the client and server application (Netscape or a Web server program) can be made to receive or transmit documents automatically (or at least after a specific time period). *See also* Client pull, Netscape, Server push.

Render

A term used in the context of many Web browsers to mean *display*, for example *'The image was rendered on the screen'. See also* Web browser.

Server push

A *dynamic document* feature of the Netscape browser that allows a Web server entity to send segments of a document, such as an image or hypertext file, to a client browser (such as Netscape). A special MIME type is used to allow data segmentation. Documents are then sent from the server to the client, and they are *updated* by the client, i.e. they are replaced, thus allowing techniques such as simple animation. *See also* Client pull, MIME, Netscape, Web server.

SGML

An abbreviation for Standard Generalized Mark-up Language. SGML is a meta-language that is used to define a wide range of document types. HTML is an *application* of SGML that is used to create such documents. SGML is itself an ISO standard. *See also* DTD, HTML, ISO.

SMTP

An acronym for Simple Mail Transfer Protocol, the primary protocol for *delivering* (or routing) messages over the Internet between hosts. *See also* Host, Internet, POP.

SLIP

An acronym for Serial Line Internet Protocol. A communications protocol used over telephone lines via a dial-up connection from the user's computer. SLIP is essentially an implementation of IP (Internet Protocol) for use over dial-up telephone lines via the serial port on a computer such as a PC, and is a popular way of accessing the Internet. *See also* Internet, PPP, TCP/IP, WWW.

Socket

A mechanism to allow processes (i.e. programs) to communicate with one another over the Internet. Sockets are the core functionality behind the TCP/IP protocol. *See also* Internet, TCP/IP.

SSL

An abbreviation for Secure Socket Layer, an open standard describing an interprocess communication mechanism used by the TCP/IP protocol over the Internet. Secure sockets have extra security features to facilitate secure transmissions over the Internet. *See also* Internet, TCP/IP.

Tags

The building blocks of the HTML language. A tag is a code that affects the layout and appearance of text within an HTML document. For example, the `<b>` tag enables character **emboldening** and `<i>` enables *italic* text. Most tags come in pairs, known as containers, so that the scope of the effect can be controlled e.g. `</i>` and `</b>` disable italics and emboldening, respectively. *See also* Container, HTML, SGML.

TCP/IP

An abbreviation for Transmission Control Protocol/Internet Protocol – the primary communications protocol used over the entire Internet network. HTTP requests are encapsulated within TCP/IP for use over the WWW. *See also* HTTP, SLIP, WWW.

Thread

A thread is defined as a single sequential flow of control within a Java program. Threads allow concurrent activities to be undertaken within a Java program, thus allowing multiple processes to be executed (effectively providing *multitasking* applications). *See also* Java.

URL

An abbreviation for Uniform Resource Locator (or Universal Resource Locator, to some). A URL is the unique address of an Internet resource – a way of specifying, in a very compact form, the exact *type* and *location* of an Internet resource. URLs allow access into Internet news servers, Gopher servers, WAIS servers, FTP servers, and even real-time (Telnet-based) resources. URLs include `http://` for a hypertext-based resource (e.g. a Web page, graphic or server script) and `ftp://` for an FTP server. *See also* FTP, HTTP, Internet, WAIS.

USENET

An acronym for *USErs NETwork* – the Internet's *bulletin board*, now containing over 15 000 different subject areas, or *newsgroups*, which users can contribute to. USENET carries text, images and audio content. *See also* Email, Internet.

Variable

A programming term that refers to a value (such as a string or a number) whose name is set using an *identifier*.

VRML

An abbreviation for Virtual Reality Modelling Language. VRML is an evolving specification for a platform-independent definition of three-dimensional spaces within the World-Wide Web. It will be designed to combine virtual reality (VR) features, networked visualization and the global hypermedia environment of the World-Wide Web. *See also* HTML, Internet, Java, World-Wide Web.

WAIS

An acronym for Wide Area Information Server, a searching tool that indexes the contents of public documents on the Internet, and which is available as a Web server at the URL `http://www.wais.com`. *See also* URL, Web server.

Web

Short name for the World-Wide Web. The term *Web* refers to the fact that information on the World-Wide Web is linked together in a *matrix*, i.e. all parts of the Web are accessible from any other point. *See also* Internet, World-Wide Web.

Web browser

See Browser, Netscape.

Web server

A program that serves hypertext documents to Web browsers such as Netscape. Examples are the NCSA Windows HTTPD program and the CERN Server. *See also* HTTP, Netscape.

WWW

An abbreviation for World-Wide Web, the hypermedia system that consists of documents encoded in the HTML language, and which is a subset of the Internet. The Web is the fastest growing area of the Internet and is expected to become the most widely used system. The WWW was the brainchild of Tim Berners-Lee and was developed while he worked at CERN, the famous particle physics laboratory in Switzerland, during 1992. Sites are linked together using hyperlinks. *See also* HTML, Hyperlink, Internet, Web.

Index